THOUGHTS OF A PHILOSOPHICAL FIGHTER PILOT

THOUGHTS OF A PHILOSOPHICAL FIGHTER PILOT

James Bond Stockdale

HOOVER INSTITUTION PRESS
Stanford University
Stanford, California

*The Hoover Institution on War, Revolution and Peace, founded
at Stanford University in 1919 by Herbert Hoover, who went on
to become the thirty-first president of the United States, is an
interdisciplinary research center for advanced study on domestic
and international affairs. The views expressed in its publications are
entirely those of the authors and do not necessarily reflect the views
of the staff, officers, or Board of Overseers of the Hoover Institution.*

www.hoover.org

Hoover Institution Press Publication No. 431
Hoover Institution at Leland Stanford Junior University,
Stanford, California 94305

First printing 1995
26   25   24   22   21   20   19   18   21   20   19   18   17   16   15   14   13

Manufactured in the United States of America

The paper used in this publication meets the minimum requirements
of the American National Standard for Information Sciences—Permanence
of Paper for Printed Library Materials, ANSI/NISO Z39.48-1992. ♾

Library of Congress Cataloging-in-Publication Data
Stockdale, James B.
Thoughts of a philosophical fighter pilot / James Bond Stockdale
      p.   cm.—(Hoover Institution Press publication ; 431)
Includes index.
ISBN 978-0-8179-9391-7 (cloth : alk. paper)
ISBN 978-0-8179-9392-4 (pbk. : alk. paper)
ISBN 978-0-8179-9393-1 (epub)
ISBN 978-0-8179-9397-9 (mobi)
ISBN 978-0-8179-9398-6 (PDF)
1. Vietnamese Conflict, 1961–1975—Personal narratives, American.
2. Stockdale, James B.   3. Air pilots. Military—United States—Biography.
4. United States. Navy—Biography.   I. Title
DS559.5S76   1995
959.704'38—dc20   95-20171
                                    CIP

CONTENTS

EDUCATION FOR LEADERSHIP AND SURVIVAL

ABOUT THE AUTHOR _____

Vice Admiral James Bond Stockdale was a true American hero. Shot down on September 9, 1965, during a mission over North Vietnam, he spent seven and a half years as a prisoner of war. Despite enduring relentless torture, intimidation, and four years of solitary confinement, he refused to capitulate, even earning the grudging respect of his captors. He ultimately received 26 combat decorations, including two Distinguished Flying Crosses, three Distinguished Service Medals, four Silver Star Medals, two Purple Hearts, and the Congressional Medal of Honor, the nation's highest award for valor. He had the distinction of being the only three-star officer in the history of the navy to wear both aviator wings and the Medal of Honor.

Stockdale retired from the military in 1979 to become president of the Citadel, a widely renowned military college in South Carolina. On his retirement, the navy established the Vice Admiral James Bond Stockdale Leadership Award, which is presented annually to two commanding officers, one in the Atlantic Fleet and one in the Pacific Fleet.

He left the Citadel in 1981 to become a senior research fellow at the Hoover Institution at Stanford University. In addition to this book, he is the author of two other works published by Hoover Institution: *Courage under Fire: Testing Epictetus's Doctrines in a Laboratory of Human Behavior* (Hoover Essays, No. 6, 1993) and *A Vietnam Experience: Ten Years of Reflection* (1984). Stockdale and his wife, Sybil, were coauthors of *In Love and War* (Harper & Row, 1984), which in 1987 was made into an NBC television movie viewed by more than 45 million Americans.

In 1992 Admiral Stockdale was an independent candidate for vice president of the United States as Ross Perot's running mate. He said he ran to repay his debt to Perot, who had worked to help free POWs in Vietnam.

In 1993 Stockdale became the first naval aviator of the Vietnam era to be inducted into the Carrier Aviation Hall of Fame. He was later the subject of *Stockdale Triumphs: A Return to Vietnam*, a documentary about his first trip back to Vietnam in 1994. Produced by Catherine O'Brien of the Stanford Video Media Group, the film received a Telly Award in the history/biography category. In the 45-minute video, he returns to Hanoi and the Hoa Lo prison—the "Hanoi Hilton"—where he was held for most of his imprisonment, discussing his prisoner of war experience and exploring the changed city.

James B. Stockdale died at his home in Coronado, California, in 2005 at the age of 81. At the time of his death he held eleven honorary doctoral degrees. His home, where he lived since 1963, has been designated a city landmark.

TRIALS BY FIRE

THE "MELTING EXPERIENCE": GROW OR DIE

Speech delivered to the graduating class of 1981 at John Carroll University in Cleveland, Ohio.

YOUR PRESIDENT [FATHER O'MALLEY] and I have a mutual friend, a Boston thoracic surgeon who has a great sensitivity for issues concerning the meaning of life and the nature of man. It's easy to understand how a man who spends the best part of his busy days at the pressure-packed juncture of life and death could become absorbed in philosophical thought. But this doctor doesn't let it go at that. He refines his thoughts through reading and shares the best of his high-quality professional articles, those bearing on the human predicament in general and human ethics in particular, with Father O'Malley and me and a few others. Well, all this bears on how I'm going to spend the next fifteen minutes because it follows that any of us in the Dr. Eugene Laforet network could expect our colleagues to have some pretty strong notions about ethical systems and their formulation. I've been asked to expose some of mine today.

Pressurized experiences have a way of giving us an overload of dilemmas that can't wait for a waffled solution. We seem to be continually in the position, described by Dr. Alfred North Whitehead, of not being able to bring half an umbrella to work just because the weatherman says there's a 50 percent chance of rain. When Dr. Laforet gets a person's chest opened up, he has to cut here or cut there in a finite interval of time. He can't waffle. Students at John Carroll University have to take the scheduled exams and pass or flunk, ready or not. Life seems to become compressed, running ahead, as if being watched on a movie screen, with the projector set on high-speed advance.

But in these circumstances, as your attention is channeled, as you concentrate, you can sometimes sense that you're undergoing a "melting" experience. Some of your inhibitions and preset feelings, fears, and biases melt as you come to realize that, under the gun, you must grow or fail—in some cases, grow or die. A sort of transformation takes place under pressure—under what the alchemists of the Middle Ages called the "hermetic."

The hermetic idea is old, having come down from ancient Egypt and Greece and been colored by Christian sacramental teaching. It was a twofold concept. It meant something sealed off—hermetically sealed, as we say. And it also meant magic, particularly magical transformation. You put something in a crucible or a retort and you subjected it to certain pressures like heat or doses of sulphur or mercury. If you were lucky or wise or both, some kind of creative transformation would take place. In physical terms, this referred to the changing of base metals into precious ones—lead into gold.

But the top-grade alchemical philosophers were not content with mere physical crucibles and crystal retorts they could hold in their hands. They were aiming at even more important things. Paracelsus thought it might be possible to create a human being (homunculus) in the laboratory—something people today are again getting uneasy about. The higher alchemy aimed not at mere physical change but at moral and spiritual transformation. The crucible and retort became symbols of creative growth. Fire and the twin elements sulfur and mercury came to represent the outside pressures exerted upon the human soul in its confined place. In extreme cases, the fire might be of hellish origin. But if the soul in question were strong enough, not mere passive matter, that spirit might undergo an alchemical change— a metamorphosis of the spirit in which the ordinary stuff of humanity could turn into something precious, emerging as if from a tightly sealed cocoon.

This alchemy comparison may sound farfetched, but it contains a hint of the sort of process of intellectual and even spiritual transformation I'm going to talk about today. A person's ethical notions tend to crystallize in the hermetic. Mine did. The pressure chamber in which my most deeply felt ideas were forged was not a surgical operating room, not a pressure-packed classroom but a prison cell.

Prisons have been crucibles of both degradation and creative impulse throughout history. Like most pressure chambers, they seem to draw out the very best and the very worst in mankind. Writers have attributed prison inspiration to Boethius, Cervantes, Dostoevsky, Solzhenitsyn, and dozens of other ex-convicts who later made their marks in the world. But, in many cases, the main inspiration was obtained through reflection, through the opportunity their prison experiences provided for uninterrupted thought, time to reorder their lives while languishing.

I have had periods of more or less stress-free imprisonment, even in solitary confinement. A fellow prisoner, a math scholar, once did me the tremendous favor of passing to me (and I mean by that putting it through the concrete wall between us with our tap code, as I memorized it) an arithmetic formula of expansion that, in a remarkably few iterations so simple that they could be performed with a stick in the dust, would yield natural logarithms to three or four decimal places. After weeks of thought, I reconstructed the process of going from natural logarithms to logs of base ten. I slowly became the world's greatest expert on the exponential curve; I dusted off the construction of a log log duplex deci-trig slide rule in my head. (No pencils or papers were allowed in the cell; my log tables had to be etched with a nail on the concealed side of a bed board.) I became one of the few men alive to truly understand why any number raised to the zero power necessarily had to be unity, why zero factorially is unity, and so on. I spent months and months in deep concentration and, at one point, could have written a pretty good advanced mathematics text. I knew the logarithmic-exponential picture inside out.

You might find it interesting that after I'd been home about two weeks I was so disillusioned at the contents of a freshly received letter that I almost cried. It was just a short letter from my young son's prep school math teacher with a casual request for a brief, written summary of all it took to build a slide rule in prison. He obviously had devoted very little reflection to the comprehensiveness of mathematical development it entailed. I chose not to do it, and I hope you can understand my frustrating dismay with the commonplace insensitivity of this "big easy world of yakety yak," as I sometimes maliciously thought of it those first weeks out. More about disillusionment later.

Those stress-free prison experiences occurred only late in the game—only after the North Vietnamese ceased trying to extract propaganda and other material from us (a heaven-sent reprieve, which took effect only after President Nixon came into office and reversed the previous administration's misguided policy of keeping known instances of communist brutality against American prisoners secret from the American press). My mathematical thoughts came from the stress-free period. The ethical thoughts came from the period when the pressure was on—extortive pressure, torture pressure—pressure to the limit to get us to contribute to what turned out to be their winning propaganda campaign beamed at the American man in the street, pressure to the limit to get us to inform on one another. These last two ideas were tied together as integral parts of the extortion system.

I'm not here to tell war stories today, but I must give you just a little more descriptive information if I'm to get across what I mean by the melting experience. The central strategy of the extortion system involved not only the imposition of loneliness but of fear and guilt—fear of pain and guilt at having betrayed a fellow prisoner. We were all in solitary confinement and solemnly warned that any attempt to communicate with fellow Americans, by wall tap, by signal, by whisper (you name it), would be evidence of our ingratitude for "the humane and lenient treatment of Ho Chi Minh." The rules of the game were that such ingratitude gave the North Vietnamese the moral justification for pommeling the communicator while his arms were simultaneously squeezed with tourniquets, shutting off the blood circulation until he submitted. Their system was designed to produce the propaganda and information they wanted whether the American chose either of the two obvious ways to go: stay off the prisoner communication tap code network and eventually become so depressed after a couple of years that he would presumably be willing to buy human contact at the price of collaboration with the enemy or join the American communication network, that is, join the American covert civilization, get caught communicating as one eventually did from time to time, and then be put through the standard chain of events. That chain went from torture to submission to confession to apology to atonement. The atonement was of course giving away prisoner secrets—being an informer in other words—plus writing the old propaganda statement about how he had been guilty of bombing "churches, schools, and pagodas." In theory at least, we were in a no-win situation.

I think that's enough background to show that we were in a pressurized quagmire of ethical dilemmas. People were trying to use us and have us tear each other apart in the process. From this cauldron were extruded some basic ethical guideposts.

Father O'Malley asked that I talk about ethical notions of the sort that would qualify as growing within a person's interior self and not simply a set of lessons learned from without. Be assured that I'm not just building a set of guideposts for prison or for a more general military setting. My conclusions are infinitely general. From this eight-year experience, I distilled one all-purpose idea, plus a few corollaries. It is a simple idea, an idea as old as the scriptures, an idea that is the epitome of high-mindedness, an idea that naturally and spontaneously comes to men under pressure. If the pressure is intense enough or of long enough duration, this idea spreads without even the need for its enunciation. It just takes root naturally. It is an idea that, in this big easy world of yakety yak, seems to violate the rules of game theory, if not of reason. It violates the idea of Adam Smith's invisible hand, our ideas of human nature, and probably the second law of thermodynamics. That idea is you are your brother's keeper.

That's the flip side of What's in it for me? If you recognize the first as an expression of virtue and the second as an expression of vice, as I'm sure any student of Father O'Malley would, let Bacon's distinction add relevance to my concentration on adversity on this graduation day of joy: "Adversity doth best induce virtue . . . while luxury doth best induce vice."

I need to tell you that in prison it soon became clear that the only way to go—for peace of mind, for mental health if you will, as well as for practicality—was to forget that business about lying low and staying out of trouble by not communicating. Everybody had to get on the line and take the torture after being caught because we had a civilization to build, a civilization of Americans behind walls, a civilization of political autonomy that had the courage to rule itself responsibly with its own laws without contact with the parent country or its government in Washington for eight years. (Thank God.)

When I started teaching philosophy at the Naval War College, I commenced reading the literature of the Vietnam era and came across a startling essay about prisoner-of-war ethics by Harvard professor Michael Walzer. This piece appeared about three years before we were released and had as its central theme the sanctity of individual rights and how the individual prisoner had no particular obligation to bother cooperating with fellow prisoners in a clandestine organization because the poor incarcerated soul had enough to do following the orders of the captors. Walzer could not have been more wrong. To ignore a fellow captive in the pressure chamber is to betray him. Anybody who has been there knows that a neighbor in the cell block becomes the most precious thing on earth, a soul who deserves your care and cooperation no matter what the risk. I'll try to explain some of the reasons why.

When you're alone and afraid and feel your culture is slipping away even though you're hanging on to your memories—memories of language, of poetry, of prayers, of mathematics—hanging on with your fingernails as best you can and yet, despite all your efforts, still seeing the bottom of the barrel coming up to meet you and realizing how thin and fragile our veneer of culture is, when you suddenly realize the truth that we all can become animals when cast adrift and tormented for a mere matter of months, you start having some very warm thoughts about the only life preserver within reach—that human mind, that human heart next door. You become unashamed to say what you mean when your pal is being taken out for torture for being caught trying to get a message to you. You tap "God bless you, Jerry" or perhaps "I love you, Jerry."

Man's need for his fellows was certainly spotlighted in those intense circumstances. We found ourselves overcoming what is often billed as the natural selfishness of man, even the survival instinct of man, by clinging to ideas like unity over self and the spirit of other similar axioms of our organization. The sting of guilt was taken out of the program by the commonsense expedient of never keeping secrets from other Americans. No matter what we said or were forced to say under torture in the privacy of the interrogation room, we routinely put out the details on our tap code network. This was a natural for tactical defense and expediency, but its fallout in terms of expiation of guilt feelings was golden. We learned that the virtues of truthfulness and straightforwardness have their own reward.

But there was more to being your brother's keeper than being rewarded in a practical sense. J. Glenn Gray, a professor of philosophy at Colorado College until his death in 1977, wrote of that special power of comradeship to overcome man's alleged basic instinct of self-preservation. He made his observations as a foot soldier on the European battlefields of World War II and recorded them in one of his books, *The Warriors: Reflections on Men in Battle.* I was at a convocation at Colorado College (where three of my sons have gone) when the president introduced me to this man and his literature by remarking that Professor Gray was the only serious scholar of recent times to reflect deeply on how men behave in mutually shared danger, mutually shared pressure. His book and my conversations with him the year before he died corroborated what I saw in Hanoi. Gray wrote:

> Numberless soldiers have died, more or less willingly, not for country or honor or religious faith or for any other abstract good, but because they realized that by fleeing their posts and rescuing themselves, they would expose their companions to greater danger. Such loyalty to the group is the essence of fighting morale. The commander who can preserve and strengthen it knows that all other physical and psychological factors are little in comparison. The feeling of loyalty, it is clear, is the result and not the cause of comradeship. Comrades are loyal to each other spontaneously and without any need for reasons. Men may learn to be loyal out of fear or rational conviction, loyal even to those they dislike.

Gray contrasts comradeship with friendship:

> Friendship is not just a more intense form of comradeship. It is its very opposite. While comradeship wants to break down the walls of self, friendship seeks to expand these walls and keep them intact. The one relationship is ecstatic, the other wholly individual.
>
> Nothing is clearer than that men can act contrary to the alleged basic instinct of self-preservation and against all motives of self-interest and egoism. Were it not so, the history of our civilization would be completely different than what it has been.

The question is sometimes asked of those who have been in high-stress situations for long periods, "What kept you going?" "What was your highest value?" My answer is "the man next door."

What about corollaries to this single, simple, old-fashioned idea? First, let's talk about recent history. How does what I've said track with the way we Americans handled the matter of the hostages in Iran? Did we credit them with that nobility of spirit, that pride of autonomy and self-reliance, that generates within a body of people of goodwill united in a common cause under pressure?

I don't think we gave them a chance to generate that spirit. We played with them like rag dolls. We couldn't keep our hands off them, allowing American do-gooders to parade them before TV cameras on holidays, arranging for and executing piecemeal destabilizing early releases. (President Carter worked for and secured through Yassir Arafat of the PLO the parole of some U.S. Marines in the first weeks of the affair—marines whose duty it was to remain with their embassy in accordance with the Code of Conduct.) In general, we seemed to proceed from the assumption that a captive embassy staff was destined to become not a proud autonomous band but a bunch of pitiable lost sheep—children stranded at the bus station waiting for a parent to come and take them home.

Americans don't seem able to grasp the politics and psychology of terrorism and hostage taking. Here's a chance for this class of 1981 to get in on the ground floor. After the pope was shot, the papers were full of thoughtful reflections and predictions by informed people. Their message, class of '81, was that your age will be the age of terrorism and hostage taking.

A better explanation of my thoughts on the hostage issue was in the *Washington Post* on Sunday, January 25, 1981, the day the main body of hostages arrived back in the United States. I entitled my article "Extortionist Theater." I see this whole scene as a modern art form, a vile art but, like most arts, fed and supported by its audience. Of course, actors are needed too. In the recent show, America furnished both the actors and the audience. The hostages were on camera, our squeamish president was publicly agonizing and assuring the world and the Iranians that no damage would be inflicted on the theater, and the American man in the street demanded and got his daily dose of several hours of hostage soap opera. To any outlaw group or government with that natural bent for extortion, this whole scene spelled one thing: gold mine! Just swoop in and grab a group of Americans, get the show in the news, get the hands wringing and the tears flowing, and write your own ticket. Some countries know how to stop this. If you're interested, check with Israel.

A second corollary could also become a public policy issue. How does what I've said track with the well-intentioned suggestion I sometimes hear that goes something like this: You military prisoners went through hell trying to protect information that wasn't worth it and refusing to make statements against your government that were no worse than those Senator Fulbright was making. Let's get smart. Forget the Code of Conduct. Tell the world we've instructed our prisoners to say or write anything they're asked to say or write. That way we would defuse the whole torture and isolation situation.

Let me tell you that the enemy extortionists would really like that solution. With resistance brushed aside, they would just dig deeper and play even more lethal games with fear and guilt. Don't kid yourself into thinking they're going to start with an antiwar statement in a candy store situation like that. More likely, subjects for their first assigned prisoner essays would be, "Why I know that capitalism made my mother a whore" or "Why I believe it is every prisoner's duty to inform on his fellow Americans." In a prison civilization, covert or overt, a person's most prized possession is his reputation with his peers. Right off the bat, dissension would dominate the scene because most good people will just not stoop to self-imposed degradation. At least half would refuse to write anything. Who's going to order them to follow this proposed new U.S. government policy? Are you going to ask the senior prisoner to do that? You would never get me to do that. You can't get out of this predicament by making it optional either. This oftheard proposal has an inherent logic that drives captives toward destructive guilt feelings and disunity. Togetherness would go, self-respect would go, and the prison civilization would become an animal farm. It has been said that you can't legislate morality. You can't legislate degradation either. My message on this corollary is that you can't make a good man under pressure finesse evil, no matter how smart it seems.

A third corollary also focuses on conventional smartness. How does what I've said track with this fact, which I generally believe to be the truth: Well-applied torture can eventually make any man give up particular facts that the interrogating ghoul knows he knows. When confronted with this, the smart-money guys from the big easy world of yakety yak might say: "When you know your enemy is on a winning wicket, why resist?"; "It defies common sense to resist—save your strength for something important"; or "Don't fight city hall."

My point is that people of goodwill under pressure and united in a common cause do fight city hall. (Thank God.) When the cool, rational smart-money skeptics challenge the united sacrifice in this example, several answers are possible.

- A practical answer: It's the only way to go in an extortion environment—everybody makes 'em hurt him. The ghouls don't like to have to hurt everybody. They don't like to be reminded of our unity. Furthermore, when you see how frustrated it makes 'em, it makes you like to live with yourself.

- An Aristotelian answer: Man is not a package of on-off switches; he is not at his base some sort of binary computer. Compulsion and free will can coexist. To give up just because you know you can't achieve total success is a form of determinism. I don't subscribe to environmental, genetic, or any simplistic determinism. Will is the thing. Man makes his character here on earth. I am the master of my fate, the captain of my soul.

- My answer: Loyalty to the group. I have a reputation to uphold with them. I can't let them down. They are my country. They are my family. I'm not a kid stranded in the bus station trying to minimize the pain while I wait for my mother country to come and pick me up.

Finally, there is one corollary that falls out of that ecstatic relationship that comes as a surprise to most of us. I'm picking up on the suggestion that I would have more to say about disillusionment. I'm going to talk about how easy it is for a well-intentioned person to commit a cruelty of disillusionment under pressure.

It's important here to interject the fact that we in those prisons were not an unsophisticated group. We were almost all fighter pilots, all had bachelor's degrees, and more than half of us had at least one advanced degree. At least most were sophisticated enough to know that as intelligent people we should be able to cope with tentativeness and commitment at the same time, much as Aristotle would have us cope with the ideas of free will and compulsion at the same time. What I'm saying is that by and large we were able to accommodate commitment unto death and freedom of thought simultaneously. Political or religious orthodoxy was not a requirement for joining the club. But I think we all tacitly agreed that insensitivity and lack of restraint in the expression of destabilizing personal views to others were very poor form.

Nevertheless, I saw unintentional cruelty of disillusionment kill a rare sort of depressed and thoughtful man. You would never guess how. It was not messages of gloom but cheery messages of hope, persistently drummed into him month after month, that eventually did him in. He internalized and took seriously those surefire, upcoming release dates. After a number had eventually passed, his mind drifted away, he couldn't hold his rice down, and he died of a broken heart.

After I returned, I found that there are many examples of that in the literature. Some of you may have read the book *Man's Search for Meaning* by Viktor Frankl, veteran of the Holocaust and a psychologist and lecturer. He says that the big threats to morale in the crucible are not the pessimists but the incurable vocal and persistent optimists. That being so, think how much more damage gratuitous statements of political or religious dissent could do to people close to the wire. It is easy to forget that, in this age of free speech at any cost.

However, it was not forgotten in Hanoi, probably because we were all so close to one wire or another and so determined—spontaneously determined, ecstatically determined—to prevail, to see each other through, together. And we were most blessed.

John Carroll University, class of 1981, may you all be blessed.

THE ROLE OF THE PRESSURE COOKER

Lecture delivered at the University of Texas at Dallas in November 1980.

CHANCELLOR ANDREW R. CECIL's expressed wish is to center this lecture series around the theme of citizenship and moral obligation. Taken generally, my subject—education for leadership and survival—falls easily within this comprehensive category. My title—the role of the pressure cooker—projects an angle of vision that is scarcely less universal. Although it subtends a very personal arc, it points back to the Christian and classical past. I am all for the idea of progress, but I believe that all progress is stimulated by an awareness of a heritage. "It is the future that we are more likely to think of immediately when the idea of progress is brought up," says Robert Nisbet, "but it was only when men became conscious of a long past . . . that a consciousness of progressive movement from past to present became possible" (*History of the Idea of Progress*, New York, 1980, p. 323).

Let me start with the overobvious, boxed in a cliche, wrapped in some truisms. The concept of citizenship is one of the fundamental ideas of Western civilization. It is an idea born with the Greeks more than twenty-five hundred years ago. It is an idea fundamental to the American republic. It is an idea historically linked to two others: freedom and organization. At its highest, citizenship achieves a balance between these two elements necessary to the survival of society. At its best, citizenship finds an equilibrium between two essential ingredients—that of rights and that of duties. When the idea of citizenship is losing its grip, one or the other of these elements becomes eroded. Either freedom is on the losing end, or the sense of duty, of obligation, goes down the drain. We are living at a time when the idea of citizenship has been seriously weakened. We have a strong sense of the rights of a citizen. But we've lost much of the sense of the corresponding duties and obligations of citizenship. Meanwhile, the state behaves in a paradoxical manner. We find ourselves in what the philosophers call a dialectical situation. Responding to popular demand for freedom and equality, the bureaucracy of the state, swollen to the proportions of a titan, enacts battery after battery of laws and regulations to ensure that freedom and equality. Result: the state's liberty is impaired as is that of its citizens. Like a giant Gulliver the state lies on the ground, struggling to move against the bonds of the very measures it has taken to ensure freedom and equality. For "freedom and equality are sworn enemies," say Ariel Durant and Will Durant in their little book *The Lessons of History,* "and when one prevails the other dies" (New York, 1968, p. 20). This is a hard saying. I will let you decide what measure of truth it has.

One of the primary duties of citizenship is its duty to education. By education I don't mean just schooling. The idea of education is broader than that, important though schooling is. Schooling is a necessary element of education but not sufficient completely to define it.

Marriage and family life are education. Sport, play, and entertainment are education. Religious training is education. Friendship is education. Military service is education. Any and every encounter with nature and society is education. Some social scientists call education in this comprehensive sense "acculturation." I prefer to call it more simply "experience."

Now there is an element in education that I consider of crucial importance. There are learned names for the many varieties of this element, and some of these we might talk about as we go on. But for the moment I'll use the word "stress." Another name for it is "pressure." Stress or pressure in education and in life has had bad reviews. I want to give it a good one. Doctors used to say stress was bad for you—one of the evils of competitive society—and should be avoided. Nowadays some doctors say a moderate amount of stress is good for you, particularly the kind that comes from physical exercise. And there's a whole school of running doctors like George Sheehan who get a kind of mystical experience from running a marathon and write books about it (Sheehan, *Running and Being*, New York, 1978). But all doctors say if you're planning to get into this, get a stress test first.

Stress is essential to leadership. Living with stress, knowing how to handle pressure, is necessary for survival. It is related to a man's ability to wrest control of his own destiny from the circumstances that surround him or, if you like, to prevail over technology. Tied up with this ability is something I can express in one word, "improvisation." I mean man's ability to prepare a response to a situation while under pressure.

George Bernard Shaw said that most people who fail complain that they are the victims of circumstances. Those who get on in this world, he said, are those who go out and look for the right circumstances. And if they can't find them they make their own.

To wrest or not to wrest control of one's destiny is a subject discussed by the Durants in that little book I mentioned. In the chapter of their *Lessons in History* called "Growth and Decay," they state that what determines whether the challenge of history will or will not be met depends upon "the presence or absence of creative individuals with a clarity of mind and energy of will [almost a definition of genius], capable of effective responses to new situations [almost a definition of intelligence]." I think the Durants' creative individual with energy of will, capable of effective responses to new situations, is the man I describe as one who can improvise under pressure.

My pitch is that if the energy of will and creativity necessary to improvise under pressure can be taught, they are best learned in a stressful regime—in a crucible of pressure, whether that crucible be a classroom or a total environment.

I suppose my coming down on the side of stress is no surprise to this audience. My life has been that of a military man, and pressure has been my constant companion. I began with a service academy education back in the time when every teacher had to register a grade for every student at every class meeting. That may not have been the best of all educational systems, but it was a stressful one. Afterward, I lived in stress for thirty years, as a fighter pilot, experimental test pilot, and prisoner of war. My last navy assignment was the presidency of the Naval War College, where I taught "Foundations of Moral Obligation." Later I became president of a college that for 140 years has educated young men in a stressful regime—the Citadel.

My lifetime of experience in the pressure cooker, whether hemmed in by the iron laws of aerodynamics at forty thousand feet on the flight test ranges over the Mojave Desert, or hemmed in by the iron laws of extortion in the prisons of Hanoi, has led me to conclude that once one learns to accommodate the shocks of a stressful existence, his adrenalin, will power, and imagination are going to start churning to provide the maximum performance of the human mind. The generation I taught at test pilot school at the Naval Air Test Center at Patuxent River, Maryland (John Glenn was one of my classmates), could have stepped right out of the pages of Tom Wolfe's book *The Right Stuff.* In those days of the early 1950s, the exciting subject was supersonic flight. I taught an academic course in thrust and drag in the high subsonic and lower supersonic flight regimes, and I can honestly say that the intellectual mastery of the graphs and the physical laws behind them were more efficiently taught to my students in the stress of actual flight in a cockpit at forty thousand feet than in the classroom. By saying that, I am not just referring to the difference between the classroom and the lab but rather to the more mentally stimulating of the two environments.

But I don't want you to think that I am holding up my experiences under stress as a simple model of education for excellence and survival. I'll tell you more about those experiences in a moment, but first I want to broaden the screen a bit lest you think that stress and pressure are tied in a beneficial way to one way of life alone, however important they may have been in that life, which happened to be the life of a military man subjected perhaps to more direct and dire pressures than most. I want you to see with me that our whole culture, even what we call Western civilization itself, is founded on the sufferings and greatness of human beings and human societies under pressure.

It is a commonplace to say that our moral heritage has two sources—Judaic and Greek. The source book of the first is the Bible and the tradition of Judeo-Christianity associated with it. The origins of the second lie in the library of poetry, drama, politics, and philosophy of the Greek writers whose works have come down to us. If you are going to talk about justice, you had better begin with Job and Socrates.

If ever a man was in a pressure situation, it is Job, the man from the land of Uz. Here is a man, once prosperous and happy, who has been struck by terrible misfortune. He has at a stroke lost sons and daughters, servants, and possessions. He has been infected with a loathsome disease. Once a rich man, he now sits on an ash heap, naked, scraping his flesh with potsherds. He asks, "Why me, O Lord?" For he believes that the Almighty has caused or allowed these calamities to come upon him and that it makes no sense. He, Job, is a good man, a just man. What has he done to deserve this evil? Job wants to talk to God about this. Is he not a just God?

Now, as we know, God does not answer Job in the terms Job would like. God does not acknowledge Job's virtue nor does he admit the situation is unfair. Instead, clothed in a whirlwind, he points to the awesome dimensions of the universe and asks Job if he, finite creature, could do anything like that. Can Job create the sea, guide the courses of the stars? Where was Job when God created heaven and earth?

In answer, Job is silent. He bows and puts his hand over his mouth. His silence is the silence of faith, of endurance. Job was put under stress greater than nearly any man could take, and he stood the test.

Theologians have found many exalted lessons in the story of Job. One of them is that we should not try to measure the standards of the infinite with those of the finite—they are incommensurable. The lesson I take from Job is simpler. Life is not fair. There is no moral economy or balance in the nature of things such that virtue is rewarded and vice punished. The good man hangs on and hangs in there. It is significant that the nearest Plato comes to a definition of courage is in the dialogue of *Laches* where Socrates is talking to a general under whom he served whose motto is "Courage is endurance of the soul." The Greeks admired the bold stroke, the audacious dash, but reserved top credit for the man that holds on under pressure. They knew by bitter experience what stress situations are. They knew what it means to break under pressure and what it means to hold on. On the battlefield, says Aristotle, the greatest pressure is fear of death and the temptation is to run away. But the courageous man holds on.

Plato's most compelling portraits of Socrates in the dialogues show him handling himself under supreme stress. Defending himself on a capital charge in court before hostile judges, Socrates resists their pressuring him to renounce teaching and inquiry. In prison, he resists pressure from his rich pupil Crito, who had the means and the bribe money, to escape. (Athenians, "children of the laws," would thus not be disillusioned by his failure to abide by the state's verdict, even though unjust.) With death only hours away he has the equanimity to advise his family and to discourse to his pupils on the soul—on the reasons why a good man should not fear death. (*Apology* 29–30; *Crito* 50–51; *Phaedo* 67–68.)

The Greek city-state itself was a bit like a pressure cooker. It was small, and life was pretty constricted within it. The pressure set up jealousies and envies, both internal and external; this was one reason these political entities were always fighting with one another and exiling or deposing their own leaders. The Greek city-state was always in danger of being attacked by its neighbors, which is why military training was so much a part of the Greek citizen's life. It is true that some city-states at certain times used mercenaries or hired armies. But in general the latter were considered inferior and untrustworthy when the going got tough. The citizen army was at the heart of Greek city-state defense. Socrates did his military service in the Peloponnesian War, saw action at Potidaea and the siege of Delium, and passed up a decoration for valor so that another man might have it.

Education in ancient Greece came down hard on physical training. This training had an aesthetic purpose. A body in good shape was fair to look upon. More than that, Greek gymnastics aimed at victory—victory in war and in the competitive games of peace. Greek gymnastic exercise was advantageous for military proficiency. One of the famous Spartan exercises was dancing—in heavy armor. This helped develop the agility a man needed to wield his offensive weapons, the spear and short sword; it also developed the finesse to sidestep the thrusts of his enemy. The philosopher Alfred North Whitehead, while teaching at Harvard, said that if Plato were to come to our country today, he would first ask to meet not a philospher but a championship-class boxer.

In times of peace—and there were few—there were several periodic competitions among the city-states. The Olympic Games were the most famous of these contests. In fact, these games were so important to the Greeks that, if at war, they suspended hostilities for the duration. Today some educators talk about the evil effects of competition on our children, of the need to avoid developing a competitive spirit in our youth. But the Greeks, whose humanism these same experts profess to admire, were the most competitive people that ever lived. They wanted to excel in everything. Their motto was *ai en aristeuein*, "always to be the best." Their public games included competition not only in racing, jumping, javelin throwing, boxing, and wrestling but also in musical, poetic, literary, and drama contests. In one of the best-known and most fun-filled dialogues of Plato, *The Symposium*, the scene is a party celebrating the prize the host Agathon has just won for writing the best tragedy. To the Greeks the heart of the game was *agon*—competition, stress, pressure, struggle to win. (Later we'll see a contemporary scholar's comment on *agon* in education.) They like to point out that the philosopher Heraclitus, to them already an ancient and legendary figure, had claimed that both music and science had their beginning in stress—the world itself composed of opposite forces, tensions pulling against each other, like the strain of a drawn bow, resulting in a comparative stability or permanence, as the strings of a lyre give forth harmony when they are pulled two ways, stretched in harmonic proportions over the sounding board of the instrument by the pegs and the tailboard fastenings. The beautiful repose of the Greek temple was seen by the intelligentsia as the product of perfectly calculated architectural stress.

Far more ancient than the dialogues of Plato or even the philosophy of Heraclitus is Homer's great story of Odysseus, soldier and navigator. In the *Odyssey* we read of his long captivity under Calypso and his twelve-year voyage, fraught with a score of deadly perils, from that rocky island, where he was held enslaved, to Ithaca, where his faithful wife, Penelope, and his son Telemachus were waiting for him. We all know Homer's trick of tagging things, men and gods, with a characteristic label: the wine-dark sea, the gray-eyed Athena, the rosy-fingered dawn. To Odysseus Homer assigned the trait of resourcefulness, the ability to improvise in a pressure situation. *Polumetis*, Homer calls him, full of survival tricks, never at a loss no matter how lethal the situation may be. A familiar episode in the story illustrates Odysseus's resourcefulness under stress. Held captive in his narrow cave by the one-eyed giant Polyphemus, Odysseus knows that he and his men are doomed to a horrible death. (That's a fair amount of pressure. Doctor Johnson told Boswell that, when a man knows he's going to be hanged in a month, it concentrates his mind wonderfully.) Odysseus had only a couple of days. He waited until the giant was in a drunken sleep, then took a stake he had hidden in straw, heated it, and plunged it into his captor's one eye, blinding him so that the Trojan war veteran and what was left of his crew could escape. Odysseus, the resourceful, kept his head; he had the ability to improvise under pressure.

A more profoundly moving story lies at the base and heart of Christianity itself—the death of Jesus on the cross. By comparison, Socrates' death was merciful and dignified. Death by crucifixion was very cruel. Reserved for slaves and the most ignominious of criminals, this mode of execution killed by the downward drag of the body weakening the chest muscles so that life was slowly extinguished by gradual and painful suffocation. What the stress was on that man who hung there is hard for us to imagine—maybe not quite so hard for those of us who have experienced physical torture. The Gospel story tells us that despite the pressure to defend himself at his trial, Jesus did not do so. On the cross, he kept silent in the face of his tormentors' jokes. He did cry out, "I thirst" and, when the anguish became more than a man could bear, "My God, my God, why has thou forsaken me?" But at the end he said, as one would speak of a duty discharged, a mission completed, "It is finished."

Ernest Hemingway, hardly a model Christian, wrote a story called "Good Friday" about the aftermath of Calvary. Some Roman soldiers who were in charge of the execution are drinking and talking of the events of the day. One soldier mumbles over and over, "I tell you, he looked pretty good in there today." No accident that Hemingway's moral ideal was "grace under pressure." He tried to see that his heroes measured up to it.

In Italy, in the early centuries of Christian Rome, a man named Boethius was imprisoned by his emperor, Theodoric the Ostrogoth, and executed on a charge of treason in A.D. 524. Boethius was both a statesman and a scholar. He had been prime minister to the emperor. His scholarly works would have an immense influence on subsequent medieval philosophy. His commentaries on Aristotle's logic became standard texts in the universities. According to Boethius's description of his imprisonment, he sits there in captivity lamenting his misfortune, the loss of his honors and riches, the confiscation of his library with bookshelves of glass and ivory. Suddenly a beautiful lady appears to him. She is Lady Philosophy. She comforts him by telling him that the world is governed by divine wisdom, not by blind chance, that we must not give too much importance to Fortune, for she is a fickle lady, taking away with one hand what she has given with the other. We must not become upset when she takes good things away from us; they were never ours to begin with. True happiness does not come from externals, she reminds him, but from within. True, life with its sudden falls of fortune is no easy thing. But would a good soldier fighting a tough battle stop to say to himself how unhappy he is? A wise man like Boethius ought not to bewail his struggles with fortune any more than a brave soldier should be scared by the noises of battle. Lady Philosophy reminds the prisoner of the wisdom of Socrates—that no evil can befall a good man.

Boethius wrote his book while in prison. It was published after his death and became one of the great Christian classics—*The Consolation of Philosophy.*

About four hundred years ago a Spanish officer lay in prison, a captive of the Moors of Algeria. He was a veteran of the battle of Lepanto, the last great naval fight in which ships were powered by oars. The Turks had been encroaching on the Mediterranean with the aim of seizing Cyprus from Venice. But Don John of Austria, leading the ships of Spain and the Venetian republic, destroyed the Turkish fleet in a fierce engagement from which this Spanish officer emerged a cripple. He got no glory out of it, for he was soon captured by Algerian pirates and held captive for five years with several of his comrades. At first he was profoundly depressed in his captivity but gradually discovered in himself the power of leadership, the ability to organize and to direct men. He kept his comrades busy with tasks that took their minds off their sorry condition. He organized six elaborate escape attempts, all of which failed. At last he was released and returned to his native land of Spain, where he expected the king to recognize his services. But the king and the people were tired of wars and battles; they wanted to hear no more about it. Embittered, the officer withdrew to his home and began to scribble a comic story about a witless don who fancied himself a knight-errant of old and rode all over Spain seeking to conquer giants and rescue damsels in distress. The story grew under the fingers of his one good hand, and at last it was published under the title *Don Quixote*. The officer's name was Miguel de Cervantes.

The Stoic philosopher Epictetus was foremost among my consolations in the pressure cooker of Hanoi. Like Cervantes he was a cripple. Unlike the author of *Don Quixote*, he had been a slave until a generous master set him free so that he could teach philosophy in ancient Rome. How I got to know Epictetus I explained in a letter I wrote in 1975 to Joseph Brennan, then professor of philosophy, Barnard College, Columbia University, who had written to me asking about the comfort and strength philosophical readings had given me throughout my eight years in prison. I expanded these thoughts and added to them later in an article I wrote for the *Atlantic Monthly* titled "The World of Epictetus" (April 1978). For what follows I'll draw on the letter. (The full text is in J. G. Brennan, *The Education of a Prejudiced Man*, New York, 1977.)

> I came into the navy as a Naval Academy midshipman in 1943 at the age of nineteen. For the next twenty years or so I was a rather technically oriented person. I was a seagoing destroyer officer, an aviator, a landing signal officer, a test pilot and academic instructor at the test pilot school, a many-times-deployed fighter pilot, and ultimately a squadron commander of a supersonic F-8 Crusader outfit.
>
> In 1960 I was sent to Stanford University for two years of politics/history/economics in preparation for later assignments in politico-military policy making. I grew generally indifferent to the subject matter and noticed that in many courses my interest would peak at about the time the professor would say, "We're getting into philosophy—let's get back to the subject." I had more than adequate time to get the expected master's degree and suggested to my adviser in my second year that I sign up for some courses over in the philosophy corner of the quadrangle. He was

dead set against it—thought it would be a waste of my time. He said, "That's a very technical subject—it would take two terms to learn their peculiar vocabulary." Finally, after I persisted, he said, "It's up to you."

It was my good fortune on that first morning, as I wandered through the halls of the Philosophy Department, gray-haired and in civilian clothes, to come by an open office whose occupant asked if he could be of help. When I told him that I was a graduate student technically in the humanities but with no formal philosophy background, he could scarcely believe it. When I told him I was a naval officer, he asked me to have a seat. He had been in the navy in World War II. His name was Philip Rhinelander. As a Harvard lawyer he had practiced in Boston for several years before Pearl Harbor, volunteered for war service at sea, and thereafter taken his Ph.D. at Harvard. After tours as a dean at Harvard, he was back in the classroom at his own request. He was in the midst of his two-term "personal" course: "The Problems of Good and Evil." This he had built upon the lessons of the Book of Job ("life is not fair"). He offered to let me enter the course and, to overcome my shortcomings of background, to give me an hour of private tutoring each week. What a departure from other departments! (In some, Ph.D. candidates sat outside their adviser's office for hours on end awaiting a ten-minute conversation.) I loved Rhinelander's class and particularly our hour together each week. I remember how patient he was in trying to get me to realize the full implications of Hume's "Dialogues on Natural Religion."

As we parted after our last session, he reached up to his bookshelf and said something like, "As I remember it, you are a military man—take this booklet as a memento of our hours together. It provides moral philosophy applicable to your profession." It was Epictetus's *Enchiridion*.

That night I started to peruse my gift. I recognized nothing that applied to the career I had known. I was a fighter pilot, an organizer, a motivator of young aviators, a martini drinker, a golf player, a technologist—and this ancient rag talked about not concerning oneself with matters over which one had no control, et cetera. Charitably put, I thought it irrelevant. Nevertheless I read and remembered almost all of it—if for no other reason than that it was given to me by a man I respected as a human being, a scholar, and a teacher.

About three years after I had said good-bye to Rhinelander, while in the midst of my second combat tour against North Vietnam as a wing commander, I pulled off a target one September morning in the midst of heavy flak when all the lights came on (fire warning, hydraulic failure, electrical failure, etc.). As I sped over the treetops it became immediately apparent that I had lost my flight controls—by reflex action I pulled the curtain and ejected and was almost immediately suspended in the air 200 feet above a village street, in total silence except for rifle shots and the whir of bullets past my ear. So help me, in those fleeting seconds before I landed among the waiting crowd I had two vivid thoughts: (1) Five years to wait (I had studied enough modern Far East history and talked to enough forward air controllers in the south to appreciate fully the dilemma of Vietnam—I turned out to be an optimist by two and one-half years) and (2) I am leaving that technological world and entering the world of Epictetus.

The world view of the Stoics, Professor Rhinelander had joked, was that their environment was a buzz saw in which human *will* was the only salvation. I was to spend more than four years combating a veritable buzz saw (until the torture and extortion machine was set in idle in the late autumn of 1969) and over three more years of simple deprived detention of the sort one would expect in a primitive hostile country. All told, four years were to be spent in solitary confinement, nearly half of it in leg irons. Throughout, until 1970, every effort was to be made to break my will, to make me a cat's paw in propaganda schemes. Real or fabricated "violations of the established regulations for criminals' detention" (e.g., tapping on the walls to another prisoner) would result in torture, with the end aim of sequential (1) confession of guilt, (2) begging for forgiveness, (3) apology, and (4) atonement (signing an antiwar statement). A similar sequence would be set up with *particular* gusto if I were found to be exercising leadership of others via the tap code ("inciting other criminals to oppose the camp authority").

The stress situation was thus framed in the above context. I was crippled (knee broken, partial use of arm); alone; sick (weight down 50 pounds); depressed (not so much from anticipating the next pain as from the prospect of eventually losing my honor and self-respect); and helpless except for will. What conditions could be more appropriate for Epictetus's admonitions? As a soldier, I had bound myself to a military ethic:

> *Enchiridion* 17: Remember that you are an actor in a drama of such sort as the author chooses—if short, then in a short one: if long, then in a long one. If it be his pleasure that you should enact a poor man, see that you act it well; or a cripple, or a ruler, or a private citizen. For this is your business—to act well the given part; but to choose it belongs to another.

I was crippled:

> *Enchiridion* 9: Sickness is an impediment to the body, but not to the will unless itself pleases. Lameness is an impediment to the leg, but not to the will; and say this to yourself with regard to everything that happens. For you will find it to be an impediment to something else, but not truly to yourself.

I was dependent on my extortionists for life support and soon learned to ask for nothing to avoid demands for "reciprocity":

Enchiridion 14: Whoever then would be free, let him wish nothing, let him decline nothing, which depends on others; else he must necessarily be a slave.

I could stop misery at any time by becoming a puppet; was it worth the shame?

Enchiridion 17: If some person had delivered up your body to some passerby, you would certainly be angry. And do you feel no shame in delivering up your own mind to any reviler to be disconcerted and confounded?

Relief from boils, heat, cold, broken bones was "available" for the asking—for a price. What should I say?

Enchiridion 24: If I can get them with the preservation of my own honor and fidelity and self-respect, show me the way and I will get them; but if you require me to lose my own proper good, that you may gain what is no good, consider how unreasonable and foolish you are.

Epictetus was not the only valuable philosophic memory in my predicament: Job (Why me . . . Why *not* me?), Descartes' bifurcation of mind and body, and many other readings were invaluable. Some of my prison mates had deep religious convictions that served them well, some drew resolve from their concepts of political virtue, and so on in a broad spectrum of varying levels of sophistication. I thought of God, and I thought of country, too, and that helped. But my "secret weapon" was the security I felt in anchoring my resolve to those selected portions of philosophic thought that emphasized human dignity and self-respect. Epictetus certainly taught me that.

Prison is not the only sealed-off place in which development of the spirit under pressure may occur. Any ship is a cutoff world under stress, and it is no accident that Melville's great American novel *Moby Dick* rose from the close confinement of its author in a succession of whaling and naval vessels that did not bring him back to these shores for three years. The cockpit of the plane, the command center, the chess board, the sports arena—these and other closed spaces can be the scene of creative transformation of self. In science there is the laboratory, its test tubes and crucibles; in religion, the ark and the tabernacle. I need not mention that the miraculous development of human life itself takes place in the sealed-off space of the womb.

I am not claiming that we should base education on training people to be in prison, but I am saying that in stress situations, the fundamentals, the hard-core classical subjects, are what serve best. I'm not the only prisoner who discovered that so-called practical academic exercises in "how to do things" were useless in that fix. The classics have a way of saving you the trouble of prolonged experiences. You don't have to go out and buy pop psychology self-help books. When you read the classics in the humanities, you become aware that the big ideas have been around a long time, despite the fact that they are often served up today in modern psychological "explanations" of human action as novel and "scientific." We didn't have to wait for Horney, Erikson, and Maslow to give us the notion of self-fulfillment or self-actualization. They were there in Aristotle's treatises on psychology and ethics all along. Of course, modern psychotherapists have to touch them up a bit to bring them up to date by injecting a heady dose of personal individualism. This would have puzzled Aristotle. He would not have understood what good it does to discover "the real me." He thought that self-realization could not be achieved without service to the community, in his case, the city-state. His time was not what Tom Wolfe calls a "me" generation.

Can we educate for leadership? That's a tough question. It's related to—it's really a part of—a similar question: Can moral values, can moral excellence be taught? There's a great deal of concern about that today. We hear that we must get back to teaching moral values to the young. But can they be taught? Socrates raised the question in the *Meno* and declined to give a straight answer. His pitch went something like this: It seems that moral values can't be taught, for if they could, why is it that fine men like Pericles, who have given their children the best home environment and schooling, have no-good sons? "Up to the present at least," he said, moral excellence must be considered as something we are endowed with, a gift from the gods, like personal beauty or blue eyes and curly hair. But that "up to the present" is important. Socrates does not close the door entirely on the question. Maybe if we could work out a science of the good, in which a model state based on justice will help us understand how to educate for the good, we might just do it, we might just be able to teach something about moral excellence and make it stick. So Plato follows the *Meno* with the *Republic*, in which he constructs just such a model state in which each is given his or her due. I say her advisedly because women as well as men will receive top education in Plato's ideal city-state.

Aristotle has a lot of common sense to offer on this question of the teaching of moral excellence and leadership. His answer to the question has been taken up into the Western tradition, modified by Locke in the seventeenth century and by Rousseau in the eighteenth, then shaped by our own founding fathers, particularly Thomas Jefferson, author of our Declaration of Independence. We are not born good, but we naturally are adapted to become so. And this adaptation means building character by habit and training on a basis of free choice. "Neither by nature nor contrary to nature do the moral excellences arise in us," Aristotle says, "rather we are adapted by nature to receive them, and made perfect by habit" (*Nichomachean Ethics*, 1103a 24–26).

Aristotle was much interested in the role of stress and pressure in life situations because of his profound concern with the distinction between actions that are performed in force situations and those that are freely chosen. There are some actions in which the agent plays no part, he says, and gives the examples of hostages taken prisoner and a man tied up so that he cannot move. A true human act is one in which intention and free choice are present. But he was especially interested in situations in which compulsion and choice can coexist. Even though I may be a prisoner or a hostage, some measure of freedom remains to me. In our situation in Hanoi we were helplessly *confined* and at the mercy of the enemy. Yet a crucial measure of freedom remained to us. We could collaborate with the enemy or refuse to do so. True, he had the power to make us confess to shameful things by torture. (The method was simple—arms tied behind the back and the rope progressively tightened as blood circulation was stopped until the strongest man would scream in pain like a baby.) But we still have the power to make him begin all over again the next day. Time and again one of our men would come back from interrogation ashamed because he had given up information under torture. By the tap code we'd tell him that we had done that and worse. "There are some instances," says Aristotle, "when a man acts improperly under a strain greater than human nature can bear and which no one could endure." But he adds, "Yet there are perhaps also acts which no man could possibly be compelled to do, but rather than do them he would accept the most terrible suffering and death." (*Nichomachean Ethics*, III, 1110a 23–28.) In Hanoi I realized that my captors had all the power. I couldn't see how I was going to keep my honor and self-respect intact. The one thing I held on to was my knowing that if you don't give up, compromise, and literally "spill your guts," you can't be had. Compromises pile up when you're in a pressure situation in the hands of a skilled extortionist. You can be had if you make that first compromise, offer to make that "deal," or "meet them halfway."

It may seem strange for someone with a deep commitment to the humanities in education to defend the old plebe year practices at Annapolis, the U.S. Naval Academy. That's a rough year. The midshipman is studying under great pressure, and he is constantly subjected to personal stresses that some might think of as pointless harassment. But that year of education under stress was of great personal survival value to me. About a month after I returned from Vietnam, one of my former prison mates came running to me after a reunion at the Naval Academy. He told me with glee, "This is really great, you won't believe how this country has advanced. They've practically done away with the plebe year at the academy, and they've got computers in the basement of Bancroft Hall." I thought, "Hell, if there was anything that helped us get through those eight years it was plebe year, and if anything screwed up that war, it was computers."

To me the greatest educational fallacy is that you can get it without stress. The student revolts in the colleges and universities of the 1960s forced faculty and administrators to back down, to take away requirements, to call off pressures, make things easy. No more required hard science. No more required foreign languages. "Take-home tests" and cozy chats took the place of rigorous final examinations. Students were allowed to take what they wanted. What they wanted was social science, urban development, psychology. What they didn't want was history, mathematics, physics, formal logic, classics, and modern foreign languages. Any reform demanded and secured was always in the direction of easing pressure, lowering standards, diminishing rigor—never increasing it. Result? More than a decade of poorly educated young men and women. In response to the economic pressures of the 1970s, the faculty knuckle-under process has begun to turn around. But it will take a lot of turning before education gets back on the rails.

There is a fascinating essay by Dr. Walter Ong in *Daedalus* magazine titled "Agonistic Structures in Academia" (*Daedalus*, no. 4, fall 1974). His purpose is to offer background material that would help educators analyze the campus struggles of the 1960s. One of the most important factors involved, says Ong, is the disappearance of a stabilizing stressful enmity that for sixteen hundred years had pitted students against teachers in ceremonial combat. Ong quotes an old German who in the late 1960s was teaching in a public high school in New York. After a trying day in class, he was heard to exclaim, "Ach, these boys want me to be their friend; they should know that the teacher should always be their enemy."

Until recent decades, ceremonial combat in the educational process had been part of Western culture. The student-teacher face-off had been standard since the early stages of the Christian era. Saint Augustine described the standoff methodology in his *Confessions*. Dialectic—the struggle of opposites—was the standard method of education in the universities of the high Middle Ages and the Renaissance.

Dr. Ong describes these agonistic structures as composed of four elements. The first was that of oral disputation. Students recited; they seldom wrote papers. They stood and defended their theses in loud clear voices, or they attacked the school solutions. The professor was the sounding board, the sparring partner, and in the end the judge with authority who awarded the palm of praise or delivered the knockout blow. It was a dialectical process of argumentation through opposites, a ritual by which students learned subjects by fighting over them.

A second element was invariably a harsh physical regime. Classes started in darkness at 6 A.M. or before. The rules of behavior were strict. (Has anyone ever seen a schoolmaster portrayed in Renaissance art without his trusty bundle of switches at his side?) A third element of this agonistic structure was the pressure of constant translation; all this oral disputation was conducted in the tribal language of intellectuals, Latin, the language of doctors and lawyers and metaphysicians. This language requirement in itself imposed a discipline, a structure, and a stressful learning situation. Ong says that the achievement of learning Latin, that tightly disciplined language, well enough to argue in it—indeed to defend one's academic reputation in it— became a sort of puberty rite for the Western-educated male in almost every century of this Christian era save our own. The fourth element was the all-male character of this educational operation. Ong says that coeducation was incompatible with any of the elements above. I suppose that might be challenged by some educators today, but I am encouraged when I remember that today most advanced feminists will defend the viability of the single-sex college, male or female. Ong's position seems reasonable to me when he argues that the agonistic style took shape in response to uniquely masculine needs.

The agonistic way, including tests of manhood, has all but passed from the modern scene. But for what it's worth, as viewed by one who has presided over a single-sex institution where rites of passage are still observed, the self-imposed stress of a structured, disciplined, semiautonomous student hierarchy yields many good results. Education there becomes an irreversible process that equips its graduates with certain items of what some would call emotional baggage. Picked up along the way are concerns with loyalty, with commitment, a capacity for passion, for idealism. Such a stressful educational environment spurs a growth of conscience and also of salutary egoism.

Jacob Burckhardt, the nineteenth-century Swiss historian, thought well of "that enigmatic mixture of conscience and egoism" he called honor. Although from many standpoints egoism is an impurity, and conscience alone would be nobler, he nevertheless acknowledged the utility and power of the blend. Egoism gives conscience staying power.

"Honor," writes Burckhardt, "is often what remains after faith, love, and hope are lost" (*The Civilization of the Renaissance in Italy*, London, 1929, p. 428).

From my own experience, I think he's right. A sense of honor under pressure can outlast them all.

PRISONER OF WAR

1982

MY "WORLD OF EPICTETUS," I soon learned, was a world in which chivalry, if it ever existed, was dead. I entered a physical world, and I got the hell knocked out of me from the moment my feet hit the ground. The world of Epictetus was also a hard-nose, political world. I had my leg broken in the street by a mob just after I landed. My leg was either going to get medical aid or remain rigid and deformed for the rest of my life. After some weeks in prison the man in charge of the prison camps took note of my refusal to make a statement critical of the United States and set me straight on priorities. "You have a medical problem and a political problem. Politics come before medicine in the DRV (Democratic Republic of Vietnam). You fix the political problem in your head first, and then we'll see the doctors." The leg was never fixed.

I'll never forget my Christmas Day conversation with that same senior Vietnamese officer three months after I had been shot down in September 1965. He said, "You are my age, you and I share the military profession, and we have sons the same age, but there is a wall between us. The wall is there because we come from different social and political systems. But you and I must try to see through that wall and together bring this imperialist war of American aggression to an end. We know how to do this, but you must help me, you must influence the other American prisoners. Through propaganda (not a 'bad word' in communist circles), we will win the war on the streets of New York. All I ask is that you be reasonable. You will help me. You don't know it yet, but you will."

A week later I heard the church bells of Hanoi ring in the New Year 1966 at midnight. I was shivering without a blanket, legs in stocks, hands in cuffs, lying in three days of my own excrement. That was only the beginning. I became immersed in a system of isolation, of extortion, of torture, of silence. Any American who from his solitary cell was caught communicating with another American, by wall tap, by whisper, you name it, was put back in the meat grinder to go from torture to submission to

Reprinted with permission from the Fall 1982 issue of the *American Educator*, the quarterly journal of the American Federation of Teachers.

confession to apology to atonement. That was a hard life, but I'm proud to say that torture became about the only route to propaganda for them because we met the challenge by communicating and taking the lumps, by organizing, by resisting in unison, by giving them nothing free, making them hurt us before we gave an inch, by fighting "city hall."

LEADERSHIP IN
TIMES OF CRISIS

1984

SEVERAL YEARS AGO I found myself cooling my heels in the offices of NBC television in New York, waiting for a stage to be set up for the filming of a public service talk show in which I had been invited to participate. I had arrived several mintutes early, and an accommodating receptionist suggested that I might enjoy visiting with one of the NBC executives while I waited. Agreeing, I was escorted into a magnificent suite and on into the larger inner office, where a dozen TV screens were embedded in the wall, all videos on, all sound off. The suite's sophisticated master was standing behind his large desk, arms folded, keeping an eye on the television world so to speak, ready to turn up any audio should something catch his eye. He was not of my generation; he was a younger man with a modish haircut and a turtleneck sweater under an expensive sport coat. I sighed to myself, "Here's fifteen minutes shot."

Not so. The man stuck out a friendly hand and said, "I'm Lester Crystall, president of NBC News." (Our acquaintance continues; in March 1983 Crystall stepped down from the NBC post to become executive producer of the *MacNeil/Lehrer NewsHour*, a post he still holds in 1995.) My navy uniform gave him a lead-in for the opening of an impromptu conversation neither of us had anticipated: "Do you think the navy is being well served by the national news media?" Startled, I muttered something agreeable, then immediately regretted that I had missed a golden opportunity to get on a soapbox.

"Well let me tell you," Crystall was already saying, "I think that in an important way, the television news industry is doing the whole country a continuing disservice. We constantly reinforce a bad idea that we helped invent—the idea that the key to being a good citizen, a discerning voter, is to know where all the candidates stand on all the *issues*. The issues are given the center of the stage, and the politician is cast as their suitor. We have made the expression 'so much for philosophy, let's get down to issues' a maxim of conventional wisdom. And at news time every evening, all networks project scenes of harassed men and women being nailed down by stubborn interviewers who insist on quick answers on where their victims stand on gun control, abortion, and so on and so on. It's as though the merits of a political leader are known only if he is first carved up into twenty or thirty sections, each representing his ten-second position on every news item of the day, and then his being reassembled and analyzed as a composite whole, as a 'Mr. Blockhead' build-it-yourself educational toy. Because this fractionation and reassembly of a candidate lends itself to simplified, marketable news theater, we have taught a nation to analyze people in this very shallow way."

Crystall continued. "What's important is not a person's current views on transient issue, but his *character*. Thinking back, I have seldom been surprised at a position held or action taken by a political figure. Once his true character is grasped, his policies and actions are almost always predictable fallouts. To test this idea, I went back and studied the Lincoln-Douglas debates in detail. And let me tell you, Douglas was all issues. He pandered to the mob on every little issue of 1858—and had our current style of television coverage prevailed in those pre–Civil War years, we would have made him the darling of America. We could have got him elected and the country ruined in one simple operation. Abraham Lincoln on the other hand was weak on some issues and indifferent about quite a few others. But you can't read the speeches he wrote and not get the message that he was all character. It comes through, even amid his somewhat off-color jokes."

About that time I was summoned to go down to a stage to be filmed discussing Shakespeare's famous soliloquy in *As You Like It*, "All the world's a stage," with Lynn Redgrave, General Andrew Goodpaster, and a couple of his West Point cadets. (What did we think of Shakespeare's characterization of a soldier: "full of strange oaths . . . jealous in honor, sudden and quick in quarrel"?)[1]

But I never forgot those words with Crystall—though it's hard to reconstruct his list of examples of hot issues of that day years ago, issues that made or broke candidates in the 1976 elections. Today the list is completely different—nuclear freeze, Central America, draft registration. In a year from now the list will again be different. And yet it will be a big deal when put to candidates who will serve in office in 1985–1989 terms—terms in which the main issues to be faced will not even have surfaced by the time of their election.

Isn't Crystall right that *character* is what counts in leadership? Character is probably more important than knowledge. It was so in the case of Lincoln. Of course, all things being equal, knowledge is to be honored. People who at the drop of a hat can give the last word on "the U.S. and the third world," "the U.S. and the world economy," "the U.S. and the Soviet Union" are valuable and sometimes good candidates for leadership roles. But what I'm saying is that whenever I've been in trouble spots—in crises (and I've been in a lot of trouble and in a lot of crises)—the sine qua non of a leader has lain not in his chesslike grasp of issues and the options they portend, not in his style of management, not in his skill at processing information, but in his having the character, the heart, to deal spontaneously, honorably, and candidly with people, perplexities, and principles.

But discussions of ideas like character and heart have to be well ordered lest they slide into flabby generalities like strong character, weak character, good hearts, soft hearts, and all the rest. To avoid that quagmire of rhetorical fuzziness, I'm going to delineate the personality traits of several common types of American public figures, then bang such traits against a worst-case crisis predicament, and finally have a look at how they fare under the gun. The method, like that of the old alchemists, is to base judgment only on the outcome of tests conducted over a hot fire, to draw conclusions only after you have brought out with heat and pressure the *essence* of what's being tested. To isolate essences, I will evaluate typical sets of character traits while exposed to obligations of leadership under the greatest heats and pressures I know—those demanding the generation and maintenance of that moral ascendancy indispensable to nurturing others to prevail with pride under the guns of an extortionist political prison.

I am affiliated with Harvard psychoanalyst Michael Maccoby in an organization called the American Leadership Forum. A few years ago he wrote a popular book entitled *The Gamesman* based on considerable data he had acquired in a study of how new technology was affecting society. Much of this data came from in-depth interviews with 250 top-level business executives, commencing in 1969 in a project called Technology, Work, and Character. With a lot of historical background, Maccoby set down four sets of character traits, each set being commonly found in one of four types of leaders who at least until 1976 had historically run America. We all know many examples of each of the four types in our midst right now—they've always been around. But by a kind of economic determinism, each of these archetypes had his day in leadership limelight roles in particular historical periods. Maccoby named these the Craftsman, the Jungle Fighter, the Company Man, and the Gamesman. I'm going to use these models up to the point where I develop a "fifth man," whose time has now come.

Ben Franklin is Maccoby's prototype of the craftsman, and craftsmen prevailed as the leaders of American society from the Revolution until the national banking and credit system emerged soon after the Civil War. This character type is self-contained, inventive, thrifty, resolute, sincere. But Maccoby doesn't play with plaster saints. Craftsmen, like all men, typically have certain negative traits: they are generally obstinate and suspicious and, expecting no favors or handouts from anybody, are often given to hoarding and stinginess. Their motto is "God helps those who help themselves." You know them today as people like Hyman Rickover and Jimmy Carter.

But Benjamin Franklin's type gave up center stage as the Industrial Revolution enveloped America after the Civil War. It was Andrew Carnegie and his jungle fighters who then became the prime movers of our country. But whereas the craftsman is *not* a game player, not a man who devotes his energies to one-on-one competition but rather to mountain climbing, to pitting himself against the world as he strives for self-improvement, jungle fighters *do* play games. They play zero-sum games—the winnings and losses at the table always adding up to zero. The jungle fighter sees his universe as having a finite amount of business out there, and he strives to get his share— sometimes more. He is tough but, like the craftsman, is also a man of conscience and heart—not the soft heart, certainly not the bleeding heart, but the Old Testament heart (about which more later). He works for himself, for his company, and frequently for his community and country. He can sit at a board table and figuratively decapitate incompetents with ease. But he looks them in the eye as he does it. And he can grieve for them as he sends them on their way. He is bold; he is paternalistic (like old Henry Ford, like old Tom Watson); he is authoritarian; he is intensely competitive.

After World War I, when public relations images and agencies became a fact of life, the jungle fighters' industries, railroads, and banks became more like government bureaucracies than the freewheeling entrepreneurial enterprises they had formerly been. And those tough old competitors themselves were gradually displaced by the less abrasive "company men." Like the jungle fighters, the company men were paternalistic and authoritarian. But unlike those pioneers of industry and finance who were motivated primarily by competitive zeal, these company men, our psychoanalyst believes, were more typically motivated by a fear of failure. Maybe the country sensed that; popular authors pictured them as just warmed-over jungle fighters lacking even the prime virtue of their predecessors—guts. (During the 1950s *The Man in the Gray Flannel Suit* and *The Organization Man* sold very well.) But their most recent progeny (Eisenhower, Jerry Ford) were characteristically honest and cautious men of conscience. They looked men in the eye when they fired them. They were "men of the heart," possessing qualities with an emotional content: a sense of commitment, a sense of loyalty, a sense of humor, spontaneity, and intellectual honesty at the gut level.

In the early 1960s, a fourth leadership style emerged. John F. Kennedy and his whiz kids took center stage explaining that we had made this whole business of running a country too hard. Maccoby identifies practitioners of this style as "the gamesmen." The gamesmen, impatient under the yoke of their paternalistic and authoritarian fathers, and educated more often than not in the game-theory-oriented elite business schools in the country, turned over a new page in leadership practices. The gamesmen believe that if one properly analyzes the "game" of life, the "game" of management, the "game" of leadership, one sees that it is not necessary to frame the problem as a zero-sum game. Rather, in their minds, American life can be analyzed as just one big game in which any number can play and win. "Join the meritocracy!" "On to the moon!" "On to Vietnam!"

Now, these gamesmen were relaxed, objective, open-minded, detached, and cerebral. Such emotional baggage as commitment or conscience they deemed unnecessary, inefficient, and overweight. "Play your cards rationally to win, drop the emotional baggage, and go to bed and sleep like a baby without remorse." Some bothered with love and families; many gave them a tentative try and quit when they found them too burdensome, too hard to deal with close up. Maccoby said that there was a theatrical production that typified the leaders of each of these four American eras and that the drama of the time of the gamesmen was portrayed in the movie *The Sting*. You might remember that screenplay; in it, fair, competitive, cooperative swingers, with the aid of teamwork and technology, destroyed the emotional, hung-up, authoritarian Godfather.

The gamesmen, concluded psychoanalyst Maccoby, were basically "men of the head": cool intellectual types, walking calculating machines. Men of the head do many things well, but they usually have trouble coping with unpleasantness. Having confrontations is such a close-up thing, and it's so uncomfortable, so personal, so creepy to have to actually look at emotional faces while you talk to people. These cool, flexible, accommodating guys don't like to discipline people, and they don't like to look people in the eye when they fire them. (It's so much cleaner and easier just to reorganize and eliminate their jobs—"Sorry about that.") Moreover, the typical gamesman craves to be admired, can't stand not to be loved, and that is a great leadership weakness. True leaders must be willing to stake out territory and identify and declare enemies. They must be fair and they may be compassionate, but they cannot be addicted to being loved by everybody. The man who needs to be loved is an extortionist's dream. That man will do anything to avoid face-to-face unpleasantness; he will sell his soul down the river for praise. He can be had.

And the gamesman can have *you*, too, if you are at his bidding and get caught out on the point when he confronts the unexpected, is threatened with facing unpleasantness, and gets cold feet. Although these gamesmen sail under the banner of compassion and benevolence, by being unable to face up to unpleasantness they pull the rug out from under law and tradition and affront the sense of fairness that good men intuitively possess. I digress with a few true stories about how modern political leaders, seeking public adulation, pulled the rug out from under some good men left out on the point.

I used to keep a list of all the American government's own violations of that Code of Conduct that that government's presiding gamesmen sent us military aviators off to war, bound to uphold. The gamesmen inherited that code. It was old and it was good; it set forth rules befitting honorable conduct of men in battle and in prisoner-of-war camps. During the early 1960s, as these gamesmen were positioning the country to enter the fighting in Vietnam, we were continually admonished to take that code seriously and prepare ourselves to uphold its demands. (Just before the Tonkin Gulf events of August 1964, I remember reading a particularly strong admonition signed by Cyrus Vance demanding "a positive and unswerving acceptance of, belief in, and devotion to the spirit and letter of the Code of Conduct, and the recognition that the code is a binding military obligation.")[2]

You can imagine the dismay of those of us who were shot down in enemy territory and then spent seven or eight years and no small amount of blood, sweat, and tears upholding that code in Hanoi prisons, out of touch with America, hanging in no matter how tough the going got, to come home and find that stringent codes had long been ignored back in America itself. Rather than obey its own laws, our government had avoided unpleasant confrontations by opportunistically putting all that honor and discipline stuff on the back burner.

For instance, the code specifically prohibits the making of false confessions. Some in Hanoi prisons gave their lives to avoid it. But our gamesmen dropped that obligation like a hot potato when the North Koreans demanded that our government make a false confession, a public false confession in the name of our president no less, as a quid pro quo for the release of USS *Pueblo* prisoners who had been held for less than a year. Our morale would have hit rock bottom if we had been permitted to read the front page of the *New York Times*, December 23, 1968: "The United States Government has deliberately signed what it terms a false confession of espionage inside North Korean territorial waters. . . . Secretary of State Dean Rusk said tonight that lengthy negotiation had turned up no other way. . . . 'I know of no precedent in my 19 years of public service,' Mr. Rusk said." According to the text of the statement issued by President Johnson, our negotiator "preserved the integrity of the United States." The *Pueblo* had *not* been inside North Korean territorial waters before it was captured.[3]

The code prohibits the acceptance of parole—the trading of a concession for freedom. (The concession demanded in North Vietnam was the making of treasonous statements.) We senior officers in Hanoi prisons forbade American prisoners to accept this sort of freedom. They stayed in jail, willingly and pridefully stayed in jail in accordance with our orders, our laws, which we derived from the code. Yet when the few who violated our orders and bought their way home with those treasonous statements showed up in

America, the gamesmen greeted them with open arms, made no charges, and even neglected to extend the statute of limitations so that we whose sense of decency they had offended by their conduct might present our case in court against them when we returned.

As a matter of fact, the responsibility for the discipline of all prison informers and collaborators was abdicated by our government and dumped in the laps of those of us who wrote and enforced the American laws of those prisons. Our government leaders, avoiding unpleasantness, would bring no charges even though their own lawyers (judge advocates) certified that our evidence was complete and sufficient. The cases were few, but those that were on the docket were serious and by being ignored left dangerous precedents. This is a matter of continuing interest and concern to those of us who were involved; there is a good deal more about these matters that belongs in the public domain.

Of course we were all encouraged to look on all these matters as our national leadership's commonsense response to unprecedented circumstances. But "unprecedented circumstances" has become a code word for the cop-out of authority, a code word for a politician's license to steal. By invoking that empty phrase, gutless leaders make exceptions to law, custom, and morality in their own favor on the grounds that the world is becoming new and different. Who's kidding whom? Such an "all previous bets are off" attitude undermines institutions. One man's exception is another man's betrayal.

And so it was in these cases so familiar to me that what was touted as benevolent forgiveness of the "suffering prisoners of war" was a thinly veiled case of a government's lack of moral courage under pressure. This was met by the vast majority of returning prisoners of war—certainly by all those who served most bravely in Hanoi—with an enraged demand that the score, the score of misery and pride under whose banner they had fought versus the score of self-serving pusillanimity that they held in contempt, be publicly settled. If the government had no belly for unpleasantness, hundreds of these returned prisoners of war demanded that private charges be brought to set the record straight for future wars. It was my constituency who demanded this justice and thus my duty to serve the charges. For the first six months after I limped out of prison, I spent ten hours a day trying to satisfy that demand, performing that duty. The faceless government bureaucracy was willing to supply massive investigative and legal support, even prepare the legal charges, but of course they insisted that I sign them as a private citizen. Meanwhile they remained on the sidelines, shoulders in the hunched position, palms up, smiling quizzically, while the press treated the affair not as the ex-prisoners' groundswell attempt to set correct precedents for the next war but as a simple grudge fight between individuals.

Leadership of that sort—"nice guy," detached, open, evasive, emotionally neutral, a legacy of those "men of the head"—is still de rigueur in too many high places. Never mind that it leaves it to the cop on the beat to take the gas and then to read the hate mail. Such leadership comes from people who are not able to experience reality, to deal with fear, guilt, and truth. And that kind of leader will never do if our institutions are to survive. When the going *really* gets tough, the people will read him for what he is, a threat to those institutions, and just calmly disregard him and walk away.

What, then, of "men of the heart," men having Old Testament qualities of heart, the qualities of heart Islam's philosopher Ibn Khaldun attributed to it, the qualities of heart the ancient Greek philosophers attributed to it? That heart was the center of wisdom, the shock absorber of guilt, the source of courage. (Courage comes from the latin *cor*, the French *coeur*; under "courage" Webster's says, "the heart as the seat of intelligence or of feeling.") The pre-Socratic Heraclitus said the development of the heart has to do with the capacity to face and experience reality. The capacity for that experience is also the capacity for courage. The heart wills, it is the seat of conscience, it introduces *purpose*. The heart is not a neutral processor of data.

In that same age-old sense, the head *is* neutral about knowledge. Ibn Kahldun wrote that no amount of knowledge of the head by itself can give a sense of what is good, what is true, or what is beautiful.

Solomon said to the Lord in a dream: "Give therefore thy servant an understanding heart to judge thy people, that I may discern between good and bad." And the Lord replied: "Lo, I have given thee a wise and an understanding heart; so that there was none like thee before thee, neither after thee shall any arise like unto thee."[4] It is not enough that a crisis leader be rational, flexible, open-minded, and cool under stress; without those hearty qualities with an emotional content—spontaneity, compassion, sense of humor, loyalty—he rings hollow.

No one can develop a strong heart, a hard heart, if he is not capable of experiencing the pain of guilt, of admitting to himself that he has acted in a way that has been harmful to others, of being able to repent, and of being able to stand the full experience of reality. The prophets have told us that it is only the hard heart that can properly repent. If we have leaders who have not developed hard hearts, leaders who cannot face up to guilt and use it as a cleansing fire, we are under the sway of people who cannot act on hard truth and real experience, and believe me, they are a hazard to navigation.

Simple "nice guys"—soft and friendly and always assuring everybody that they feel it "way down here" for the little folks—were hazards to navigation where my data came from. And of course those data came from that very confined, pressurized, intensely heated laboratory-like cauldron of personality distillation—the extortionist prison where, as in the hermetically sealed retorts of the alchemists, essence and change are highlighted, accentuated, and observed on a faster-than-life time base.

There is no way our government, let alone a university, could afford a leadership laboratory like that. You would need a score of human subjects—all of high intelligence, nearly identical in cultural backgrounds, all being well educated (in our case, thirty- to forty-five-year-old males, all aviators with college degrees and most with advanced degrees from good universities)—all facing a common danger of the most destabilizng sort, that is, the destruction of their personal reputations. Such threat of destruction would be backed up by a force of skilled tourniquet-wielding maulers with unlimited rights of torture—all subjects first undergoing about a two-year solitary confinement, a "softening up" period before the experiment proper started, then each subject being locked in a concrete box ten feet by four feet, in leg irons, able to communicate only by clandestine wall taps.

At that point the subjects' group project would be assigned: to establish and maintain a prison society that breeds unity, pride, mutual trust and confidence, and high-mindedness. The idea of the experiment would be to collect data over a two- or three-year period, data that would provide insight into the nature of leadership in times of crisis and allow the pinpointing of leadership character traits that succeed or fail in crisis circumstances.

Clearly soft hearts will not do. A crisis leader must be able to handle fear. A crisis leader must be able to handle guilt. A person is thrown into a political prison either to have his mind changed or to be used or both. People with experience know that the tools of the trade in an extortion operation are only secondarily the infliction of pain and the condemning of people to months of isolation; those are just catalysts for the one-two punch that lies within all effective systems of compulsion—the one-two punches of fear and guilt. That fact has been part of the wisdom of the ages. In the second century, the Stoic Epictetus was lecturing in the area of Epirus on the eastern shore of the southern Adriatic: "For it were better to die of hunger, exempt from fear and guilt, than to live in affluence and with perturbation."[5] Eighteen hundred years later, Carl Jung, Swiss protégé of Sigmund Freud, was describing the process as destabilizing victims with fear and then polarizing them with guilt. He who would prevail when these forces are set upon him must handle that fear and guilt or die or—worse—collaborate.[6]

In Hanoi, the inducement of fear was not subtle. Physical abuse to the point of unconsciousness was commonplace. But what haunted the prisoner was not pain but the threat of disgrace. One learned that the maintenance of *moral* authority was crucial to minimizing an interrogator's gains in the eyeball-to-eyeball, hour-after-hour, one-on-one sessions. You learned that to keep from being had you had to develop a private reservoir of willpower, spirit, and moral ascendancy from which you secretly drew solace when the going got tough. That reservoir had to be yours alone, with no access ever given to foe or friend. It was a trinity: you, where you lived, your power source. From it you had to generate a personality that kept all outward signs of fear or guilt obliterated, contained within you where you could deal with them properly, alone. (I used to perform a ritualistic chant under my breath as I was marched to the interrogation room with a bayonet pricking the middle of my back: "Show no fear, show no fear; don't let your eyes show fear.") To handle fear, you had to become a sort of knight of selfhood, as playwright Robert Bolt described Sir Thomas More in his play *A Man for All Seasons*: "Thomas More, as I wrote about him, became for me a man with an adamantine sense of his own self. He knew where he began and where he left off, what area of himself he could yield to the encroachments of his enemies, and what area to the encroachments of those he loved."[7]

The handling of guilt was generally a more formidable problem. Of course I'm *not* talking about guilt vis-à-vis our military duties in the war; that problem did not exist. Of course the North Vietnamese took a crack at trying to make such feelings exist. From the very first we were tortured to follow their script of our being remorseful for having bombed their "schools, churches, and pagodas." But that sort of statement was so patently unreal and so ludicrous that it left no psychic scars on the way through us. True debilitating guilt has to be based on reality, and the big reality in Hanoi on the guilt score was that many of the American prisoners there had been needlessly shot down while following Washington-issued, lock-step operation orders dictated by politicos who had grown more concerned about creating a national image of compassion than saving American airplanes and lives. We had no feelings of owing any Vietnamese remorse. My friend and prison mate Jim Kasler was a Korean War fighter ace against the MiGs at the Yalu and veteran of scores of bombing missions in North Vietnam. He described the maneuvering restrictions put on him as leader of the war's first raid against Hanoi's oil storage tanks in an article in the *Air University Review*:

> The operations order had also directed that all attacks would be executed on a south-to-north heading to preclude tossing a hung bomb into the city of Hanoi. Approaching from the north, we [Kasler was leading a flight of sixteen supersonic Thunderchief fighter-bombers] had to make a 180-degree pop-up maneuver to strike the target as ordered. What the attack order meant was that every aircraft would be rolling into the bomb run at the same spot, heading in the same direction. Not too smart from the pilot's viewpoint, but in the interest of protecting civilian populations such orders were commonplace in Vietnam. (Ideally, attacks should be on

divergent headings to confuse the gunners and thus prevent them from zeroing in on one spot.)[8]

Our feelings of guilt were not about what we did to the Vietnamese but about what they were forcing us prisoners to do to each other through torture—their shutting off the blood circulation in our arms and beating us while our heads were stuffed into suffocating, claustrophobia-inducing positions until we "submitted" and gave the names of cocommunicators, the duties of specific camp mates in the clandestine underground American prisoner organization, and so on. Like as not, as soon as this material was extracted, we involuntary informers were whisked out immediately and isolated in a separate location where we would eat our hearts out in solitude in the months that followed—cursing our inabilities to stand more pain, feeling remorse for the harm we were sure was being visited on those most precious beings in our lives, our friends back in the cell block from whence we had come.

This feeling of rottenness was made all the worse by the degrading dictatorship-of-the-proletariat rules of procedure in those dungeons. An American had to bow at the waist ninety degrees whenever meeting any Vietnamese guard or officer. He could never look at the sky but always had to keep his eyes cast toward the ground. When brought to interrogation, he was to take the inferior position—on the floor if the interrogator was in a chair and so on. All in all it was designed as a guilt-inducing and debilitating environment, against which one had to work at the very point in time when one was trying desperately to muster courage and keep his spirits up.

In that make-or-break situation, one learns that there are two self-destructive routes to degradation: to become consumed by guilt on the one hand or to practice self-delusion and deny its existence on the other. To become consumed is to lose all willpower; when you feel yourself sinking into that funk, you have to force yourself to pull out of the slump by emphasizing the reality of the situation: "After all, I *was* tortured." But that reality can be exaggerated into fantasy and followed over another cliff: when you start denying *any* personal responsibility, you are on another mud slide to self-destruction. In that case, you know in your heart of hearts that you could have done better, and you know that there is no one magic point in time when you are suddenly transformed from a person of free will to a blameless victim of outside compulsion. Would that life were so simple; we all spend our most important hours in that ambiguous zone, part volition, part compulsion. (It was none other than Aristotle who told us that compulsion and free will can coexist.) Honest men in prison know that there is no such thing as "brainwashing" or "breaking." These expressions of self-delusion never find use behind bars. They are just unfortuante metaphors that allow people outside prisons to be less uncomfortable in discussing human limitations.

To either hide from guilt or let it consume you is a gamesmanlike escape route from the truth—and he who cannot bite the bullet and use that guilt for its intended purpose, as a searing fire to cauterize the wound, as a goad to better resistance next time, is doomed. He who cannot cope with reality himself is certainly lacking the heart to lead others through crises.

In times of crisis the wise and courageous handling of the twin fires of fear and guilt has historically been one of mankind's greatest challenges. All too many who can't face up to dealing with them forthrightly have discovered the cheapest escape route of modern times: jump on the bandwagon of a social determinism that holds that all men are victims of their environment, that moral decay is the natural product of hardship. In that world everybody escapes responsibility for his actions, and guilt not only ceases to be a problem, it becomes an ornament of the chic affectation. (Many of these social determinists delude themselves into ascribing nobility to feeling guilty about having power or wealth.) The notion that human beings are always victims of their circumstances is an affront to those bold spirits who throughout history have spent their lives prevailing over adversity.[9]

In my data bank, the facts show that the more the degradation, the more the pain, the more the humiliation, the more the human spirit was challenged, the better it performed. A sense of selfless unity, a nobility of that spirit that seemed to run counter to conventional views on survival instincts grew up among us. It became commonplace for one man to risk greatly to save another. I don't believe it *always* happens that way. There are stories of those in crisis who savagely turn against each other—all against all. Whether the best or the worst in men emerges as they face crises together swings on the quality of leadership available to them.

I say "leadership available to them" because people in true crises usually beg for leadership—seldom is it a case of some authoritarian master imposing it on them. Although conventional wisdom has it that the human condition is optimized when each individual has a maximum of autonomy, when true crisis prevails, when life really gets chaotic, when the dividing line between good and evil ceases to be clear-cut, when no consensus exists as to what is the right and what is the wrong thing to do, people demand to be led, regimented, and guided. The neophyte senior spending his first month in a cell block, grasping after a fashion the great dilemmas of human choice on every hand, typically launched his career of giving prison orders by whispering under his door something like, "In this situation where we're being forced to do things against our will, all I can ask is that you do what you think best." About two days later, said senior would be accosted by juniors with outrage: "You have no right to dump these decisions in our individual laps; we deserve to live in a sensible society in which we have some idea about what is considered unavoidable and what is considered totally repugnant. Tell us just exactly what specific enemy demands you want us to refuse and take torture for. It is not fair for you to proclaim that all should try to do good; you owe it to us to set down rules of behavior and tell us just exactly what the good is."

Anyone who has lived in a severe extortion environment realizes that the foremost weapon of the adversary is his manipulation of his victim's shame. If when the people call for a leader in extremes, a guilt-ridden wimp (one who manufactures guilt for which there is no way to atone) takes the seat of authority, they are doomed. Only if a man with a hard heart answers is there hope.

This "fifth man," this hardhearted leader who can deal with fear, guilt, truth, and reality, is one who would come across in the prison society as a moralist. I do not mean a mere poseur, one who sententiously exhorts his followers to be good. I mean one who has the wisdom, the courage, indeed the audacity, to elucidate just what, under the circumstances, the good *is*. This requires a clear perception of right and wrong and the integrity to stand behind one's assessment, to persevere when the going gets tough.

In 1940, as the British were being crowded toward Dunkerque, the seaport in the far north of France, a message was received in London from a certain element of those British forces about to be involved in the long-shot mass evacuation attempt. The message was made up of just three words: *But If Not*. A sharp-eyed biblical scholar saw it immediately as a quotation of the three key words in a scripture story of ultimate commitment. The words were lifted from the Book of Daniel, chapter 3, where the conceited and domineering King Nebuchadnezzar was laying down the law to Shadrach, Meshach, and Abednego: either serve Nebuchadnezzar's god and worship the golden image he had set up or get thrust into the fiery furnace.

The king gave the three a chance to think it over, and they answered as follows:

> O Nebuchadnezzar, we have no need to answer you in this matter. If it be so, our God whom we serve is able to deliver us from the burning fiery furnace; and he will deliver us out of your hand, O king. *But if not*, be it known to you, O king, that we will not serve your gods or worship the golden image which you have set up.[10]

What is needed in times of crisis are leaders with the character to stand up like Shadrach, Meshach, and Abednego when challenged. These are people with Old Testament hard hearts who can deliver the ultimate stultification and turn the Nebuchadnezzars of the world around:

> Mr. Nebuchadnezzar, we've thought your proposition over, like you said. We've decided on the furnace.

NOTES

1. William Shakespeare, *As You Like It*, act 2, sc. 7, lines 150–51.

2. Quoted from Paragraph B. (2) of *Department of Defense Directive*, 1300.7, July 8, 1964.

3. F. Carl Schumacher Jr. and George C. Wilson, *Bridge of No Return: The Ordeal of the USS Pueblo* (New York: Harcourt Brace Jovanovich, 1971), p. 86.

4. I Kings 3:9, 12 (King James version).

5. Epictetus, *The Enchiridion*, trans. Thomas W. Higginson (Indianapolis, Ind.: Bobbs-Merrill Educational Publishing, 1955), p. 21.

6. C. G. Jung, *Psychology and Alchemy*, vol. 12, 2d. ed. (Princeton, N.J.: Princeton University Press, 1968).

7. Robert Bolt, *A Man for All Seasons* (London: Heinemann, 1961), preface, p. xii.

8. *Air University Review* (Montgomery, Ala.), November–December 1974.

9. In April 1983, the FBI reported that in 1982, the worst year of the recession, national crime declined by 4 percent—the steepest decline in five years (see R. Emmett Tyrrell Jr., "The Continuing Crisis," *American Spectator*, June 1983, p. 4).

10. Daniel 3:16–18 (revised standard version).

TRIAL BY FIRE

1985

In time of peril, like the needle
to the lodestone, obedience, irrespective
of rank, generally flies to him
who is best fitted to command.
—Herman Melville, 1850

LET ME TELL you something about myself.

In 1960, I was a U.S. Navy lieutenant commander, a fighter pilot just off carrier duty, when I started the most important years of study of my life, at Stanford and at the Hoover Institution. I studied the humanities in a postgraduate program paid for by the government.

Within three years after I left Stanford, I had been shot down over North Vietnam, imprisoned in an old French dungeon in Hanoi, and become one of the first heads of government of a covertly organized colony of American prisoners of war—a colony destined to remain autonomous for nearly eight years.

During this period I thanked God for those twenty-four months of history, politics, and philosophy at Stanford and Hoover. And I was grateful, too, for the practical lessons in leadership at sea I had had up to that time.

In that atmosphere of death and hopelessness, stripped of the niceties, the amenities of civilization, my ideas on life and leadership crystallized. I returned home with a simple, almost sparse concept of what qualities a leader should have. *And I believe with utmost conviction that these traits are right.*

A CRISIS LEADER

I would like to share my views with you. But let me make one point first. I think these criteria are important because our changing times demand the kind of person who can lead in troubled times. Down the road, locating these individuals will be crucial to the welfare of all sectors of our society.

I'm not talking about our "nominal" leaders who may look the part, who say the right things, who indeed may be the right people in calm waters. I'm talking about the leaders who, to use Melville's phrase, "in time of peril" come out of nowhere to control the flow of events: the businessman who rises to the top to keep a company afloat during a depression; the warrior who takes command of a decimated battalion, rallies its spirit, and makes it whole again; the mayor who gets the bankrupt city back on its feet.

Frequently, these are not the people the public was acclaiming before the fire started. These are the *natural* leaders to whom others instinctively turn in times of crisis, who become the leaders through trial by fire.

What are the true qualities we're looking for? Let me examine just five.

Must Be a Moralist

First, in order to lead under duress, one must be a moralist. By that, I don't mean being a poseur, one who sententiously exhorts his comrades to be good. I mean he must be a thinker. He must have the wisdom, the courage, indeed the audacity to make clear just what, under the circumstances, the good *is*. This requires a clear perception of right and wrong and the integrity to stand behind one's assessment. The surest way for a leader to wind up in the ash can of history is to have a reputation for indirectness or deceit. A disciplined life will encourage commitment to a personal code of conduct.

Must Be a Writer of Law

Second, there are times when leaders must be jurists, when their decisions must be based solely on their own ideas of fairness. In effect, they will be writing "law." When they're on the hot seat, they'll need the courage to withstand the inclination to duck a problem. Many of their laws will necessarily be unpopular, but they must never be unjust.

Cool, glib, cerebral, detached guys can get by in positions of authority until the pressure is on. Then people ease away from them and cling to those they know they can trust—those who can mete out just punishment and look their charges in the eye as they do it. When the chips are down, the man with the heart, not the soft heart, not the bleeding heart but the Old Testament heart of wisdom, the *hard* heart, comes into his own.

Must Be a Teacher

Third, every good leader is a good teacher. He is able to give those around him a sense of perspective and to set the moral, social, and particularly the motivational climate among his followers. This is not an easy task. It takes wisdom and self-discipline; it requires the sensitivity to perceive philosophic disarray in one's charges and the knowledge of how to put things in order. I believe that a good starting point is that old injunction "know thyself." A leader must aspire to strength, compassion, and conviction several orders greater than required by society in general.

Must Be A Steward

Fourth, a leader must remember that he is responsible for his charges. He must tend the flock, not only cracking the whip but "washing their feet" when they are in need of help. Leadership takes compassion. It requires knowledge and character and heart to boost others up and show them the way. The Civil War historian Douglas Southall Freeman described his formula for stewardship when he said you have to know your stuff, to be a man, and to take care of your men.

Must Be a Philosopher

A fifth requirement of a good leader is a philosophical outlook. At least he should understand and be able to compassionately explain, when necessary, that there is no evidence that the way of the world assures the punishment of evil or the reward of virtue. The leader gives forethought to coping with undeserved reverses. As he is expected to handle fear with courage, so also is he expected to handle calamity with emotional stability or—as Plato might say—with endurance of the soul.

Humans seem to have an inborn need to believe that virtue will be rewarded and evil punished. Often, when they come face to face with the fact that this is not always so, they are crushed. The only way I know to handle failure is to gain historical perspective, to think about people who have successfully lived with failure. A verse from the Book of Ecclesiastes perfectly describes the world to which I returned from prison: "I returned and saw that the race is not always to the swift nor the battle to the strong, neither yet bread to the wise nor riches to men of understanding, nor favors to men of skill, but time and chance happeneth to them all."

THE LIGHT AT THE END OF THE TUNNEL

These are my views, based on my professional and personal experiences, my own trial by fire. As we look for the leaders of the future, I believe that the criteria I have listed will give us leaders who do not *follow* public opinion but *transforming* leaders who can implant high-minded needs in place of self-interested wants in the hearts of their people.

One of their tests will be the ideals they inspire in their followers. And the other will be their own fortitude and behavior. The key to our future leaders' merit may not be "hanging in there" when the light at the end of the tunnel is expected. It will be their performance when it looks like the light will never show up.

OUR PERSONAL AND NATIONAL RESOLVE

Speech to the American Society of Newspaper Editors,
San Francisco, April 8, 1987

I CAME UP WITH THIS TITLE from a flat-footed start in the two minutes between answering Neil Morgan's initial contact phone call and his deadline to go to press with the program. It might give you the idea that I am going to talk about the *abstractions* (religion, patriotism, and so forth) that I think our personal and national resolve ought to be attached *to*. Not so. Such talk is the preserve of preachers and political orators, and I am neither.

I am going to talk about resolve *in itself*—its nature, how expensive it is (what it takes out of you), what it takes to generate a reliable quantity of it, how it must be selectively focused, how indispensable it is to prolonged, competitive campaigns of human will, personal and national. I don't like to hook it to abstractions because it's seldom in abstractions that its major staying power lies. And when it comes to resolve, staying power is the name of the game.

That comes as a shock to many. People like to think that abstractions drive our lives. Take it from me, you can't get off the stage of an ex-POW-type talk until you finally concede to the questioning audience that, yes, it was principally God and the American ideal that carried you through. Now I think for many of my comrades, and probably for most, those are very

Vice Admiral Stockdale's speech was entered into the *Congressional Record* of April 23, 1987, by Congressman Robert H. Michel of Illinois, following this statement in the House of Representatives.

Mr. Speaker, one of the genuine heroes of the Vietnam War is Vice Admiral Jim Stockdale who endured and survived years of torture, solitary confinement, and endless interrogation at the hands of Communist Vietnamese after he was shot down in North Vietnam.

Jim Stockdale recently made a speech [April 8, 1987] on the subject of "Our Personal and National Resolve" to the American Society of Newspaper Editors. While it concerns his own experiences as a navy flier—he is the only person to have personally witnessed all of the events leading to what became known as the "Tonkin Gulf incident"—and his survival at the hands of Communist torturers, what he has to say about the necessity for resolve—in human beings and in nations—can teach us a lot about our own problems and particularly about this nation's resolve as it faces a militant and highly motivated adversary.

important considerations. But as I learned, and probably as you know, and as literatures tells us, resolve's power frequently lies in objective roots.

My friend Glenn Gray, before he died a notable professor of philosophy, spent World War II on the battlefields of Europe interrogating German prisoners and scribbling in a personal journal, which years later he published under the title *The Warriors: Reflections on Men in Battle*. He talks of the mysterious growth of comradeship among men who would never be friends and have nothing in common but common danger. Not often, but occasionally in prison, I would get a relayed tap code message from a new shootdown: "I've got to have something to hang on to. What do you think I should hold as my highest value in here?"

My stock answer, and one I believed in more strongly every day I was there, was, "The guy next door. Protect him. Love him. He is precious. He is your only link with our prison civilization in here." Over the years our prison civilization, tied together with those thin strings of surreptitious and highly risky wall taps, *became our country*, our family. So when you as newspaper men might ask, "Wouldn't bad news about your homeland decay your resolve? What if a big scandal broke? Wouldn't that pitch you into the depths of despair?" my reply would be, "Probably not." But of course we had a degree of protection from outside influence in our little "country"— protected from the bad news in the press because the Vietnamese insisted on translating your articles into their own pidgin English phrases, thereby robbing them of much of their credibility. And protected as well, as we marshalled our resolve, from interference by what had by then become a pusillanimous government in Washington. Suppose I had had to check with them before I ordered us all to take torture before complying with this or that Vietnamese edict. It would have blown their minds.

The only time I ever saw real anger at news in the prison was when we were told on the loudspeaker, convincingly, that McNamara and Johnson had quit and that the bombing would stop. That was personal. That was betrayal.

But even that had little or nothing to do with the level of long-term *resolve* of the vast majority of our prison gang. By then, we *were* the world, as we saw it. Our secret orders had gone out to all Americans in North Vietnam (with over nine-tenths support): "Accept no amnesty, no early release, we all go home with the last man." That *did* blow Washington's mind. A few years ago I got a five-page, single-spaced letter from William Bundy trying to unravel it.

Where *were* the roots of this kind of resolve? Certainly the roots were not cerebral, in our heads; the roots were emotional, in our hearts. When you're down to the wire, you can't afford to play with intellectualism. And when you're living with the carrot and the stick you have to force yourself to repel arguments from reason.

I have a hunch that, in most cases in this type of situation, the roots of resolve have most to do with ego, conscience, personal honor, "over my dead body." But it's hard to get a man under pressure to open up on that. Each develops his own formula and seals it in his breast. Strange commonalities grew up among men who came to devote their lives to clinging to self-respect with their fingernails—building, building, building resolve. No one would talk about it there. No, you don't find men exchanging philosophical confidences on death row. More than once I have spent an afternoon daydreaming in a dark cell—to suddenly have revealed to me some marvelous truth of the heavens that I felt the tremendous urge to share with my neighbor. When I got into the subject, his answering taps for each word grew more hesitant and withdrawn. I was getting into his private territory. And he clearly didn't want to get involved in mine. He had worked out a balance that was keeping him even with the interrogators and the ropes, and my insights, which he was nicely rejecting, would have been only threats to his equilibrium, destabilizers of his web of resolutions that he had compounded to live by in times of crisis. The core of his resolve was his alone, not for public consumption.

What he was building was what I came to call, what I named in that prison, "moral leverage." Moral leverage is sort of like a very clean conscience, except it's active, not passive. It's a power source. It is nothing modern or sophisticated; rather it is the simple, even *primal*, power source of human nature. It is a gut feeling that you develop that tells you that you are clean and you are right and that you are ready to carry your mission to the ends of the earth. Like all simple primal powers of man, it gets generated only when he is pushed to the extreme. In a political prison (and in my view political prisons for the individual and wars for nations *are* the extremes that cry for primal power), it is what is needed to salve closed the chinks in your moral armor, those gaps that alone give the commissar access to your inner self with his extortionistic crowbar. I am using the word "moral" here in the fundamental sense Clausewitz uses it in *On War*:

> It is not the loss in men, horses, and guns, but in order, confidence, cohesion. . . . It is principally the moral forces which decide here.

Concepts of morality were always in the shadows of the North Vietnamese prisons. In the ordinary sense, what was moral to them was usually immoral to us, but the *subject* lurked, always. I am not saying they honored our moral positions; but even as they wiped them aside, if they detected conviction, consistency, and personal honor, their eyes sometimes betrayed the fact that they were inwardly moved. Communists are trained to keep an eye on the moral high ground. But in running that political prison, they kept an even sharper eye out for hints of *shame* in us. Shame they loved because it was their best leveraged entry point in working toward a false confession. (And I don't need to remind you that political prisons are built around the need to get false confessions.) The commissar needed that entry point to start feeding in the fear and guilt, feeding in those pincers, that spearhead all breaking of human will. So you learned to get up in the morning and say to yourself "God, help me keep my conscience clean."

Power as a political prisoner comes from building layer upon layer of convictions that are hard to assail. You lie awake at night memorizing and concentrating on position points that you can maintain for hours, eyeball to eyeball with your interrogator, not blinking or betraying fear or guilt, yes and position points you can maintain in the ropes. Because on all important issues, unless you fold, those ropes are going to come. And as we all know, that's serious business, for it's in the ropes that death visited some.

And that's why I've spent so much time on the prison scene in this talk because *there* it becomes clear, clear for all to see, that a wise man sailing into harm's way needs a lot of emotional baggage but cannot let shame become a part of it. Shame is excess in circumstances that call for resolve. It wearies resolve. The point, then, is to do nothing shameful, nothing unworthy of yourself. Because if you do, and you are in any way honorable, it will haunt you and corrode your will. These are simple but very true, very powerful, very important facts.

And it came to me on more than one occasion, as I checked and rechecked my private package of moral leverage in that filthy solitary cell as I waited for that inevitable showdown torture session, that it is not an intolerable analogy to compare a leader taking a nation into war with a political prisoner building resolve, preparing himself for what lies ahead. Each is going to see blood and be surprised at it each time, each is going to have to look the opposition in the eye and convince himself and them that he is conscious of where he is going and prepared for the consequences, and each is going to be exposed to every temptation to back out, cop out, for lack of moral leverage, and leave a lot of people out there swinging in the wind.

Resolve worthy of laying your own life on the line in the torture room, or putting your country's soldiers into combat, should be founded on a rock and ingrained in your heart. Nothing less.

That's the way I think about resolve. Heavy as it is, draining as it is, it isn't the sort of thing you spray around on things you would just vote for. We can all conceive of a universe in which most of the things we would merely vote for (approve of) might be served just as well by other choices. But can you conceive of a universe in which it would be worthy of you to be cowardly or maleficent, vicious or wanton, or utterly without charity? Of course not.

Resolve is too expensive to waste on trivial things and too precious to throw away on anything you don't believe to your bones to be worthy of you. On the other hand, the things we do consider worthy of ourselves demand it.

In other words, what we dispense resolve on depends on how we feel about ourselves. How we behave and think depends on who we think we are. If we have a low opinion of ourselves, if we *deserve* a low opinion of ourselves, our resolve is not likely to flourish. For contrast, look at Socrates. Socrates thought it unworthy to himself to pander to the Athenians because all they could do was extend his life, and pandering to extend his life was an affront to his own sense of behavior worthy of him. His resolve was, as with all of us, directly tied to his own self-respect and the terms on which he could preserve it.

So what about national resolve? You've got it. It's too valuable, it's too hard to come by, it takes too much out of us, to commit it to any cause that is not worthy of our nation. And if you agree with me that what goes for a man going into torture (i.e., his need for resolve) should apply to a leader sending his troops off to shed their blood (his need for resolve), you'll see I'm saying quite a lot about what's worth going to war for. Intellectualism won't cut it, bureaucratic maneuvering won't cut it, arguments from reason are insufficient. To profess resolve means you are willing to make the cause part of you, part of the nation. It must come from the heart of the leader, from the heart of the nation.

Who was tracking the heart of the nation as we dabbled in Vietnam as war clouds gathered over Southeast Asia? Who was keeping his eye on our moral leverage as we tripped the switch that locked us into that war for keeps? Let's talk about moral leverage and that Tonkin Gulf Resolution, that *engine* of the war.

At the time I was shot down in September 1965, the Tonkin Gulf was still just a place. It was a place where I had had some interesting and revealing experiences a little over a year before. It was easy to talk about. Everybody I was associated with during that first week in August 1964 knew exactly what happened and exactly how this Tonkin Gulf Resolution came into being. There was no way you could hide it from a thousand ears on military duty, listening in on tactical radio circuits.

But when I came home in 1973, I quickly learned that in the eight intervening years of my absence, the story, and its management, had changed in many ways. Hearing my loose talk, a senior officer whispered to me, "You don't understand the full situation."

"Don't understand it?" I answered. "Hell, I led all three of the air actions that week; I know more about it than anybody. Who do you think's been protecting all this for eight years in a communist jail!"

But he was right. I had a lot to learn about the entirely new ways in which this pivotal event in American history was discussed. Tonkin Gulf was no longer just a place, it was a buzzword, a symbol. Different groups had affixed different packages of ideas to it. And the trend continues. To many, "Tonkin Gulf" is a buzzword for Johnson duplicity. To others, Johnson betrayal. Now to another group, which includes some of those who have their hearts set on doing away with the War Powers Act, Tonkin Gulf equates to "antiwar lies." Many strange combinations. Strange bedfellows.

I'm going to go back and talk about it just like I did in 1964 and 1965 when it was just a place and when the facts were clear, unmistakable, and distinct. Once again quickly, here's how it goes. On a Sunday afternoon, August 2, 1964, I took four F8 Crusaders from the *Ticonderoga* 300 miles up into the gulf and shot up three North Vietnamese PT boats, which had fired a couple of torpedoes at the *Maddox* and missed. Washington promptly wrote off the episode as the erratic action of a trigger-happy local PT commander. A little over 48 hours later, on a dark and stormy night, there was another call for my squadron to go up into the gulf. I answered the call, was the first plane up there, had the best seat in the house, and watched it all. This time there were two destroyers, *Maddox* and *Joy*. At first everybody seemed to think they were going to be attacked, but the North Vietnamese never showed up. No boats. No attack. False alarm. The carrier reported "no boats," of course. The destroyers reported no damage, no boats sighted, sorry about early messages that got you riled up, Washington, but overeager sonar operator and weather conditions had us confused for a while.

Giddy hilarity prevailed in pilots' quarters on the carrier and in destroyer wardrooms as we all turned in after midnight. We were all drained, relieved, laughing at the fiasco of seeing ghosts on a stormy, spooky night at sea.

Mark this down, newspaper men: In the nineteenth century, before radios, that would have been the end of it. It would have been forgotten by those involved in a couple of days, and the world would have continued as before. But nowadays, with alert Washington in instant communication with almost everybody, on top of everything, a hand on every button: Chaos. Big Deal. And the world would never be the same. The Giant had been aroused by the destroyers' early messages, and twelve hours, I say again *twelve hours*, after the *corrective* messages had started pouring into Washington from the destroyers and carrier, I blew the oil storage facilities of Vihn, North Vietnam, off the map in reprisal—reprisal *not* for the Sunday affair but for the Tuesday night nonaffair, for *repeated* attacks. (See *Vantage Point* by L. B. Johnson.)

Well, what did I think after that? Remember, I had not had those communist prison lessons on how tendentious issues turn on moral leverage yet. And being brought up in the world of technology, expediency, and bureaucratic squeeze plays, I must confess I didn't think a hell of a lot about it. I knew Washington knew I had blown up the big oil tanks on a false pretense. (I had some important visitors come see me on a secret trip from Washington some days later, as readers of the book [*In Love and War*, by James and Sybil Stockdale] will remember.) But I was only a forty-year-old fighter pilot, new to the ways of the world in high places. Vietnam was a tinderbox situation; I felt sure the war was going to start anyway. Washington thought so too. (The previous May, William Bundy had prepared the resolution to get Congress aboard—it was a "fill in the blanks" document. Here was an opening in the Tonkin Gulf, so "make it the Tonkin Gulf Resolution and get the war started, in earnest.") When you are facing an inevitable event, why not see that it is triggered on *your* time schedule instead of the enemy's? Why not opportunistically interpret mixups as provocations?

Of course I wised up in prison. As this moral leverage concept seeped into my consciousness, it finally dawned on me that government leaders who use official secrecy as a weapon to start wars under false pretenses destroy themselves—in particular their ability to maintain the self-respect and *resolve* necessary to keep a nation on track and safely through to victory. Even to lie there in the leg irons and follow the world news by reading through the propaganda crap of Hanoi Hanna, you could not miss the central fact that as the months wore on the Johnson government was losing confidence *in itself*. That was the *bitter* pill, particularly if you knew its roots and saw it coming, as I did.

Quite a change from those happy days when LBJ, sitting on August 5, 1964, before a stack of conflicting messages could get a laugh out of the line: "Well, boys, I guess we'll never know what happened, will we?"

I sometimes think of myself as the phoenix arising from the ashes to answer that question. In my absence complicated battles had raged in Senate committee rooms; tactics of each side changed time and again. Those Washingtonians who kept trying to prove there had been boats out there on that Tuesday night after all centered their "proof" on certain North Vietnamese intercepted messages that supposedly described what *U.S. News and World Report* later called a "phantom battle." (See the article of twelve full pages in the issue of July 23, 1984. Two years of study went into it.) I am the only person in the world who was an eyewitness to both the actions of the real PT boats on Sunday and the "phantom battle" on Tuesday night. These messages that McNamara introduced as proof before the Senate in February 1968 present a picture of Tuesday night in the gulf that literally no one who was there recognizes. But when I finally got to see the messages, they exactly describe what a Vietnamese observer would have reported of my real PT boat episode of Sunday the 2d. I can track my own airplane right through the battle. Just a mixup of messages?

Well, of course I didn't know how all this fiasco, this modern management route to the start of the Vietnam War, all worked out till I got back from prison. What did that young intelligence officer in the TV movie last month tell James Woods when he ("I") asked him in 1973, "What ever happened to that Tonkin Gulf Resolution?"

I remembered his researched reply and wrote the line in the book. He said:

> I was still in high school on August 7th, 1964, when it was enacted, so didn't actually follow it too closely—the whole issue became a political football while you were in prison. Fulbright's committee in the Senate had big hearings about it, everybody became disillusioned with it, and finally sick of it, and it was Nixon who finally declared the thing null and void, repealed it. But by then it was 1971 and most people wanted to forget about it. I don't know, it just kind of went away.

To me, that sums up the Vietnam War. The legacy of "the best and the brightest." Talk about going out with a whimper! No understanding of moral leverage; no pretense of resolve. What the hell kind of a scale of values has this twentieth-century world lured us into? Those whiz kids and their mentors played games with the great goodwill of middle America, squandered it, "got religion," bugged out, left a generation of their sons face down in the mud, and got away with it. They bragged about running a war without the emotional involvement of the mob, the men on the street. They decided it was best to keep the American public in the dark and rely on their own "creative thinking."

As a matter of fact, the "game play" in the Tonkin Gulf was hailed by the American game theory elite as an artful piece of politico-military manuevering. This game theory crowd are the people who like to think you can move adversaries around by clever feints and bluffs as you would an intelligent opponent in a game room situation and thereby save lives as you make gains with the military potential—sending tacit signals by the use of arms and making war more humanitarian, they would say. By 1966, Harvard economics professor Thomas Schelling, whose book *Strategy of Conflict* I had dutifully read in graduate school fours years before (and laughed at, in hindsight, as I saw the scene in Hanoi), was in print with a new book on military strategy, *Arms and Influence* (Yale Press, of course). This one memorialized LBJ's finesse in the Tonkin Gulf in those August days. These three sentences capture the spirit:

> If the American military action was widely judged unusually fitting, this was an almost aesthetic judgment. If words like "repartee" can be applied to war and diplomacy, the military action was an expressive bit of repartee. It took mainly the form of deeds, not words, but the deeds were articulate.

I would call it an articulate rendering of a resolution that plumb ran out of resolve and plumb got us off on the worst of all starts in a war. It gave us a false confidence in escalation theory and a guilty conscience. How much longer are we going to let these egghead theorists drive us into these blind alleys?

I say let us be aware that resolve and commitment and moral leverage, the only glue that ties America's sons to their leaders, cannot be displaced by throw-away concepts of finesse and trickery. These are not worthy of us, and because they are not worthy of us we cannot rely on them. The deepest human resolve is not built on self-deception, rationalization, or cuteness. It has its roots in the finer elements of human beings and of their countries. Thus—resolve to stand for what is worthy of us, to live so that our own best conscience is not offended. Only this will perpetuate the best of us and our institutions for generations still to come.

IN WAR, IN PRISON, IN ANTIQUITY

1987

THE BEST EDUCATION, the best preparation for a full and successful life, surely entails a proper blend of classical and contemporary studies. While we pursue the keys to the kingdom of modernity—studies in political science and economics and high technology—we need to understand the importance of a broad background in the readings of antiquity, those readings that form the basis of our civilization. In time of duress, in war especially, is that classical background important.

Achieving that magical combination of ancient and modern grounding took me half a lifetime to improvise. I grew up as a veritable prince of modernity; as a young man I was a test pilot, flying supersonic fighters when they were headline news and sharing a schoolroom with future astronauts. Then, at thirty-seven, too late for graduate school in high tech, a turn in my life took me to the quite different atmosphere of the study of moral philosophy. By that I mean old-fashioned philosophy—Socrates, Hume, Mill—mixed with literature with moral overtones—Shakespeare, Dostoyevsky, Camus, and the like. I was deeply exposed to the thoughts and actions of men of the ancient past, of mankind dealing with Ultimate Questions.

In the course of my study of moral philosophy I have been privileged to have wonderful mentors. One was Phil Rhinelander at Stanford. Another was Joe Brennan of Columbia. He came to the Naval War College when I was its president to help me introduce moral philosophy there. Those two mentors, despite their differences, had a great deal in common; each had one foot in modernity, one in antiquity. They gave me much. They led me to a treasure of striking insights such as this one by Mark Van Doren: "Being an educated person means that given the necessity [after doomsday, so to speak], you could refound your own civilization."

The Stoics said that "Character is fate." What I am saying is that in my life, education has been fate. I became what I learned, or maybe I should say I became the distillation of what fascinated me most as I learned it. Only three years after I left graduate school, I participated in the refounding of my own civilization after doomsday, when the giant doors of an Old World

Reprinted from *Parameters* 17, no. 4 (December 1987).

dungeon had slammed shut and locked me and a couple hundred other Americans in—in total silence, in solitary confinement, in leg irons, in blind-folds for weeks at a time, in antiquity, in a political prison.

That refounded civilization became our salvation. Stripped to nothing, nothing but the instincts and intelligence of the ancients, we improvised a communication system dredged up from inklings of a distant past (actually the tap code of Polybius, a second-century Greek historian with a flair for cryptography), and lived on comradeship in a polity that would have been a credit to Polybius's Athens. The spiritual power (not necessarily religious) that seeped into us as we surreptitiously joined forces against our common enemy came as a surprise.

In my solitude the impact of this unexpected spiritual power sometimes caused me to wonder. Does modernity (post-Enlightenment life under big governments and big bureaucracies, constantly competing to remake the world in the image of the new) deaden our noblest impulses? Does it smother or atrophy the power of the human spirit, the power of human nature? Do the readings of ancient times, the classics, serve merely to give us insight into the events of the past? Or do not the texts of those self-contained cultures of antiquity portray human power in all its vibrant potential? Do they not contain evidence of a more imaginative and fundamental grasp of the essence of being human than can be found in the twentieth-century texts that have since joined the classics on the humanities shelves?

In Homer's immortal epic *The Iliad*, as Hector is about to leave the gates of Troy to fight Achilles—knowing, as he must have known, that he would lose and he would die—he says good-bye to his wife and baby son at the gates, and the baby starts to cry, frightened by the nodding of the plumes on his father's shining helmet. Some would think the tale of the Greek-Trojan war to be an irrelevant relic of bygone days. Some would think it should be stricken from the reading list because it glamorizes war. Some would think that now at last, with reason to guide us, we can scoff at a warrior's suicidal obligations. But others of us react quite differently, seeing in that scene a snapshot of the ageless human predicament: Hector's duty, his wife's tragedy, Troy's necessity, the baby's cry.

My reaction, of course, is the latter, not only because I am a romantic by nature, but because by the time I first read *The Iliad* I had lived in antiquity (and I am not referring to the lack of electricity or plumbing). I had lived in a self-contained culture, a prison culture I watched grow among men of goodwill under pressure. I knew what it was to be a human being who could be squashed like a bug without recourse to law, and I knew that the culture, the society, that preserved me had to be preserved or nobody had anything to cling to. I knew that civic virtue, the placing of the value of that society above one's personal interests, was not only admirable, it was crucial to self-respect, and I knew that to preserve that culture, sometimes symbolic battles had to be fought before real battles could start. I knew that obligations, particularly love and self-sacrifice, were the glue that made a man whole in this primitive element, and I knew that under the demands of these obligations being "reasonable" was a luxury that often could not be afforded.

I also knew during this prison existence that I was being shown something good—that life can have a spiritual content one can almost reach out and touch. I suppose it can always have that, but I was used to the idea of it being fuzzed up, powdered, fluffed, and often ridiculed here in manmade modernity, where changing the world takes precedence over understanding it, understanding man himself.

The same message comes through in the writings of Fyodor Dostoyevsky, Arthur Koestler, and Aleksandr Solzhenitsyn. They've been where I've been. So had Miguel Cervantes. This future author of *Don Quixote* was a young officer in the Spanish army taken prisoner after the Battle of Lepanto in the sixteenth century. He spent seven years in an Algiers political prison. Same story: "Confess your crimes," "Discredit yourself," "Disavow your roots." He was tortured to disavow Christianity; he could get amnesty and go home if he would disavow it. I was made much the same offer. I was to disavow "American imperialism." Good boy, Cervantes, you hung in too. You knew how this age-old game is played. Political prisons are not just sources of fables of the past. They could just as easily inspire the literature of the future. Unable to tolerate dissent, totalitarian governments must have them. How else to suppress and discredit their enemies within?

You know, the life of the mind is a wonder—the life of the mind in solitude, the life of the mind in extremis, the life of the mind when the body's nervous system is under attack. If you want to break a man's spirit, and if your victim's will is strong, you've got to get physical. Sometimes you might think that you can unhinge strong people with psychological mumbo jumbo. Sorry, there is no such thing as brainwashing. But even physical hammering will not alone change all hard-set attitudes. The real method to jellify those attitudes, that is, to extract those seemingly heartfelt "confessions," is the artful and long-term imposition of fear and guilt. Solitary confinement and tourniquet-tight rope bindings are mere catalysts for the fear and guilt conditioning. Remember, I'm talking about strong-willed victims. They're going to make you hurt them. They know from experience that the compliance extracted by brute force is in no way so spiritually damaging as that given away on a mere threat. And they have learned from experience that in the end it is a spiritual battle. The leak in the dike always starts from within.

How does the mind of the victim respond to these challenges? How did we respond in those North Vietnamese prisons? Realize the situation here: They've got man in a laboratory test that no university in the United States could set up. They're not going to leave him in a room just to fill out a bunch of questionnaires or give him some innocuous maze to work his way out of. They're going to boil the *essence* out of him as a chemist would heat and pressurize a specimen to study its properties, its nature, in a laboratory. What is the nature of man? What surprises does human nature have in store under these conditions?

First, regarding the loneliness, the solitude: It's not as bad as you think. Don't forget, the time factor is stretched out way beyond most psychological experiments. There was a professor at Stanford who got national attention several years ago for locking some students in the basement of a library for a few days and then writing a book about his observations on their behavior. I laughed when I read it. You don't know the first thing about a person until he has been in the cooler for a couple of months. He has to first go through the stage when he is preoccupied with going insane. That's a normal prelude without lasting significance. Figure on that phase lasting for the first three to four weeks. It ends when it suddenly dawns on him that he'll have no such luck; he's stuck with himself. Almost everybody then sets himself up in a ritualistic life. Something deep-seated in human nature likes, feels safe with, repetition—a time for this, and a time for that, repeated regularly every day. You get to thinking about how liturgies of worship must have gotten started in some prehistoric clan.

Your mind drifts to many anthropological questions. How do institutions and governments get started? Are they the product of a man on a white horse? Does some powerful person impose rule: "We gotta get organized; here are the tribe's rules; break 'em and I'll cave your skull in." I doubt it. When you're scared (and that's probably why people grouped into those first crude polities—fear of predators, human or otherwise), you don't feel the urge to take charge. And when you're expected to, by virtue of heredity in clan or tribe, or seniority, for sure, among military prisoners, on first contact you seem compelled to say something becoming a well-brought-up American boy, like, "In these circumstances when you are being threatened or tortured to do things that offend your very being, I can't bring myself to order you to do this or that. Everyone must have the autonomy to choose the best of the alternatives facing him. Do the best you can and God bless you."

How civilized and compassionate! But it will never sell. Those fine young people in trouble won't let you get away with that. Their response is sure to be something like this: "You have no right to piously tell us each to seek out the good, and then back out of the picture. You are in charge here, and it's your duty to tell us what the good *is*. We deserve to sleep at night, feeling that at least we're doing *something* right in all hewing to what our leader says. We deserve the self-respect that comes with knowing we are resisting in an organized manner." As the veteran prisoner Fyodor Dostoyevsky aptly noted, "Man's most deep desires in life under pressure are not for a rationally advantageous choice, but for an independent choice." On the parade ground, all the rankers vie for leadership, to be out front; but in a political prison, being the boss means you're the first guy down the torture chute when the inevitable purge starts. In that place, the drive for discipline and organization starts at the bottom and works its way up. Maybe it always does when lives and reputations are at stake.

How about the handling of fear and guilt? Those are determining forces in any life. You can't accomplish anything without a little of both ("fear of failure" can keep you going once you get started), but if you let them get out of control, they'll tear the very core out of your being.

Did I say a little guilt—a feeling of inadequacy with regard to your duties—was a good thing? Most modern psychiatrists would have us float around on a pink cloud of emotional tranquility, free of conscience's nagging, but you've got to have a goad if you're going for anything big. In Arthur Koestler's *Arrival and Departure*, the brain of a restless young southeast European exile, who is determined to get back into the fighting of World War II, is given a spring housecleaning by a psychiatrist, who finds him hiding in Portugal in 1940. "What's eating him?" his friends all want to know; "he's seen enough war," they conclude. Predictably, the psychiatrist finds the problem in his past, a troubled childhood, and after clearing him of his hangups (she thinks), she awaits him on a ship with tickets that will take them both to a safe, carefree life in America. At that point he runs aboard the ship only to divulge the shocking news that he has just signed up with British Intelligence to be parachuted as an agent behind enemy lines. Old prisoner Koestler writes him a notable farewell speech: "The prosperity of the race is based on those who pay imaginary debts! Tear out the roots of their guilt and nothing will remain but the drifting sands of the desert."

There's power in feelings of guilt.

Yet there's devastation when it rises to such levels that it consumes you (remember, in your wartime prison cell you're waiting to be picked off by the first vulture to interrogate you), or when it creates self-delusion ("after all, I *was* tortured; maybe something came over me; my poor performance must not have really been my fault; I must have been broken or brain-washed"). Such rationalizations won't play well in the cold light of day when you're edging yourself out on the thin ice separating you from a nervous breakdown. And a nervous breakdown you cannot afford in this place. So there you are, wretched, about to sink into the Slough of Despond—bow first or stern first, depending on which crutch (consuming yourself or deluding yourself) you elect to use. Either will guarantee you the loss of your self-respect; that being all you have left, you have to learn to just sit there in your solitude and throw away both crutches and heal yourself—there's no outside professional help available. You have to deal with guilt, eat it, if you will. You can learn to use its fire for what it was intended, a flame that cauterizes your will to make you stronger next time. Of all the challenges guilt brings in a political prisoner's life, working off the feeling of having brought harm to a fellow inmate is the most demanding.

Later, out in public, you have no recourse but to join in the inevitable discussion of your so-called agony in prison: "How was the food?" "Did you get any fresh air?" "Were you warm enough all the time?" "Did you have any feelings of friendship for your captors?" "How was the mail service?" But when you get one old political prisoner alone with another, they exchange tales of a quite different nature, of nervous exhaustion, uncontrollable sobbing in solitude, the wages of fear, and the feelings of inadequacy, of guilt. It doesn't do to discuss these matters with strangers; they put you down as some kind of wacko.

But believe it or not, as time wears on in solitary you get better at dealing with these matters. The ultimate accommodation with them comes from focusing intensely on leading a very, very clean and honest life, mentally and otherwise—and you find yourself being consumed in a strange, lasting, and unexpected high-mindedness. By this, I don't mean "joyfulness," and I particularly don't mean "optimism." (In *Man's Search for Meaning*, Viktor Frankl makes the point that babbling optimists are the bane of existence of companions under stress. I totally agree with him—give me a pessimistic neighbor every time.) What I mean by the setting in of high-mindedness is the gradual erosion of natural selfishness among people of goodwill facing a common danger over time. The more intense the common danger, the quicker the "me-first" selfishness melts. In our situation, at about the two-year point, I believe most of us were thinking of that faceless friend next door—that sole point of contact we had with our civilization, that lovely, intricate human thing we had never seen—in terms of love in the highest sense. By later comparing notes with others, I found I was not alone in becoming so noble and righteous in that solitude that I could hardly stand myself. People would willingly absorb physical punishment rather than let it fall to their comrades; questions arose in my mind about the validity of the much-talked-about instinct of self-preservation. Solzhenitsyn describes his feelings of high-mindedness in his gulag writings in words like these:

It was only when I lay there on the rotting prison straw that I sensed within myself the first stirrings of good. Gradually it was disclosed to me that the line separating good and evil passes not between states nor between classes nor between political parties but right through every human heart, through *all* human hearts. And that is why I turn back to the years of my imprisonment and say, sometimes to the astonishment of those about me, "Bless you, prison, for having been in my life."

Was I a victim? Not when I became fully engaged, got into the life of unity with comrades, helping others and being encouraged by them. So many times, I would find myself whispering to myself after an exhilarating wall tap message exchange: "I am right where I belong; I am right where I was meant to be."

In all honesty, I say to myself, "What a wonderful life I have led." No two of us are the same, but to me the wonder of my life is in escaping the life Captain McWhirr had programmed for himself in Joseph Conrad's *Typhoon*: "to go skimming over the years of existence to sink gently into a placid grave, ignorant of life to the last, without ever having been made to see all it may contain of perfidy, of violence, of terror." And the author adds, "There are on sea and land such men thus fortunate—or thus disdained—by destiny."

Always striving for true education is the best insurance against losing your bearings, your perspective, in the face of disaster, in the face of failure. I came home from prison to discover something I had forgotten; in my old Webster's collegiate dictionary I had pasted a quotation from Aristotle: "Education is an ornament in prosperity and a refuge in adversity." I had lived in the truth of that for all those years.

THE ASCENT:
CLIMBING THE PYRAMIDS
OF NAVAL AVIATION _____

Address to Tailhook Association, 1988

SOMETIMES WHO WE ARE is more clear to perceptive outside observers than
to ourselves. Let me read a passage about a couple of naval aviators flying
combat in Vietnam in 1967:

> A man may go into military flight training believing that he is entering
> some sort of open-air technical school where it is possible to acquire a
> certain set of skills. Instead he finds himself in a *fraternity* that encloses
> his whole life, as if he has taken vows and promised to sacrifice all to its
> requirements. He is faced with the undreamed-of task of climbing a
> pyramid that is miles high and extremely steep, and the idea is to prove
> at every inch of the way up that he is one of the elected and anointed ones
> who have a certain rare quality (which is never named but universally
> admired) and that he can move higher and higher and ultimately, God
> willing, one day—he just might be able to join the special few who reign
> at the Apex.
>   The idea is to put your hide on the line and then to have the moxie,
> the reflexes, the experience, the coolness to pull it back in the last yawning
> moment—and then to be able to go out again the next day and the next
> day and every next day and do it all over again—and, in its best expres-
> sion, to be able to do it in some higher calling in some action that means
> something to thousands, to a nation. At the Apex in military flying has
> always been the business of flying fighter planes in combat, and navy
> fighter pilots could argue that they raised the ante highest of all. In
> addition to the rigors of high-performance flight, they offer a little death-
> defying drama routinely, at least twice a day, during Carrier Ops: On top
> of everything else, including combat itself, there is the little business of
> launch and recovery . . . out on that heaving greasy skillet.

Published by permission of the Naval Aviation Museum Foundation, from *Foundation*
10, no. 2 (fall 1989). Publisher, Progress Printing. This article is a slightly modified version
of a banquet speech Admiral Stockdale delivered to the active and retired navy carrier
pilots' fifteen-thousand-member Tailhook Association in 1988.

Those passages are from an old *Esquire* magazine article by Tom Wolfe (written before he was famous) talking about the apex of flying in my generation—a story about two guys flying in wartime as an F-4 crew off the *Coral Sea* from Yankee Station in the summer of 1967—developing a theme that he later coined as "the right stuff" in his book of that name.

There are several generations of naval aviators today. I specifically mention three: generation 1, whose apex in flying took place in World War II; generation 2, whose apex took place in the Vietnam War (recognizing that both the above generations had members who flew in Korea as well); and generation 3, the "center of gravity," the largest group—those whose first war is yet to come. (And again, I recognize that some in generation 3 have flown in adventures in the Middle East, the Persian Gulf, and Libya.)

In my opinion, being at the apex does not refer to rank. It refers to one's lasting reputation as a reliable stick and throttle pilot. It's a distinction that belongs alike to senior aviators like Jim Russell or to my friend who was flying fighters in his fifties, Diz Laird, or to Tommy Blackburn of Fighter Squadron 17 (a natural if there ever was one).

My pitch is aimed at generation 3 from generation 2—my philosophy of flying in war. Generation 1 knows a lot about this subject, and I think they will agree with my ideas about what your daydreams should be if you eventually want to inch your way up that steep pyramid toward the apex.

And the bottom line is that *nothing* will be as important to climbing that pyramid as your ability to *improvise* on your feet, to adapt effortlessly, naturally, almost thoughtlessly, to changing circumstances.

How do you get so you can do that? I have some antiestablishment home exercises that you'll have to do secretly because they are somewhat out of whack with the peacetime mood:

- Pull the covers up over your head after you go to bed and secretly think about a life that is not run "by the numbers."
- Secretly, get used to thinking *big, basically*, and *simply*. There used to be a guy at Patuxent River—first as a navy pilot and then back to Test Pilot School (TPS) as a civilian test pilot. His name was Bud Holcombe. He had made his navy reputation at Pax as a dead stick landing expert, taking up each modern jet in turn, shutting down the engine and "writing the book" on the best way to dead stick it in. I was with Bud at TPS, and he could see that I was preoccupied with trying to memorize lists. I was fidgety, with little previous jet experience, trying to remember exactly the recommended air start procedures of the seventeen or so new airplane types I was learning to fly. "Forget checkoff lists," Bud said. "If you look at an airplane

like a bunch of switches to be memorized, you'll kill yourself. Think basics! What do you need to start an engine? (1) air (get the nose down), (2) fuel (meter some in), and (3) fire (get some sparks going). Think big and basically and don't get rattled, and you'll live forever!"

- And lastly, and the hardest for some: *Develop a sense of history.* Get it into your head that when the war starts, all that preceded it shrinks into insignificance. Know that when the war starts (and, believe it or not, not all our vaunted aviators are quick to pick up on exactly when that happens), you must shift yourself immediately into that frame of mind urged by that old World War I U.S. Navy recruiting poster: "Don't *read* history, *make* it!" And to make history well, you've got to develop the habit of you, *yourself alone,* keeping track of the state of play about you, of knowing exactly where the ball is on the playing field. Why? So you can *capitalize on the moment!* You have to stay mindful of when the name of the game has changed, mindful that intuition then plays a bigger role than ever before, and fully aware that the chips are irrevocably down and that your actions will be in the record books for posterity.

Now all this preparation—all that buildup of resolve in your gut—has to be done on *your* time because in peacetime we're all trapped in a feeling that life is just one damned checkoff list. "Fill out this form!" "Fill in that square!" "Get this on your record." And meanwhile we're asked to believe that this monster organization (in which we're all but cogs) will somehow grind out some grand form of *progress*!

Well, in war, progress is bunk. Opportunities don't roll in like a saturating fog bank. They come as *incidents.* Life in war is *episodic.* And the man who scales the pyramid has thought of that beforehand and mentally prepared himself to make the most of each episode from the moment it first reveals itself.

War goes in spurts, and you've got to be there with the *right stuff* when the moment strikes. Please bear in mind that

- I'm not talking about "getting checked out"
- Or "getting in the groove, the mold"
- Or "going to Yankee Station and getting the dope on the routine"

We all do that sort of stuff all the time. What I'm talking about is getting ready, when the situation arises, to be able to pick up on the fact when the *mold,* the *rut* you've been taught to churn down, is *broken,* out of phase with the state of play on the field, no good anymore. And to know when it's time to run the gap with intuitive trail blazing.

Don't worry, I'm not going to walk you through the Vietnam War. That's boring and foolish; no two wars are alike. I'll just offer you a few snapshots that will illuminate *principles*. And in all these snapshots, there will be that juxtaposition of (1) the creative guys who recognize new situations, have a sense of history, and (2) the guys whose personal plans would have worked out better if things had stayed the way they were—those who "just love" that old groove, that old rut.

Snapshot 1: August 5, 1964—the day the Vietnam War started. (History had been warming up all summer. I was skipper of VF 51, and we had deployed on the *Ticonderoga*, spent half our time flying over Laos from *Constellation*, then back on *Tico* for the same, plus the Tonkin Gulf episodes—you had to be pretty slow not to be braced for the coming moment.)

My phone call from ship's ops: "You are leading the first air strike against North Vietnam, give me your pilot lineup."

The names rolled off my tongue as though they were wired into my genetic program. I never had consciously thought about how I would suddenly answer such a question. The squadron rank structure, my fitness report pecking order, all went out the window in my mind. *This* was serious for a change! I had to have people who wouldn't "blow it." I guess in hindsight they had to have emotional stability first, be good on the handlebars second, and, oh yes, to know *what day* this was—be able to put a red hydraulic pressure warning light behind them if it came on en route to the target—and to keep quiet about it. Forget that new exec! He can't improvise worth a damn! He can't even get a flight rendezvoused unless everything goes perfectly, always by that *damned book!* This is no flight for people strapped to books! Oh, yes, I had gun cameras brought to the ready room. "I'm taking one," I told my "go" pilots. "This is going to be a historic flight, but they're optional." (These cameras markedly reduced forward visibility in the Crusader, and I was a little set back when I realized that I was the only one to take one.)

Clouds! We were taking the A-1 Spads—and that meant we had to proceed to an offshore rendezvous point by flight—and the weather was socking in. (This would be the first and last time we took the Spads into major North Vietnam targets; but today I judged the North Vietnamese wouldn't be expecting us, and those Skyraiders were worth the risk. What a bomb load they carried!) We self-imposed total radio silence. We all sensed that we had to keep our lips sealed with those vulnerable Spads getting ready to lumber down the chute. We navigated for a spot behind a shielding mountain offshore. Sheer luck! All F-8s, A-4s, A-1s, photo F-8—all found the same hole at the same time, and down on the petroleum-oil-lubricant (POL) storage tanks we went!

Fire! All bombs smashed into the oil tanks (the flak didn't start till the Spads were pulling off clear). Red flames to ten thousand feet!

Later, "experts" differed as to whether this was "actually the war starting point" or not. Let me tell you, when you are there, shoulder to shoulder with red flames shooting to ten thousand feet, coming out of a city of fifty thousand people, you know you are seeing a war start. You don't have to consult a "strategic expert."

"Don't read history, make it!"

All pilots home, elated. Restrike being manned; we are diverted to the wardroom. (There is not a single oil tank still standing over there in Vinh, no reason to restrike, but that's what time lags will do for you with Washington running everything eleven hours away. The new executive officer [XO] is leading our element. Damn! No time to stop that now.)

Backslapping happiness in the wardroom. The staff intelligence officer seeks me out. "Everything seems to have gone great. Bad luck on the photo Crusader, though. Camera malfunction and very little coverage of the POL tank damage."

"Try this gun camera film," I say, stooping over and recovering the camera cartridge from my pocket. "It's not usually very good quality, of course, but surely I was pointing at the burning tanks with my trigger down most of the time."

I'm taking my first bite into a sandwich when the intelligence officer comes walking up, shaking his head. "You won't believe this," he said, "but I gave your film to the chief of staff and he said 'throw it over the side, I just processed a flash message about gun camera film from Washington. Told them we had none. Can't afford to be inconsistent.'"

Wow! Must have thought inconsistency would look bad on his record? Yuck, yuck—live and learn. No sense of history? To make matters worse, my XO was so late getting the flight organized amid the restrike chaos that he apparently felt justified in declaring himself "low state" just short of the beach and left unescorted wingmen in flak while he hovered offshore. The junior officers (JOs) were disgusted. I put him on the first carrier on-board delivery (COD) to naval air station Cubi Point with orders to await disposition of his case.

There you have it! War starts. Skill, competence, guts, nerve, careerism, fear, cowardice—all mixed up in one big fat ball. And nobody seems to take time to sort it all out.

I'm not targeting that exec; I'm telling you to expect such things to happen when *your* war starts. He was not built for war. It had nothing to do with his quals. He was qualified for everything: he had screened with a sheaf of 4.0 fitness reports; he just wasn't worth a damn when the bullets started flying. So what's new? Cases like this pop up after every long period of peace, we're told. But it's frustrating to try to handle such cases justly in the beginning of a war when *justice* means doing nothing but Bureau of Personnel (BuPers)–type paperwork for two months! (I never did get around to finishing it; I had immediate orders to take command of an air group on another ship. I don't think the XO cared either way; his friends later told me that he was just secretly glad to be out of the whole combat flying business.)

Read Jack Broughton's book *Going Downtown*. Jack is my age and no amateur: West Point graduate, retired air force colonel, lots of combat flying in Korea, former leader of the Thunderbirds, F-105 wing commander at Takli during 1966 and 1967. (Actually, he was the *deputy* wing commander, but it's clear from the book that his boss didn't particularly relish leading his pilots "downtown"—better to "let Jack do it.") As a matter of fact, the number of totally qualified senior pilots who arranged *not* to go "downtown" is one of the more interesting things you learn from this book. And don't let anybody tell you that pilot age is the problem.

Broughton has a sense of history. He knew that pounding Hanoi with heavy bombs that summer of 1967 was the *only* American military activity that was truly hurting old Ho Chi Minh. But listen to what he says about how the pilots themselves sorted out: "Not everyone who had the basic credentials was up to these downtown missions. We had a few who could *fly* okay, but were just *not built* for the task at hand." And that task at hand included repeatedly watching comrades and their aircraft being instantly turned into golden blobs of flame by missiles, flak, and MiGs. One relatively senior pilot who just refused to fly in Package 6 anymore made Jack so mad he found himself *hounding* his legal officer trying to keep the guy from returning home with his wings intact. Finally the legal officer said, "Don't you see that 'the book' is written to *protect* guys like this?" Wow!

Or read *Over the Beach*—a recent tale about my old *Oriskany* Air Group 16 at war throughout its seven combat cruises. Same story. Misfits are exposed. And they, too, escaped to hide in the system—one found a nice spot as an aeronautical engineering duty rear admiral! And another returned to his desk in BuPers and got promoted to captain! All services have trouble with that. I never will forget coming home from eight years in prison and being told that the navy would be coming out with some real tough policies about moral integrity. I was delighted and thought we were actually going to have servicewide dialogue about pilots who chicken out over the target and prisoners of war who cop out and accept parole. And then I saw the policy paper: nothing but a bunch of crap about fiscal accountability. Is that as deep into personal integrity as the system can afford to get? The matter of dealing with deep personal motivations is going to get more and more critical when the psychological stresses of air combat increase as higher-performance and very expensive aircraft are being shot at with evermore lethal munitions and as our legalistic society closes in on people with the guts to try to put unsuitable-for-combat aviators in their place.

But to those good guys flying to Hanoi in those last few weeks of the summer of 1967, the whole seven-year air war seemed to be compressed into a single decision point. It was then when those with a sense of history, a recognition of the moment, came forward with their very best. Between July and October that year, the *Oriskany* had 40 percent of its total deck load shot out of the sky. Cal Swanson was right in the eye of that storm as skipper of a Crusader squadron. Captain Wynn Foster, my wingman when I was shot down and later skipper of VA 163, left his severed right hand and arm, intact almost to the shoulder, lying on the starboard console of his A-4 cockpit while he successfully pulled his ejection curtain with his left. He told me that in the last *month* of that summer 1967 push, VA 163—a twenty-one pilot, fourteen-plane squadron—lost ten airplanes, with nine pilots killed or wounded. In the whole war, seven Navy Crosses were awarded to A-4 pilots. In August 1967, four of those seven were given to *Oriskany* pilots—three of them in VA 163 that both Wynn and I were shot down from earlier. They were "striking while the iron was hot"—giving their all in what they felt was "the final push."

Oh, that it could have been so treated in Washington! At that very turning point, at the moment when the British consul general in Hanoi, John Colvin, observed that "Hanoi was no longer capable of maintaining itself as an economic unit nor of mounting aggressive war against its neighbor," Washington ordered the bombing stopped. "Miserable pissants in Washington," I screamed to myself as our bomb concussions ceased to rattle my cell and I was hauled off for two years in leg irons.

And nowadays we are reading documents that prove that more than a year before that great push of the late summer of 1967, Robert McNamara had written the war off as a lost cause. It took him that year of lag time to get his way. Too bad for the two hundred carrier aviators and crewmen who were killed or captured that year.

But let's hope it won't be that way ever again. You in generation 3 have still got to hone your instincts to know when the big push requires your all. I travel with the San Francisco 49ers football team. Bill Walsh read *In Love and War*, mailed copies to his NFL football coach friends, befriended me, and takes me along as a companion. I'm in the locker room before the game, at the half, and on the sidelines throughout it. Those professional athletes are by and large easygoing guys. They have an inbred knack of always keeping track of where the ball is on the field and have honed their "big push instincts." But like you and me, they are amenable to hanging loose and shooting the breeze on the sidelines till the moment of truth approaches. Then suddenly onlookers like me are left standing alone. The sideline troops have instantly picked up the scent of imminent opportunity and taken their distance. Each player seeks to be alone with his thoughts and starts to pace back and forth like a cat. Each *feels* that moment coming when he will have to produce the *right stuff* on just three or four plays if he wants to inch his way up professional football's steep pyramid to the apex. That instinct to know when it's time to push is universal. Daydream about it! Develop it!

During that summer of 1967, the 212 American pilots in the jail cells of downtown Hanoi, under those bombs that Jack Broughton and Air Group 16 were raining down, were also instinctively realizing that "now is the time to push."

I'll finish with a snapshot of my group in Hanoi: the city was in disarray—all water mains broken, electricity off most of the time, no public transportation, people scared to death. (We weren't. We knew that those guys up there dropping bombs knew where *we* were.) Torture was at its peak, and our underground organization was in fully integrated operation, meeting, as we liked to say, "force with force."

But later in August, things went awry. A brand-new navy shootdown and friend I came to respect very highly was placed "cold" in one of the deep dungeon cell blocks reserved for us old "blackest criminals," as the North Vietnamese called us. At the strategic moment that same evening, when we had lookout coverage, we whispered to him under the door. As with everybody else new, we gave him the communication instructions, my underground rules (in acronym form—"take significant pain before you do a, b, c, or d") and, as I always insisted, gave him my name and rank as leader of the underground.

Little did we know that owing to an unprecedented shootdown overflow, he had not even had the initial torture! Later that night, when they had a vacancy in the torture room, they hauled him out. He properly refused to do a, b, c, or d on demand and, in the melee that followed, let slip the remark, "What you ask is improper and specifically forbidden by my *commanding officer!*"

"Aha!" they said. That got their attention. For no matter what else is going on in a communist prison, everything stops when they have proof that there is organized prisoner opposition. They called for the commissar, and the question was put, "Just who is your commanding officer?" Of course under the pain that was promptly applied—pain that not even my favorite linebackers on those San Francisco 49ers could have resisted—they got my name. And a prisonwide purge for details was started. Bones were broken and Americans were killed.

Later snapshot: I am in a dark isolation cell, naked, blindfolded for the past month, my knee rebroken, hunching around with hands cuffed behind, trying to get a wink of sleep after dark while the loudspeaker outside blares Russian martial music as the whole country warms up for the fiftieth anniversary of the Bolshevik Revolution. Talk about being plugged into history!

You should know that the history of the war as seen from Hanoi consisted of two separate wars. This war I am recounting was about to end when Lyndon Johnson threw in the towel and stopped all bombing the next year, 1968. It had lasted three years and two months. It was the big one, the long one. In it the U.S. Navy lost 211 carrier airplanes over North Vietnam, and in them were 275 air crewmen. Forty-eight percent of those crewmen were never heard of again. Nine percent were recovered by search and rescue operations. And 43 percent of us wound up in Hanoi prisons, a few dying while there. In that war over hostile jungle territory, ejecting with a good chute meant you had a fifty-fifty chance of survival. You in generation 3 remember that; it's likely to be the same in your war.

Then began a three-year and two-month hiatus—a period as long as World War II in which there were no bombs and, so far as we prisoners could tell, no American actions that would in any way affect our fate. Then came the short one-year plus second war, culminating in that beautiful December 1972 plastering of Hanoi with B-52s, something that could have been safely done and produced the same result—North Vietnam's virtual surrender—seven years earlier, in 1965.

But don't get the idea that we who lived that war out in Hanoi gained nothing to show for it. We did not come up empty-handed. We learned the hollowness of much of the conventional wisdom we had brought in with us. Like being committed to "surviving at any cost," for instance. I'll let the old master Solzhenitsyn do the talking here. Let him tell it as he learned these same lessons in the gulag.

"Survive at any cost," he kept repeating to himself at first. But as he got into the underground (and anybody worth his salt does so), he realized that to survive at any cost was as often as not to survive at the cost of someone else—at the cost of a comrade. The way to survive at any cost could be to become a stool pigeon and carve out a comfortable niche for yourself.

The turning point in anybody's life, he said, is when you come to that fork in the road where you have to decide whether to risk your life or to lose your conscience. One road leads up, one down. To survive at any cost is to think me first, to lose your conscience, to take the low road. To *support others* at any cost is to risk your life, to take the high road. He chose the high road, and from that comes the name of one of the closing chapters in his book about the gulag, "The Ascent."

He also had always been told that "it is the *result* that counts." In the high-mindedness that eventually comes to you as you preserve your conscience, he learned, as did we, that it is *not* the "what" but the "how." It is not the result, but the *spirit* with which you pursue your just ends that *really* counts. So I say, "Bless you, prison, bless you, shootdown, bless all the close shaves, all the torture, and all the hairy night landings, and those ready room memories, for having been in my life." Some of my friends left navy flying early and went out and made big money—but in hindsight I wouldn't trade places with any of them. There is no doubt in my mind that to have been diverted from this naval aviator's life would have been to be disdained by destiny. You all know as well as I do that it's worth the trip.

ON PUBLIC VIRTUE

1988

THOSE WHO STUDY the rise and fall of civilizations learn that no shortcoming has been as surely fatal to republics as a dearth of public virtue, the unwillingness of those who govern to place the value of their society above personal interest.[1] Yet today we read outcries from conscientious congressmen disenchanted with the proceedings of their legislative body and totally disgusted with the logjamming effect of their peers' selfish and artful distancing of themselves from critical spending cutbacks, much-needed belt-tightening legislation without which the long-term existence of our republic itself is endangered.

The sad fact is that today such artful dodging of controversial questions is the road to reelection. It is not that a conspiracy of the selfish engineered such a turn of events but that an evolution of governmental practices over time has made it easier for a legislator to stay on the fence and appear faultless. In the articles about the current national deficit predicament, we read that an exponential rise in public relations opportunities and techniques, with the resultant lure of extremely valuable, career-enhancing personal video coverage, has had its effect. This first generation of politicians since Pericles actually to be seen by their electors, we are told, is hooked on upbeat and safe thirty-second spots. But the stampede for self-advancement at the expense of the national interest is now with us in many matters other than the national deficit and concerns much more than personal publicity. Even the patriot with instincts to stand up and be counted for what he knows in his bones is right but unpopular has reason to ask himself why. The press regularly covers what this swing portends for national solvency, productivity, and other domestic economic issues. I will address how the trend toward sitting tight and playing it cool affects my calling: the profession of arms and the conduct of war.

It is crucial for the United States in the 1990s to reverse civilian government officialdom's steady drift toward shirking its duties to civic virtue, public virtue, the habitual taking of personal responsibility, and the placing of the overall good of the body politic above personal ambition and gain.

Probably no character trait was so universally identified by our Founding Fathers as essential to the long-run success of the American experiment as selfless public virtue. In those days of decision, almost all of them were quick with pleas for its encouragement and institutionalization. For instance,

John Adams, in a letter to his friend Mercy Warren, author and sister of revolutionary leader James Otis, wrote: "Public Virtue cannot exist in a Nation without private, and public Virtue is the only Foundation of Republics. There must be a positive Passion for the public good, the public Interest, Honour, Power and Glory, established in the Minds of the People, or there can be no Republican Government, *nor any real liberty.*"[2]

The connection between liberty and public obligation probably occurred naturally to those who founded the United States. Many of them were exceptionally well read in political history and theory. The founders' debates were salted with easy references to Locke, Hume, Machiavelli, and Montesquieu as well as the ancients: Aristotle, Senecca, Marcus Aurelius, and that second-century Greek who was the great historian of the early Roman Republic, Polybius. That Roman Republic and its ethos, particularly during its first three hundred years, were a natural model for our founders' dreams. Like ours, their republic emerged from monarchy; like ours, the people of its early years were mostly free farmers. And although war had been the most dramatic feature of the life of the early republican Romans, their historians described how the development of Roman character was formed by institutions with which our revolutionary forebears could identify: the family, the religion, the moral code, and to a lesser degree the school, the language, and the literature of the society.

Polybius (who died when the republic was a mere 386 years old, before it had become corrupt) praised the Roman government as the best in the world and described the honesty of the Roman people as superior to that of his own countrymen. Their army, "the most successful military organization in history," never lost a war and brought a city-state a mere twenty miles square to the status of conqueror of the whole of the Mediterranean world.[3] So it might be considered natural that during the formation of our government, when constitutional issues were being debated, the famous and not famous on both sides of the issues wrote under Roman pseudonyms (Publius, Camillus, Brutus, Cassius). George Washington was so taken with the character of Cato the Younger in Joseph Addison's 1713 play *Cato* that he made the Roman republican his role model. He went to see *Cato* numerous times from early manhood into maturity and even had it performed for his troops at Valley Forge despite a congressional resolution that plays were inimical to republican virtue. Washington included lines from the play in his private correspondence and even in his farewell address. According to historian Forrest McDonald, the life-giving principle of both Cato and his country's government was public virtue.[4]

My central point is this: in late twentieth-century America the lack of the republican virtue that our Founding Fathers so strongly felt was key to national harmony and longevity is creating internal distrust, ineptitude, and frequent failure in our foreign affairs and military employments at least as serious as those in our long-term national solvency and productivity. This point was forcefully laid bare at a Paris conference to rethink Vietnam in which I participated in December 1987.

This Paris conference was a tripartite event to reflect on the French and U.S. Indochinese wars since World War II. It was held a block from the Arc de Triomphe in the International Conference Center, where Henry Kissinger signed the final agreement of January 1973 on the Cessation of War and Restoration of Peace in Vietnam. About two hundred people attended, all by special invitation. Fifty or so were designated speakers. Translator headphones could be set to French, Vietnamese, or English.

From the first session it was clear that the conferees were most interested in the Americans' war (1964–1973). It also immediately became clear to all in attendance that our conduct of that war (the topic of the first session) is still, even among Americans, a matter of considerable confusion and angry dispute. Most participants in the war feel betrayed by one force or another, and certainly none of the high-level participants who spoke at Paris showed any interest in putting the war behind them. There were just too many fundamental breaks in national integrity that deserve to be aired. And they all come down to one thing: we can't afford to fight any more wars without a thoroughgoing national commitment in advance.

We Americans on that first panel were a varied lot but all quite knowledgeable. Two were high-government on-scene officials: William Colby, director of the Phoenix pacification program in Vietnam and CIA official who later headed the agency, and Ambassador Robert Komer, former assistant to President Lyndon Johnson in charge of pacification in Vietnam in 1967 and 1968. One was a professor of political science and an author: Guenter Lewy, a student of the Vietnam War who writes on international legal aspects of the conflict. Three were senior combat participants in the war: Colonel (ret.) Harry Summers, a combat infantry veteran of the Korean and Vietnam Wars and now an author, Clausewitz scholar, and syndicated columnist; Major General (ret.) Mike Healy, combat commando in World War II and Korea, founder and commander of the U.S. Army Special Forces, who served in Vietnam five and a half years; and myself, Vice Admiral (ret.) Jim Stockdale, in Vietnam as a combat aviator for two and a half years and prisoner of war in Hanoi for seven and a half years.

So far as I know, no person in this group had any prior grudges against any other, and each seemed to speak from the heart when he drove home points that had welled up inside him as he devoted the best years of his life to the all-out pursuit of his nation's aims as he understood them. Each made cogent points with which almost none of the others could agree. The war went on so long and through so many phases that each one's honestly held views had a lot to do with his vantage point in the Vietnam fighting and the era he represented. In brief, people came down on different sides of such basic issues as whether the nationally accepted route to victory was seen as (1) working on the local level as counterinsurgency instructors and fighters to get the South Vietnamese on their feet, (2) focusing on what Clausewitz called the center of gravity, the North Vietnamese army, while the locals worried about the guerrillas, or (3) using our technical advantage in an early, quick, and unconstrained conventional air and possibly amphibious assault on North Vietnam's power base. The conflict between the first two options brought us to the question of whether we were there to fight a people's war or a soldier's war. One participant remarked, "In 1959 the Communists launched a 'people's war,' to which we Americans [incorrectly, he thought] replied with a 'soldier's war,' which our pacification experts, starting in 1967, tried to slowly transform into a 'people's war'—which found itself facing a North Vietnamese 'soldier's war' by the time Lyndon Johnson gave up and abandoned the cause."

This is not to say that victory would have been particularly difficult or that the problem lay in poor coordination of military efforts. What it does say is that since the Untied States has given up declaring war and started sending armies forward on what will obviously be a prolonged campaign without a national consensus behind them, things have not gone well. Those who believe that U.S. war-making procedures as they have evolved since World War II provide built-in restraint by fencing in our overseas commitments to those that the traffic will bear in a running constitutional battle between Congress and the commander in chief need only see one of these yearslong conflicts laid out and analyzed at such a conference to be convinced that warfare by grudging compromise is a disaster. Our Constitution as written protected our fighting men from shedding blood in pointless exercises while a dissenting Congress strangled the effort. But what has evolved, apparently to everybody's satisfaction but those soldiers, affords them no such protection.

What the traffic will bear nowadays in an overseas threat to U.S. national interests is almost never the old-fashioned, forthright military intercession of times past, when we appeared at our friends' gates as a volunteer fire department prepared to climb the hills to windward to cut fire lanes to protect their homes. Now our internal debates—and we must have internal debates every step of the way because we allow Congress to sit on the fence, ready to take individually advantageous positions ex post facto—take the form of a morality play. (As Kissinger asked at the Paris conference, "Can anybody think of a more absurd concept than humanitarian aid for guerrillas?") From the outset, U.S. support of the noncommunist side of area squabbles is usually cast in compassionate paternalism, which can come back to bite us. We immediately find ourselves in the hearts-and-minds business, at the grass roots, trying to help our friends help themselves. Suddenly we are partners in matters not directly connected with our national interest; we are mired down in our friends' internal affairs (Washington's bureaucracies quickly supplying organizations to meet these ill-considered obligations), and we find we are not the fire department but the rich uncle, ready to mind hearth and home and shoulder the blame for all that goes wrong.

The problem with sneaking into wars in dovish poses and getting off to a misleading start in missionary roles was illuminated on the last day of the conference in an event billed as a conversation with Henry Kissinger. Both my wife, Sybil (herself a conference participant), and I have great respect for Kissinger. I owe my freedom to him and President Nixon. And Sybil, who was founder and chair of the National League of Families of American Prisoners and Missing in Southeast Asia during the war, had bimonthly meetings with him for years. Ever since she has spoken of him as "the most honest man in Washington" during those years. (He never told the wives of those listed as prisoner or missing falsehoods about the prospects of peace, whereas a misleading cheery optimism they knew to be false was standard fare for most politicians.)

On that December day in Paris 1987, Kissinger took us back to the situation when President Nixon entered office and Kissinger became national security adviser in January 1969, inheriting from the Johnson administration (1) 500,000 American troops in place in South Vietnam (1,200 of whom were killed in action during the first month of the Nixon administration), (2) a bombing halt that had been in effect for months, and (3) a fully organized activist U.S. antiwar movement. This last was an unusual problem because it was backed by the very members of Congress who were largely responsible for the ill-defined role of our armed forces in Vietnam. Kissinger explained his prolonged negotiations with the North Vietnamese representative, Le Duc Tho, particularly those parts that took place after our December 1972 B-52 bombings had brought Hanoi back to the conference table (to the very room in which Kissinger then spoke). Of their final agreement of January 1973, Kissinger said, "I believe it was not a glorious agreement, but it was one that could have been maintained."

Kissinger later solicited questions from the floor, "particularly from the Vietnamese in the room." (These Parisian anticommunist Vietnamese made up about a third of the attendees.) Their questions were shockingly rude. We Stockdales couldn't believe our ears because the questions (almost all asked by young Vietnamese women who read from printed slips handed to them by Vietnamese men just before the session) implied a U.S. responsibility for a final settlement among the Indochinese people that had never occurred to us in all the ten years of our total commitment to the venture. Moreover, the questions had a sharp personal edge to them, and it was clear that Kissinger was being targeted by an organized ad hominem assault that puzzled and offended us greatly. For example: "Dr. Kissinger, I was but a little girl during the war; I am a boat person. Please tell us why you delivered Vietnam over to the Communists." "Mister Kissinger, do you think Vietnamese history will clear you? If yes, what kind of a man are you? If no, what have you been doing to alleviate the sufferings of your involuntary victims?"

Although wincing at first, Kissinger held on to his good humor and evinced no anger. "Free Vietnamese should have the right to ask unfriendly questions," he said. His voice was steady and cool as he half-jokingly said he did not know how to respond to questions he had already answered (it being obvious to all present that the writers of the questions had imperfectly anticipated his preliminary remarks). He continued. "The tone of what I am hearing reminds me of that which I listened to in this hall fifteen years ago [from Le Duc Tho]. It is not in the interest of free Vietnamese to use the arguments of those trying to destroy them."

The Vietnamese seemed to be saying that the United States owed them another war. As for Kissinger as the source of Vietnam's downfall, one must start with the Johnson administration; it had written off the whole effort as early as the summer of 1967.[5] McNamara, in a widely publicized statement years later, said that he had become convinced that the enterprise (as he was running it, one must assume) was hopeless over a year before that. His fundamental change of mind has been traced to August 1966.[6]

Nevertheless, President Nixon pressed the war from 1969 through 1972 despite gloomy prospects left by the destabilizing changes of pace it had undergone before he came into office, and then he had the courage to mine Haiphong harbor, bring the B-52s to Hanoi, and force the North Vietnamese, at least temporarily, to give up. Kissinger told the audience his only regret was in not doing the mining and bombing of 1972 immediately when he and Nixon came into office in 1969.

Kissinger calmly answered questions from the floor until they played themselves out and then candidly explained the events of early spring 1973 in which the Vietnamese seemed to find his betrayal of them. "We never had expectations that the North Vietnamese would respect the accords," he said, "but we judged that an agreement would rally a consensus in Congress. We never dreamt that we would be unable to enforce the agreement."

I was in the process of being released from prison in those days, returning to the United States with the rest of the U.S combatants in Southeast Asia that spring. In early April 1973 President Nixon invited me to visit with him in the Oval Office. We spent an hour and fifteen minutes alone there during the late afternoon of April 9. We of course discussed my prison experiences as leader of the underground, but in time the subject changed to his preoccupation with ongoing North Vietnamese violations of the agreement they had signed that January. The president said he was seriously considering reinstituting B-52 bombing, now that U.S. personnel were out. He asked if I would publicly support him if he bombed. I said yes, and I would have done so wholeheartedly for the man who had extricated us prisoners from seemingly hopeless circumstances. My notes made immediately after the meeting show surprise that he even asked.

Sybil and I had privately discussed these revelations from the president back in the spring of 1973, and they flashed back into our minds as Kissinger continued his talk in the Conference Center in Paris fifteen years later: "We had scheduled a meeting in Paris with the North Vietnamese in May 1973, and we planned a full month of bombing in preparation for it" (that is to say, bombing the North Vietnamese to force them to keep the word they had given only four months before). He then explained that in the crucial month of April 1973, John Dean had gone to the federal prosecutor. Six weeks later President Nixon was effectively powerless, and Watergate had sealed the fate of Vietnam.

And then came the most bitter pill of all. Kissinger brought up what he called the final error in his calculations: "I suffered from the illusion that this [January 1973] agreement would unify the American people, that the peace movement would be gratified that we had reached settlement and that others would be gratified that we had maintained honor. It did not occur to me that the people who opposed the war would have an interest in proving peace could not be maintained." On August 15, 1973, the Congress of the United States decreed that there would be no more funds for U.S. military action of any kind in Indochina. What made it impossible to enforce the peace settlement, said Kissinger, was what made it impossible to fight the war: a minority of vocal Americans who wanted the United States to lose the war.

Talk about a lack of public virtue! Our fighting forces in the Vietnam War were working against public apathy, congressional institutionalized indifference, and the self-righteous vindictiveness of a powerful group of demonic haters. Benjamin Rush, physician, political and social reformer, signer of the Declaration of Independence, pioneer in the treatment of the mentally ill, father of American psychiatry, had all the credentials to be correct when he scanned our 1787 Constitution as a member of its Pennsylvania Ratifying Convention. He noted that the drafters had worked hard to protect the American public from the tyranny of the government but perhaps not hard enough to protect us from the tyranny of one another: "In our opposition to monarchy, we forgot that the temple of tyranny has two doors. We bolted one of them by proper restraints; but we left the other open by neglecting to guard against the effects of our own ignorance and licentiousness."[7]

Is the United States to go down the tubes of paralyzing self-interest? So far, this has been the fate of the best of the world's civilizations—even Rome, though not until it had run out of enemies that kept forcing it back to unity, vision, and heroism.

The United States has plenty of challenges ahead, glasnost or no glasnost, and the chances are good that they will awaken our best natural impulses. My certainty here comes from my own intense personal experiences within a society under stress. In a microcosm of the United States, a little group of U.S. pilots clandestinely organized a tightly wound society in a political prison. I'll never forget my panic when, as frequently happened, that society was rent with the jailers' purges that tore it apart. When you're left stranded, alone, with nothing to cling to, no friends, no culture, no protection, you develop some mighty warm feelings for the group you left behind and learn why it's in your best interest to maintain the unity of your society, your nation, as a value higher than your personal interest.

But it's unfair to our fighting men to wait for natural impulses to repair the gap left in the Founding Fathers' plan for national unity in time of prolonged combat. War declarations may be irrevocably passé and the War Powers Resolution too tight a tether on our president's maneuvering room. But some compromise that makes Congress go on record before yearslong military campaigns start has to be put in place. There has to be a better solution than leaving the self-sacrificing soldier's peace of mind to the whims of Washington infighting. I've heard too many decorated veteran warriors from Vietnam say, "Our government better figure out some way to make it clear that they mean business next time, or I'm through with soldiering." They are sick of being told that their lives have to be provisionally committed to a half-baked plan because it's the only way the president can, in the national interest, get around adverse congressional sentiment.

These men were brought up pledging allegiance to the flag of a United States of America, which from its beginnings was committed to a separation of powers. From maturity they knew the strengths of this form of government, which balances the legislature against the presidency. But they also sensed, as did our Founding Fathers and the six generations that followed, that its weakness was a tendency to become fickle when the point of no return has passed, when the fat was in the fire and the troops were in the field. Over those generations a national confidence had grown up, particularly through those personal commitments documented by congressional declarations of war. Even without those declarations, there was a history within our government of a broad base of men of public virtue who would not permit blood to be spilled in vain. If in the post-Vietnam United States the soldier is just to be told that in modern times opinions change, that he should be prepared to have commitments dropped, that he should do his job in the field and never mind that he will be fighting for a government constantly doing a balancing act against nasty opposition from within, that fighting and dying as part of a sideshow to a Washington power struggle are de rigueur in these times, this simply will not do. He is entitled to demand: "Where is that republican virtue and its emphasis on liberty and justice for all that I thought was part of what I was pledging to all of those years?" Soldiers will march off to their deaths only so long as they don't feel they have to die alone for what will be abandoned causes.

Rome sets a precedent for such causes. Heed the letter from deployed soldier Marcus Flavinius, centurion in the 2d Cohort of the Augusta Legion, to his highly placed cousin, Tertullus, at home in Rome:

> We had been told, on leaving our native soil, that we were going to defend the sacred rights conferred on us by so many of our citizens settled overseas, so many years of our presence, so many benefits brought by us to populations in need of our assistance and our civilization.
>
> We were able to verify that all this was true, and, because it was true, we did not hesitate to shed our quota of blood, to sacrifice our youth and our hopes. We regretted nothing, but whereas we over here are inspired by this frame of mind, I am told that in Rome factions and conspiracies are rife, that treachery flourishes, and that many people in their uncertainty and confusion lend a ready ear to the dire temptations of relinquishment and vilify our action.
>
> I cannot believe that all this is true, and yet recent wars have shown how pernicious such a state of mind could be and to where it could lead.
>
> Make haste to reassure me, I beg you, and tell me that our fellow citizens understand us, support us and protect us as we ourselves are protecting the glory of the Empire.
>
> If it should be otherwise, if we should have to leave our bleached bones on these desert sands in vain, then beware the anger of the Legions![8]

NOTES

1. Forrest McDonald, *Novus Ordo Seclorum: The Intellectual Origins of the Constitution* (Lawrence: University Press of Kansas, 1985), p. 71.

2. Ibid., p. 72.

3. Will Durant, *The Story of Civilization, Part III: Caesar and Christ* (New York: Simon & Schuster, 1944), pp. 34, 71, 33.

4. "It was at once individualistic and commmunnal: individualistic in that no member of the public could be dependent upon any other and still be reckoned a

member of the public; communal in that every man gave himself totally to the good of the public as a whole. If public virtue declined, the republic declined, and if it declined too far, the republic died" (McDonald, *Novus Ordo Seclorum*, pp. 70–71).

5. Jim and Sybil Stockdale, *In Love and War* (New York: Harper & Row, 1984), pp. 276, 464 n. 1.

6. Lieutenant Colonel F. Charles Parker, "The Vietnam War and Mao's Struggle for Power," *The World and I*, April 1987, p. 615.

7. Benjamin Rush, "An Address," in Hezekiah Niles, ed., *Principles and Acts of the Revolution in America* (New York: N.p., 1876), p. 234.

8. Jean Larteguy, *The Centurions*, trans. Xan Fielding (New York: E. P. Dutton, 1962), preface.

STOCKDALE'S REVIEW OF *VIETNAM: STRATEGY FOR A STALEMATE,* BY F. CHARLES PARKER

June 1988

IN 1958, a territorial squabble in the Far East, quickly and like a powerful magnet, drew two world powers into an asymetric standoff with a third. China had commenced shelling two little offshore islands they claimed as their own, Quemoy and Matsu. Because this action portended tinkerings in matters both the United States and the Soviet Union had definite but very different ideas about, matters they held as crucial to their national interests, both moved in. If China did the obvious and followed up its bombardment of the islands with an attempted invasion of Taiwan, the whole power balance in the Western Pacific would change. At that time I was operations officer of the lead navy fighter squadron of the carrier task force shadowing the China mainland week after week, poised to destroy an invasion fleet if it should put to sea. Because I had to keep up with the state of play to brief my pilots, I spent most of my time between flights puzzling over the message traffic that was pouring into that aircraft carrier from all over the world, giving hour-by-hour accounts of the unfolding international intrigue.

That was a real education for this then-thirty-five-year-old U.S. Navy officer, brought up in the cold war, conditioned to confront the communist bloc as a monolithic, seamless whole. So help me, the Soviets and the mainland Chinese were starting to act like they were more angry with each other than either one was with us; it was becoming clear that the invasion was not going to take place! The Soviets, though automatically badmouthing our fleet's action there at every turn, were harassing the Chinese to back down. Although the world then tended to think of China and Russia as two peas in a pod, "communist brothers" locked in a much-ballyhooed mutual defense treaty, it was turning out that, when it came to practical actions in the Western Pacific, the Soviets much preferred to keep their "communist brothers" in check by having the Taiwan Straits patrolled as usual by the American Seventh Fleet! That was my introduction to three-way conflicts.

Americans are not comfortable in three-way conflicts. We like to think of two "teams" in opposition—in business, in sports— they versus us. When, depending on the issue, one of the teams splits out so that each of its segments hates the other much more virulently than the "opponent," it makes us nervous. Three-way conflicts are common in the Far East. Take for instance the American public's confusion about the fighting in China at the end of World War II. We found it hard to understand how we could be allied with China to beat the Japanese and suddenly have two Chinese segments (Nationalists and Communists) spending most of their time fighting each other. Either one of them would rather have had the Japanese win than have the balance tripped against them in their feud with each other.

I became so interested in what I had seen transpire in the Taiwan Straits that I got the navy to send me to graduate school at Stanford for my next shore duty. After a year of course work, I spent another in the library of the Hoover Institution on War, Revolution and Peace on that campus, pouring over modern Soviet and Chinese documents, writing a 1962 master's degree thesis I entitled "Taiwan and the Sino-Soviet Dispute."

There is a whole field of scholarship that has to do with the historiography of modern communist states. Libraries such as the Hoover Institution's continually stock translations of all radio and television scripts as well as all magazine and newsprint material available to the public of the world's communist countries. With day in and day out reading, and an understanding of the ideological "party line" of each country, an intelligent researcher can learn to break through the surface propaganda and decipher the internal political issues and disputes that affect the state's wrestling with international issues. People who do this are commonly called "Sino-Sovietologists" or "Kremlinologists." The good ones' work is useful and highly respected by those involved in the diplomatic arts. F. Charles Parker, with Russian-language credentials and a Ph.D. in history, is a good one.

The same Colonel F. Charles Parker, United States Army, is also a good researcher in the labyrinths of public documents involving military affairs in the United States. He knows from experience the procedures, language, and terminology used by United States Army general staff in the "working" of national security issues.

This book is the product of "Chuck" Parker's ability to "read through" the bureaucratic language of not only Soviet and Chinese Communists but the American defense establishment as well. This book's subject, "what lies behind America's defeat in the Vietnam War," demands it and allows him in this volume to break new ground in a field cluttered with misleading tracts, skewed by misinterpretations of the phraseology in their references.

But behind the ground-breaking achievements of this volume lies an equally important factor: Chuck Parker's compulsion to know the truth, his drive to find that "x factor" that will make the story of what happened to the U.S. Army in Vietnam jibe with the gut feelings he brought home after serving there as an officer. For, in a sense, Chuck was driven to the library by the same forces that took me there in 1960: an unrequited curiosity about what prompted events he personally participated in to turn out as they did. But whereas I spent a year, he has spent a dozen years. And whereas I worked on what is already seen as a minor incident in the life of the United States, he has tackled the problem of unearthing the causes of frustration and failure that have devastated at least two generations of Americans and might well forever have marked this land.

I say at least two generations were left devastated because his was and mine was, and he is the age of my oldest son. Chuck's Vietnam experience was as a field artillery commander soon after graduating from West Point. Mine was as an air wing commander and later prisoner of war, long after graduating from Annapolis. We have many things in common but mainly dismay at the way our national reputation and self-confidence were squandered by the Johnson government's ignorance and treachery during those years (1964–1968) when it rushed our country off on the wrong foot and immediately plunged it into irreversible trouble in Vietnam.

What is uncovered is ignorance of international politics beyond belief. Chuck documents a Johnson administration, spearheaded by Robert McNamara and Harvard's "best and the brightest," rushing U.S. troops forward to contain a Chinese communism that didn't need to be contained, indeed a China that was, even at the time when McNamara was demanding the deployment of more troops than the U.S. Army could accommodate in South Vietnam, sending signals (missed by a tone-deaf U.S. State Department) begging for a U.S. rapprochement of the sort Richard Nixon later brought into being.

The world our government was setting their brace against was a world that had ceased to exist. It was the world of long ago Korean War days, the world of a monolithic communism in which a frenzied China might any time, without warning, drive its hordes into the forces of the nearest "imperialist aggressor" and in which a more mature Soviet Union could be counted on as a moderating factor. Averill Harriman, Johnson's emissary to the Soviet Union on more than one occasion, returned from Moscow at a time of peak troop buildup in Vietnam assuring our leaders that "the USSR is as anxious for peace as we are." And the administration laid down a never-to-be-violated law: no B-52 bombings against Hanoi or Haiphong for fear of arousing the Chinese dragon and having it launch "human waves" over the Vietnamese border to grind U.S. soldiers and marines into the dirt.

The Johnson administration strategy was fatally flawed from the outset by its not knowing the enemies. It worked from a world model attributing motivations and attitudes to our particular adversaries remembered from its youth. The lessons of Sino-Sovietology of the late 1950s and early 1960s, so familiar to the academic elites of all political persuasions, were apparently totally ignored. Parker calls our Vietnam War a sideshow to the *main event* of international politics during those years of the mid and late 1960s: the Sino-Soviet dispute. Mao Tse-tung, long before the first U.S. adviser stepped foot in South Vietnam, had been steadily working to break away from Soviet influence. Khrushchev (and later Brezhnev and Kosygin), once our army went ashore in Vietnam, saw the U.S. troop presence near China's border as triggering pro-Soviet Chinese elements against Mao under the slogan "America is threatening China's borders." Chinese leadership was committed to the opposite view: that the United States was not a threat and that such a deal as Nixon eventually worked out could have become a reality any time, Vietnam War or no Vietnam War. So as we abstained from arousing China with our bombing (of the sort that I watched bring Hanoi to its knees in December 1972), the Soviets set about metering just the right level of armaments to the Viet Cong and the Democratic Republic of Vietnam troops in South Vietnam to keep us building up troops, forever chasing McNamara's magic "crossover point," where our inflicted casualties would creep ahead of communist troop buildups in the south and show us "the light at the end of the tunnel."

The treachery comes in with McNamara's rigid concept of how to run a war with production-line number-crunching efficiency. He, too, used an out-of-date model that allowed for no spontaneity of action and that would have horrified Clausewitz or Jomini. There was nothing obscure about McNamara's model; at the time the U.S. policy of having permanent ground forces in South Vietnam was being locked in place, he had the Joint Chiefs of Staff (JCS) appoint a group to study it and certify it as having at least a 75 percent chance of producing victory. The question went like this: Can the U.S. ground forces in Vietnam, without relying on the flow of supplies to the enemy being stopped by strategic bombing or the mining of harbors, without calling up U.S. reserves, and given a force level of 175,000 troops by the end of 1965 and troop increases beyond that as required and as our capabilities permit, win? Of course the JCS study group answered yes. Pity them. It soon became clear that another condition, unstated but lurking in the background of all discussions, was binding: that victory had to be achieved before the November 1968 national elections in the United States.

And McNamara meant business; his skills peaked in the field of constructing models (such as the one above) that provide easy tracking capability, allowing him to demonstrate whether the enterprise was proceeding above or below the time line. (This is the way a systems analyst would run a production business.) And one of his key variables was that crossover point; he had figured out that it had to be passed at such and such a time or the war would spill over into the U.S. elections years later, the big no-no. To check where he was on the crossover point problem, he assigned intelligence forces to submit "enemy troop counts in South Vietnam" from time to time.

One of the first such assessments came in on November 20, 1965, early in the war. Although the U.S. troops had reported more kills than expected on the tactical operations since the last check, and had won two rather large battles, the figures indicated that the enemy combat strength in the same period had *increased* by more than 30 percent! Big danger signal to McNamara! (Those pesky Soviets were outfitting new soldiers up north faster than we could kill them down south.)

Parker tells us how McNamara called for more and more U.S. troops, even ahead of the army's capability to utilize them. He tracked figures and trends frantically all spring and into the summer of 1966. It was in early August 1966, still early in the war, with only about 300,000 U.S. troops thus far in Vietnam, and U.S. kill ratios running ahead of prediction, when he (likely correctly, within the rigid confines of his static model) saw that he was *not* going to have his victory before the national elections of 1968. McNamara thereupon suddenly ceased his drive to accelerate the flow of inbound troops, ceased to chase the crossover point, went for a fixed U.S. "troop ceiling," and abandoned the goal of victory.

August 1966! I hadn't even been in prison a year yet, and I had six and a half more years to go!

But it was the U.S. Army and Marine ground forces in South Vietnam that deserve our pity. In due time, McNamara contrived a way to read routine continuing troop requests as "excessive military demands," and the U.S. expeditionary force therafter just grew toward the "troop ceiling" and fought for no stated purpose other than "not losing." Even though the administration ultimately caught on to how the Sino-Soviet dispute framed the circumstances the United States faced in the war, and realized the opportunities were open to derail the Soviet supply system and get U.S. efforts back on track (by mining the harbors and wrecking North Vietnam's logistics infrastructure with heavy bombing of Hanoi and Haiphong), nothing was done for *two more years* but let the troops tough it out in the meatgrinder against known, unwinnable odds.

This book will break your heart. It took the author a dozen years' work to get to the bottom line, but it was worth it. In the preface, Chuck takes us back to Vietnam. "Somehow, at the age of 23, I *felt* that something was wrong here. I felt, but I didn't know. Now I *know*."

THE BULL'S-EYE
OF DISASTER

Adapted from a speech given under the auspices of the
Rockford Institute in April 1989.

FOR OVER A DECADE now, it's been commonplace for our leaders to urge us
to put Vietnam behind us. My wife, Sybil, and I were face to face with our
good friend George Bush when he said it again at his inauguration in January.
The Congressional Medal of Honor Society has front row seats at these
affairs, and I swallowed hard when during what I would call his "plea for
unity" acceptance speech he said, "Surely, the statute of limitations on
Vietnam has run out." I was not the only one in the Medal of Honor section
who decided to take that remark with a grain of salt. New Nebraska senator
Bob Kerrey and I exchanged knowing glances.

In case you don't know, Bob Kerrey was a Navy SEAL (sea, air, land)
team leader who lost a leg on a voluntary and highly risky midnight pene-
tration of a VC (Viet Cong) island stronghold to abduct their political cadres
for interrogation. In the pitch-black melee, a hand grenade exploded right
at Bob's feet. He refused medical treatment until his gang and their quarry
were back down the high cliff, into the rubber boats, and away. Good work,
but in hindsight, all for naught.

I think Bob and I and many of our cohorts think there is much more to
be written and said before the nation puts that Indochina chapter of our
history to bed. I *know* there is material yet to be released that belongs in the
public record. The total Vietnam War story involves just too many fundamental breaks in our national integrity to be buried in the vault. It is a
package of lessons for the current age, and for the future.

I find that World War II guys, and, of course, President Bush qualifies
as a hero among them, sometimes dust off the Vietnam experience as a one-
of-a-kind mix-up in which our civilian and military leaders misjudged the
nature of the problem and, once in, sank into an unexpected quagmire that
was beyond almost anybody's practical control. From my study—and intuition—I find that impossible to believe.

I was there for ten years and taking in data all the time—one year just flying, two flying heavy combat, and seven and a half in prison—*not* "languishing," *not* "sitting out the war," as used to be said when American POW's had Geneva Convention protection, but fighting a torture battle, four of those years from a solitary cell in a penitentiary, surreptitiously commanding a secret and tricky underground organization, while regularly picking the brain of the prison-system commissar who sat on the North Vietnamese army's general staff. Altogether, I've come to realize that this talk about "surprise" at the resistance we met—at least among our senior leaders on the Joint Chiefs of Staff—is sheer bunk.

Books lead me to believe that the war held scarcely any surprises for the informed military. Their relationship with McNamara's whiz kids (who took over planning and running the war) was sort of like that of my prison pal who had come out of a dog fight in a parachute as the back seat (radar guy) of an F-4 with his front seat (pilot). The truth of the matter was that their plane came apart not as a result of enemy gunfire but because of a midair collision with one of their wingmen—a very rare event in that war, I assure you. One day years later I was sitting in a Hanoi prison cell block while my pal's pilot was describing to the rest of us his surprise, while in violent maneuvering against a division of MiGs, to feel the unexpected impact of a blindside midair! "No surprise, Boss," interrupted the popular back seater, smiling and shaking his head in the spirit of sardonic flyboy humor. "I knew what to expect right after I heard your briefing in the ready room. The flight was briefed like a midair, and it was flown like a midair."

A joke (sort of), but it was no joke with the Vietnam War as a whole. *It* was planned like a midair and flown like a midair: a perfect disaster. But the planners didn't have to go to prison. They didn't even have to fight. They didn't even know *how* to fight. They just knew how to "thread the needle"—how to get an army out there that would satisfy our elders' drive, the Establishment's drive, people like Dean Acheson's and John McCloy's *Wise Men*'s drive—to meet cold war verities, shackled sufficiently to keep the allies of the enemy below a high simmer and our own general public in the dark and calm. No emotion, please. Early in the war Robert McNamara said, "The greatest contribution Vietnam is making is that it is developing an ability in the United States to fight a limited war, to go to war, without the necessity of arousing the public ire." Can you think of any action more inconsistent with the basic idea of a democracy than the launching of *the* ultimate public endeavor, the committing of a generation of its young men to battle, the quintessential emotional experience, under the guise of their merely acting out their parts in some new sort of sterile half-speed surgical intrusion and thus well enough served without the encouragement and support of the public sentiment?

Oh, there was no doubt in the minds of the insiders, or of those of us who were out there on the firing line before 1965, that a "land battle" was what was in the works. You notice that I said that the needle threaders got an *army* out there and shackled it. Nobody who understood the problem wanted the U.S. Army out there trying to win hearts and minds in the weeds—least of all the Joint Chiefs of Staff. After two years of study and God knows how many confrontations with the president's "defense intellectuals," our JCS's final formal recommendation (made in October 1964, just before "the" war-shaping decisions were rendered by the Executive Department) hung in with the LeMay solution—to bomb Hanoi and Haiphong, back to the Stone Age if necessary; to keep the U.S. Army out of the field except as a last resort; to "isolate" the battlefield and let the South Vietnamese have at it with the Communists in a fair fight. (There are data in the files that establish LeMay's rationale as not to glorify the air force but to save the U.S. Army from ruin.) Their plan, the JCS believed, best utilized America's military power and best served its national purposes and well-being.

And take it from one who was there when the B-52s finally *did* bomb Hanoi for a few days eight years later: that would have done it. "The walls came tumbling down"; the loss of life, American *and* Vietnamese, was minuscule in comparison to the "land war" we bought into (at most, 1 percent of what was commonplace in World War II bombardments—one hundred a day in Hanoi versus fifty thousand a day at Dresden being a not-illegitimate contrast). The noisy Hanoi streets went absolutely silent. Their military officers were first thunderstruck, then obsequious, setting our guards to the unprecedented task of making the rounds of the cell blocks with hot coffee at dawn before the daily barrage started. Within two weeks, their national authorities were back at the negotiating table and, in so many words, in the process of surrendering.

The chiefs' "short war" recommendation of October 1964 was handed over to the young Establishment intellectual LBJ had asked to draft his strategy. His name was William Putnam Bundy, Dean Acheson's son-in-law. (Insecure Johnson had to have that old-boy Ivy League prestige behind him.) And according to the "twenty-five years after" books coming out now, it was William Bundy who was arbiter of most things crucial during the "war-shaping" period. It was he who in May 1964 had drafted a "fill in the blanks" congressional resolution that became the Tonkin Gulf Resolution after the events of early August of that year; it was he who cooled the JCS's idea of "keeping the pressure on with follow-up raids" while the iron was hot after our reprisal air strikes of August 5; he was a leader among those who insisted on not bombing Hanoi and Haiphong, raising the ludicrous flag of caution for fear of a China that was trying to get into America's orbit during those very early Vietnam War years—the start of China's political turnaround that took Nixon's and Kissinger's insight to recognize and capitalize on a few years later. According to a good book entitled *Four Stars*, which came out this spring, it was this same William Bundy who rejected the idea of a clean declaration of war, something that public sentiment would probably have supported in that fall of 1964—a "bright line test" that would have assured our deploying soldiers of the congressional and public support they deserved in exchange for laying their lives on the line. Bundy rejected it (says the book) to save LBJ "an embarrassing pre-election political headache in his peace-oriented campaign against Goldwater for President."

Admiral Lloyd Mustin appeared before William Bundy's war strategy working group as advocate for the chiefs' "short war" plan in November 1964. His words tersely described the distillation of JCS thinking: "Instead of working to buttress the South Vietnamese government in order to defend itself, the United States should take stern actions against North Vietnam to make that defense needless." (Over the years, the chiefs had collected lots of data, including the horror stories of Lieutenant Colonel John Paul Vann's unsuccessful attempts in 1962 and 1963 to motivate or teach the South Vietnamese to fight "Western style.") But the "short war" plan went down the tubes on December 1, 1964, in a formal meeting with LBJ and his principal advisers: Rusk, McNamara, the Bundys, Rostow, McCone, Ball, and Ambassador Maxwell Taylor. A campaign of reactive (tit-for-tat) gradualism won—the strategy of the game theory advocates who claimed that if you titted for tat long enough, you could eventually convince your adversary that his cause was hopeless (the "Prisoners' Dilemma" game). It seemed a "safer" theory—and by its implicit restriction of options to almost *none* except the stationing of our army units right down there in the jungle— it had the old "morality play" aspect of compassionate paternalism, our troops acting out the moral of those 1950s books like *The Ugly American*, helping our friends help themselves at the grassroots level; "limited war," they called it.

(If I sound cynical about grassroots support and "helping little people help themselves," I am skeptical about it from *both* the rational and emotional sides. Rationally, it is generally thought of as a poor utilization of our army's fighting power. Our troops are *not* missionaries and to cast them in such roles is to get them into positions asking for the sort of abuse Sybil and I heard being poured on America at a conference in Paris a year ago last December. I can't forget the insults of the Parisian anticommunist Vietnamese. In so many words, these leading Vietnamese intellectuals, who had sponsored the South Vietnamese government, charged America with intruding into South Vietnam's internal affairs and bringing about their country's descent into communism. In short, they claimed America owed Vietnam another war. We got so close we got pinned with the blame from both sides.)

The reason I think this rehash and analysis is worthy of your time is that it exposes the insidious dangers of that gradualistic paternalism that is so attractive to the timid. It could happen again. Remember Winston Churchill's words in his introduction to *The Gathering Storm*?

> It is my purpose, as one who lived and acted in these days . . . to show how the malice of the wicked was reinforced by the weakness of the virtuous, how the councils of prudence and restraint may become the prime agents of mortal danger . . . and how the middle course, adopted from desires for safety and a quiet life may be found to lead direct to the bull's-eye of disaster.

It's hard to believe, now, but "limited war" was a new expression in early 1965. There was lots of discussion about it—just like when its modern counterpart, "low-intensity conflict," was introduced a few years ago. Either can get confusing if you try to apply it to yourself as an individual combatant. In April 1965, a few months after our national Vietnam strategy had been decided, I was heading westward on the aircraft carrier *Oriskany*—starting my third eight-month cruise that would mainly involve flying missions over Vietnam. I was forty-one years old and had climbed to the top of navy flying—air group commander, senior combatant pilot on the ship. This was to be a full combat cruise (since we had left the United States we had heard about the marines landing near Da Nang and the start of the Rolling Thunder bombing campaign). Three things triggered a speech I gave to all my air group pilots a few days before we raised the Indochina coast. (The full text appears in Admiral Sharp's book *Strategy for Defeat*.) The first trigger was informal chitchat among my squadron commanders about whether limited war required the same low-altitude/high-accuracy bomb drop patterns as regular war. "I heard some squadrons on other ships were thinking about pulling out high," some were saying. Second trigger: an easily detectable and understandable anxiety among my pilot population as a whole—85 percent of whom were facing their first combat. The majority (the juniors) were well educated, thoughtful, and sensitive—too young to remember the national fervor of World War II. (I still vividly remembered the whispered concern among several just like them aboard the carrier *Ticonderoga* the previous summer as we eyed the still-wet bomb damage assessment photos of the flaming wreckage of the Vinh oil storage yard following our reprisal raid of August 5. "Yes, sure enough, there are *bodies* among that rubble.") The third trigger: a letter from a bright and highly respected former senior associate of mine, wishing me well on the one hand, and surprising me on the other by suggesting that I might give thought to laying off pressing for

Code of Conduct conformance of prisoners—that it was, after all, a *regular* war document.

I'll quote myself just enough to give you the drift and the tenor of the times:

> Where do you as a person, a person of awareness, refinement, and education, fit into this "limited war," "measured response" concept? I want to level with you right now, so you can think it over here in mid-Pacific and not kid yourself into "stark realizations" over the target. Once you go "feet dry" over the beach, there can be nothing *limited* about your commitment. "Limited war" means to us that our target list has limits, our ordnance loadout has limits, our rules of engagement have limits, but that does *not* mean that there is anything "limited" about our personal obligation as fighting men to carry out assigned missions with all we've got. If you think it is right or sensible for a man, in the heat of battle, to apply something less than total *personal commitment*—equated perhaps to his idea of the proportion of *national* potential being applied—*you are wrong*. It's contrary to good sense about self-protection—half-speed football is where you get your leg broken. It's contrary to human nature. So also is self-degradation. Don't think for a minute that the prisoner's Code of Conduct is just a "regular war" or "total war" document. It was written for *all* wars, and let it be understood that it applies with full force to this air group in this war. . . .
>
> If you don't agree with *all* the above, *right now* is the time to turn in your wings. It's much less damaging to your pride if you do it here in mid-Pacific now, as a clearly thought-out decision, than after you see your shipmates get shot up over the beach. . . .
>
> I hope I haven't made this too somber. I merely want to let you all know where we stand on duty, honor, and country. Second, I want to warn you all of excessive caution. A philosopher has warned us that, of all forms of caution, caution in love is the most fatal to true happiness. In the same way, I believe that caution in war can have a deleterious effect on your future self-respect and, in this sense, surely your future happiness. When that Fox Flag is two blocked on Yankee Station, you'll be an actor in a drama that you'll replay in your mind's eye for the rest of your life. Level with yourself now. Do your duty.

No one came forward to turn in his wings. By the time the *Oriskany* returned to San Diego in December 1965, its pilots had earned a record total of decorations for flight heroism. Of the 120 pilots addressed in this talk, 13 did not return with the ship. Nine were killed in action, and 4, including myself, were shot down and taken prisoner.

On the *Oriskany*'s next cruise, during the summer of 1966, five more from my air group joined us in the Hanoi dungeons—their killed-in-action list higher yet than ours. And in the summer of 1967, still more prisoners, and still more lives and airplanes, squandered running up and down the same restricted tracks in North Vietnam in that gradual escalation to nowhere. In five months of that 1967 cruise, the *Oriskany* had over half of its deck load of airplanes shot out of the sky.

So much for "limited war"; so much for the pussyfooters and needle threaders who wanted to finesse a war with game theory, without disturbing anybody important. I say to them what my North Vietnamese jailers frequently said to me: "The blood, the blood, is on *your* hands."

Those of us who entered prison early actually saw three different wars. The first lasted three years and two months—the war of reactive gradualism decided on by LBJ and his jolly gang on December 1, 1964—the war that ran its course as described above. Then there was a three-year, two-month "hiatus" war—like the "limited" war, practically as long as America's World War II—but no airplanes in the sky, absolutely no American actions that we could detect having any effect on us one way or another. It lasted from late 1968 to late 1971—I was in solitary for the first half of it, and I was brutalized more in 1969 than in any year in prison. Some don't like to hear this, but on the whole, life was easier for us in prison when America was bombing and hammering at their gates. To have our bombing "paused" was somehow considered contemptible. And then the old JCS "short war" loomed into view in late 1971—the mining of the harbors, the tactical bombing of military targets in Hanoi and Haiphong, and the climax: seemingly endless streams of B-52s bombing Hanoi and Haiphong military complexes starting on that wondrous night of December 18, 1972. In eleven days, North Vietnam was shut down completely.

That was commitment. A long time coming and, in hindsight, perhaps too late for an emotionally drained America. But for what it's worth, I believe if the October 1964 JCS "short war" plan had been accepted and put in motion during that spring of 1965—a move that would have been perfectly natural and totally possible—then we would have a free and secure South Vietnam today; we would have about forty thousand fewer headstones in Arlington Cemetery right now; and we would have all been home before Christmas 1966. What is known as the 60s—antiwar disruption and all— would never have happened.

How did we get so screwed up? The American government tried to do something the Founding Fathers knew would never work: to send ("sneak" may be a better word) armies into war without a solid consensus of public support. Hear out two of my most trusted friends:

Ross Perot, a savvy patriot in everybody's book, says, "If we didn't learn anything else from Vietnam, it is that you don't commit your men to the battlefield unless you commit the American people first. They fell just as dead in Vietnam as they did on Omaha Beach in Normandy. First commit the nation; then commit the troops."

Fred Weyand, combat general in Vietnam and former chief of staff of the U.S. Army, says, "When the army is committed, the American people are committed, and when the American people lose their commitment it is futile to try to keep the army committed."

The Founding Fathers drove a spike into the Constitution they framed, a spike aimed specifically at that crucial need for public commitment, ensuring that no soldier marches off to a war that becomes an expendable sideshow of a Washington power struggle: the provision that *only the Congress can declare war.* My constitutional law professor friends at Stanford tell me that the debates at the Constitutional Convention revealed two basic underlying reasons for that clause. The first stemmed from a consensus among the Framers that *no one person,* not the president or any other in government, was to have the authority to lead the United States into war. Thus Congress was given the obligation (*not* the optional honor) of being the watchdog in this matter. (There was debate about just making it the Senate, but the Framers decided they needed a broader base.) And there was a second reason to put Congress on the hook: it was decided that unless it unequivocally authorized a war at the outset, Congress was a good deal more likely later to undercut the effort, leaving a situation that satisfied neither the allies we induced to rely on us nor our men who fought and sometimes died.

I think it is fair to say that, generally speaking, since World War II and our subsequent discontinuance of declarations of war, things have not gone well. And we are all sick of these arguments about what is a war and what is a prolonged campaign and how do you know in advance. Yes, and tired of having to agree to the obvious: that it's neat that the president can pull off these successful flash-in-the-pan operations like the Libyan raid and the Grenada rescue and, too, the successful Persian Gulf presence, without the encumbrances of prior debate. But I don't think it is any sort of legal challenge to write a descriptive paragraph that clearly separates out the future Koreas and Vietnams from future Grenadas or Persian Gulfs. Basically, we're not talking about naval and air actions or marine team landings, we're talking about the United States Army in combat on foreign soil. And I think such expeditions (overseas wars) should be *declared* or not fought at all.

One of the obfuscating factors in getting this hammered out is the ambivalent stance of Congress. My law professor friends have drawn out for me examples of what they call the typical congressman's "studied ambiguity" on the subject. It's a fact that today the artful dodging of controversial questions is the road to reelection. They say that during Vietnam and in some conflicts since, Congress has shown itself to be consistently unwilling to end the fighting—in fact quite willing to continue to fuel it: "anything for the boys overseas!!"—but at the same time quite resourceful in scattering the landscape with rationalizations whereby Congress could continue to claim that "it wasn't really *its* war." In general, the modern congressman is quite likely to be happy to let the president call the shots on war and peace while he devotes himself to the construction of his private political bomb shelter.

I have an interesting study of different wartime congressmen's reactions to queries about their views on the Vietnam War in the light of their signatures on the Tonkin Gulf Resolution:

> "Prevent further aggression?"; "I was sure they told me they meant only aggression against our armed forces!"

> "Oh, that was only to handle further provocations against destroyers in the Tonkin Gulf."

> "I was told we were just going along with one of old LBJ's international bluffs."

> Foreign Relations Committee report: "Although it can be interpreted to authorize full-scale war, that was not our intent *at the time*."

Every day our newspapers report the details of some squabble over legislative versus executive control of foreign involvement. They are competing for the prestige of running it. I'm talking about the other end of the stick—the obligation to take responsibility for it *and stick with it* when it turns to worms. If you want to see that flip-flop acted out in spades, come to a prison camp. When there's reprisal and torture being meted out, some prisoner officers, senior and thus responsible, will shirk all leadership duties because they know they'll be spotlighted, hammered, and exposed to bad press at home. But let the heat come off, and those same rankers who had been cowering in their cells for months, even years—not answering wall taps of those seeking guidance, dodging their responsibility of command—suddenly surface and present their credentials to lead the homecoming ticker tape parade. That happened. Everybody wants the prestige of control when the heat's off, but many shuck it like a hot potato when the fat is in the fire.

American congressmen—Vietnam antiwar congressmen who were lengthening the conflict even as American bodies were piling up—were able to get off easy with their constituents despite their signatures on the Tonkin Gulf Resolution. The American public didn't hold them responsible because there was just enough ambiguity in the air about just exactly where this resolution (new word) fit in. But who can forget how quick they were to endorse this "engine" of the war that LBJ demanded in the heady times of summer 1964. The House of Representatives passed it unanimously after a total of forty minutes of discussion. The Senate had two diehards, and it took eight hours and forty minutes—but, as you might know, before a Senate chamber that was less than one-third full.

I have an aside on this. Sentiment rules the world, said Napoleon—and those on the scene when important events take place have a good vantage point to see the degree to which sentiment and image have the final say over facts. The excuse for the Tonkin Gulf Resolution was made into headlines that read like "North Vietnamese Torpedo Boats Make Midnight Sneak Attack on American Destoyers." As most of you know, I had the best seat in the house to watch that event, and our destroyers were just shooting at phantom targets—there were no PT boats there. Not a conspiracy, but a hysterical mix-up. I reported that, and Washington received it promptly, but we went to war anyway. Those early headlines, based on Washington's *word* on what happened, set the tone for the reaction of the whole country, and two days later LBJ got his blank check for whatever kind of war he wanted—*and* a magnificent boost in the popularity polls for his upcoming election. But when we pilots who were out there really snickered was when we read the superimaginative graphic accounts of the sea battle in the news magazines a week later. If you have old *Newsweek*s, *Time* magazines, or *Life* magazines of that time, look at the stories, and drawings, and remember that there was nothing there but black water and American firepower. And then, contrast that 1964 public reaction to a *nonevent* to that 1973 reaction to a *real* event, to a magnificently handled dearming of our enemy's capital city, with pin-point bombing of rail yards, transportation facilities, and missile sites and an all-time low civilian casualty rate. How did our Congress react? In the middle of it, one of our senators said on NBC TV that it was "the most murderous aerial bombardment in the history of the world." Headlines screamed it was a "Christmas bombing"—I was there and not one bomb was dropped on Christmas. It was billed as a "holocaust," a carpet bomb-ing—I was there and not one bomb was dropped downtown. But by 1973, the country had come to such a state that a vocal minority of our citizens, who by that time *did not want America to win that war*, were able to prevent the enforcement of the agreement that those eleven days of bombings had extracted from the North Vietnamese government.

What a mess! High-handed entry into the war, distrust of the JCS, mismanagement of the battle, squandering of the public trust, fifty-eight thousand of our soldiers dead with nothing to show for it! This could happen again. And we are asked to close the books and put the Vietnam War behind us? Sociologist Charles Moskos at Northwestern University predicts that won't happen until the last of the generation that the old guard mangled are quiet in their graves—in the year 2030.

In those years, and perhaps now in some quarters of our government, the ideas of "declaration" and "mobilization" seem to be thought to bring with them the idea of *moral approbation* of the project—whereas the undeclared effort, especially one not even "worthy" of national mobilization, is less official, less real, less demanding of our internal sympathies. (It's like when fifty thousand soldiers die in a *national effort* it's bad press. When fifty thousand soldiers die in an undeclared "police action," it's just "the breaks.") After losing out with his "short war" pitch, army Chief of Staff Harold Johnson (a very interesting man with whom I identify) made a push for national mobilization, not only for the manpower but for the public involvement, the public commitment.

(Harold Johnson was an ex-POW of World War II who made the Bataan Death March and who described his time behind bars as being "in a great laboratory of human behavior." I've never heard it better stated. He has been described as a skeptic, dedicated to integrity, hating absolutes, distrustful of easy solutions, dead set against U.S. troop involvement in Vietnam. He said the joint chiefs were *never* asked to vote one way or another before they were sent in—the civilians said "go" and they went—and thus was understandably heard to refer to the Department of Defense as the Department of Deceit.)

Anyway, the key player who turned off General Harold Johnson's mobilization proposal (on July 25, 1965) was ex-Supreme Court Justice Arthur Goldberg. He voices the opinion that a "mobilized" Vietnam War would make his image as our U.N. ambassador more *tainted* than would an "unmobilized" Vietnam War.

Well, I say then, from the national commitment viewpoint, that's all the more reason for the soldier to want his war declared. That's the only way he can be confident that the government really *means* it.

The worst part of all this is that in the undeclared case, it's such a *natural* thing for our very Congress (being unaccountable to the public) to turn out to be an after-the-fact agent that nullifies our fighting men's best efforts as an expendable miscue, a discard from the Washington power game. The Framers had it figured correctly. Our Constitution had to be written so as to protect our fighting men from shedding blood in pointless exercises while a dissenting Congress strangled the effort. But what has evolved in this modern age, apparently to everybody's satisfaction but that of those fighting men, affords them no such protection.

I've heard just too many decorated veteran warriors from Vietnam say, "Our government better figure out some way to make it clear that they mean business next time, or I'm through with soldiering." They are *sick* of being told that their lives have to be provisionally committed to a half-baked plan because it's the only way the president can, in the national interest, get around adverse congressional sentiment. They shouldn't have to take that.

I'm not usually on the stump. The woods are full of experts who can probably put me down in nothing flat. As the saying goes, "I don't know Washington."

But I do know some American history, and how the Framers' model for this country was that most admirable Republic of Rome. During the formation of our government, when constitutional issues were being debated, the famous and not famous on both sides of the issues wrote under Roman pseudonyms (Publius, Camillus, Brutus, Cassius). George Washington was so taken with the character of Cato the Younger in Joseph Addison's 1713 play *Cato* that he made the Roman republican his role model. Washington loved the theater and went to see *Cato* numerous times and even had it performed for his troops at Valley Forge despite a congressional resolution that plays were inimical to republican virture. Lines from the play can be found verbatim not only in Washington's private correspondence but in his farewell address. The Roman Republic and its ethos, particularly during its first three hundred years, were a natural model for our founders' dreams.

But they, as we all must, eventually fell. They fell from a decay of public virtue, from selfishness and inconsiderateness. I just don't want to see that process speeded up here.

ON HEROES AND HEROISM _____

Forrestal Lecture, United States Naval Academy
Alumni Hall, January 30, 1991.

TEN DAYS AGO, Sunday, January 20, 1991, I was sitting in a little television studio in San Francisco, an audio bug in my left ear, staring straight ahead into a little black hole called a TV camera lens, waiting to be projected into the East Coast *MacNeil-Lehrer* show. I was asking the technician for more volume as I could barely hear an Iraqi recording of an American pilot's voice, the show's first event. "My God," I muttered to myself as the volume came up, "that guy has been tortured—no question."

That was the beginning of one of last week's big stories. No picture images of pilots had been transmitted yet—and I knew nothing of what to expect on the tape. Of course in Vietnam, where new shoot-downs' statements—some tortured, some not—were frequently piped into our cells via the prison squawk box system, as leader of the underground I made it my business to develop an ear to detect which was which, to keep up with the jailers' policies. In fact many of us prisoners became expert at detecting the telltale signs of forced statements: use of words not common for college-educated, laid-back American aviators, particularly when the words were lifted right out of the enemy's political slogans; pilot sophistication levels grossly undershot—common in scripts written by non-Western neophytes in their second language—halting speech; and so forth.

Anyway, this guy, whose name and service I missed while still trying to get the volume up, was a "no doubt about it" case. He had been hammered and hammered hard. I had five minutes to mull it over while Jim Lehrer discussed Soviet affairs with Generals Wickham and Donnally on the air. Then Jim called my name and asked what I thought about the tape. I laid it out like I saw it. Those generals in the East Coast studio with him seemed relieved and readily seconded my convictions. And at that point a wrinkle, in this endless chain of wrinkles of the war in the gulf that are discovered and paraded before us daily, was institutionalized.

And of course the man whose tape I had just heard turned out to be U.S. Navy lieutenant Jeffrey Zaun, who received his diploma from this Naval Academy here in Memorial Stadium six years ago last May. His face stares out at all of us from the cover of this week's *Newsweek* magazine issued yesterday. And it is "the face of battle."

And it is the faces of many in battles throughout history, those caught up in what Clausewitz called the province of danger, uncertainty, and chance that I want to use as the backdrop of the phenomenon I want to talk about tonight. And that phenomenon is the *rising* of the *few* who discover in the course of conflict that that province of danger, uncertainty, and chance is their natural habitat, and grow to feel at home there, and come to express themselves in that environment in actions that are appropriate in almost no other line of work. I'm going to talk about heroes and heroism.

I know you midshipmen have thought about this subject—it was probably a touch of the romantic in you that initially stirred you to come to this place (certainly it was true in my case). It's just that today we're ground into the idea of egalitarianism, that it's somehow unfair, or undemocratic, to recognize, let alone admire, those uncommon and special people who over history have risen to challenges in ways totally incompatible with conventional wisdom's view of so-called instincts of self-preservation. In other words, we've become too self-conscious and embarrassed to talk about certain human behaviors limited in distribution to a highly selective few.

So tonight, I want to throw self-consciousness and embarrassment to the wind and, for a half hour or so, talk about something you should know: the history, the literature, and yes the *reality* of heroes. Let me tell you, they are out there—those of confounding selflessness and seeming immunity to fear; those with fires burning in their breasts, fires that may turn the tide for you as leaders someday. They have eluded concise definition since the beginning of recorded history. Aristotle would say only that they do exist and exist as the polar opposites of the beasts—that as the beasts are a cut below the normal human, the heroes are a cut above him, somewhere between the humans and the gods.

Heroism is an elusive subject, particularly because the hero in times of peril is often a person who theretofore had demonstrated only ordinary competencies. "Hard up the helm!" shouted Captain Claret, bursting from his cabin like a ghost in his nightdress as his U.S. Navy frigate, suddenly caught in an unpredictable wind shear off Cape Horn, teetered on the point of capsizing. "Damn you!" raged Mad Jack, hard-bitten mustang lieutenant, officer of the deck—"Hard *down* I say, and be damned to you!" Contrary orders! But Mad Jack's were obeyed. And the ship was saved.

We know this happened because Herman Melville watched this scene on deck that night as a young enlisted U.S. Navy sailor in the 1840s. He later incorporated the incident into a largely autobiographical book, *White Jacket*. Quoting Melville from said book:

> In a sudden gale, or when a large quantity of sail is suddenly to be furled, it is the custom for the First Lieutenant to take the conn from whomever

happens then to be officer of the deck. But Mad Jack had the trumpet that watch, nor did the First Lieutenant now seek to wrest it from his hands. Every eye was upon him, as if we had chosen him from among us *all*, to decide this battle with the elements—by single combat with the spirit of the cape. For Mad Jack *was* the saving genius of the ship, and so proved himself that night.

Melville even supplies us with a kind of coda, a sort of general rule of human behavior with which you may or may not agree: "In times of peril, like the needle to the lodestone, obedience, irrespective of rank, generally flies to him best fitted for command."

In telling this story, Melville produces several other eye-opening concepts. Captain Claret was not a neurotic Captain Queeg. He was not an ineffective or spineless person. He performed many command functions well, sometimes rather forwardly, once ordering a boarding party to invade a Spanish ship in port to arrest and recover his deserted leading petty officer of the foretop who was ensconced there. Courage in wielding authority from his cabin, Claret had. And that kind of courage might be called moral courage, as Clausewitz defines it—one of two kinds he contrasts in *On War*: that is, the courage of taking responsibility as opposed to courage in the presence of danger to the person.

It was this second kind of courage that Claret lacked, courage that makes one move easily in the presence of physical danger and chance. (Old Prussian Clausewitz says courage in the presence of danger to the person can come from [1] what he calls "the permanent condition, proceeding from the organism," what we would call courage in the genes, or [2] "temporary conditions, positive enthusiasms from such things as pride or patriotism." He prefers a combination of the two.)

Melville, less analytically but more functionally, says it this way:

These two orders to the helm, given by the Captain and his Lieutenant, exactly contrasted their characters. By putting the helm hard *up*, the Captain was for *scudding*; that is, for flying away from the gale. Whereas Mad Jack, with helm *down*, was for running the ship into its teeth. Scudding makes you a slave to the blast, which drives you headlong before it; but running up into the wind's eye enables you, in a degree, to hold it at bay. . . . As with ships, so with men; he who turns his back on his foe gives him the advantage. That night, off the pitch of the cape, Captain Claret was hurried forth from his disguises, and, at a manhood-testing conjuncture, appeared in his true colors. A thing which every man in the ship had long suspected that night proved true.

Melville's windup of the incident is interesting. He said that, to show "how spontaneous is the instinct of discretion in some minds in such times," the captain took no action against Mad Jack. "Nor so far as the crew ever knew, did the Captain even venture to reprimand him for his temerity." The author does not even attempt to *define* Jack the hero, nor does he feel obliged to list—make analyses of—his strengths, virtues. He merely says he was "in the saddle" in that ship. To me, that marks the genius of Melville. It took me a long time to give up on such tortured justifications and admit that heroes stand on *action alone.* "There he *is*" "You *saw* it!" "He actually *did* it!"

"Long ago and far away," you say. "Times have changed," say some military experts, some military writers. John Keegan, a British military historian, journalist, and longtime professor at Sandhurst, wrote a book about being fitted for command a few years ago. Its title was a good one: *The Mask of Command.* He made the excellent point that throughout history, at least since the time of Alexander the Great, all good combat leaders have always labored under the same five imperatives vis-à-vis the men they lead. They are the imperatives of *kinship* (taking care never to leave any doubt in the minds of your troops that you and they are, in the last analysis, comrades in arms), *prescription* (having a personal, authoritative style of laying down rules and direction), *sanction* (being perceived as a person who has, and follows, some cogent theory of reward and punishment), *action* (being able to show your men that you *do* know how to fight), and *example* (showing by your every move and whole being that you subscribe to the principle that those who impose risk should be seen to share it).

Keegan concentrated the book on the last imperative, calling it heroism. After an enlightening and thorough review of exactly how Alexander the Great, the duke of Wellington, U. S. Grant, and others handled themselves in battle—in what patterns they rode or paced during the heavy fighting, how close they approached the opposing lines, what personal mannerisms seemed natural to them as they showed their mettle, dodging bullets or spears while keeping track of the state of play at the same time—he tacked on a chapter at the end about modern times. There, in so many words, he told us that as of *right then*, 1987, *example heroism*, as he dubbed it, had to go, that in the high-tech world it had no meaning, that computers and their ilk *replace human motivation* in modern warfare, that the spirited and the phlegmatic stand as one in their presence, and, furthermore, that those given to "theatrics" (which he equated to heroism) were dangerous.

John Keegan is no flake, but his last chapter was so inconsistent with his great buildup before it, and so inconsistent with the late-twentieth-century warfare I have been involved in, that I had to believe that some fear of Armageddon was polluting his judgment. He seemed to be using any excuse to put down that old bugaboo of the dangerous influence of individual *personality* on history. Moreover, he seemed to be trying to convince the reader that there is safety in leadership by committee and that natural forces are now dictating the shaping of our lives around a harmonious antheap of universal mediocrity. (I, of course, in disagreement, share the view of Harry Truman: "Men make history, and not the other way around.")

I stuck it to Keegan on those grounds in the *Wall Street Journal* review I had been commissioned to do. About a month later, I got a nice letter from John from England, and he *almost* seemed to agree with me. He sort of expected it from me, he said.

My experience as a squadron and wing commander in Vietnam showed me that in combat, high-performance, high-technology fighter airplanes are *illuminating* the difference between the courageous and the timid, not fuzzing it up. As the air war matured, as North Vietnam's air defenses became more sophisticated, human motivation became ever*more* important in the wild blue yonder. High-tech gear does *not* have the effect of lumping every combatant into the same amorphous mass of emotion-free anonymity. The truth as I saw it, now reinforced by many new books written by experienced airborne commanders who regularly took strike groups into what we called Package 6, the Hanoi/Haiphong complex, was that failures of pilot nerve *matched* the record-breaking numbers of high-caliber flak guns and enemy fighters, to say nothing of the surface-to-air missiles they faced. Higher-tech airplanes facing ever-higher-tech opposition tend to increasingly polarize the warrior mass, with the heavy end of the fighting load being taken over by proportionately fewer and fewer of the best.

My good friend Jack Broughton, a West Pointer my age, leader, as an air force colonel in his late forties, of a record number of missions into Package 6, authored the books *Thud Ridge* and *Going Downtown*. In *Going Downtown* he wrote: "Not everyone who *had* the basic credentials was *up* to these downtown missions. We had a few who could *fly* okay, but were just *not built* for the task at hand." Jack Broughton, organization man? Hardly. His *conscience* was his guide, and when two of his majors who *were* built for the task "downtown" were about to be court-martialed unjustly, he sprang to their defense. As their operational commander, Broughton found out that the U.S. Air Force was seeking to use the majors' own gun camera film to convict them of a rule violation for firing in self-defense at an off-limits gun platform firing at them (specifically, a Soviet cargo ship moored to a Haiphong dock, off-loading munitions). He then called for and burned their film and took the career-ending court-martial himself.

Prisons, as well as air battles, are also worth a close look as incubators of authentic heroes. It was Anwar Sadat who in his memoir *Reflections from Cell 54* wrote that there are only two places in the world where a man cannot escape from himself: a battlefield and a prison cell. Prisons, torture and isolation prisons, are ripe for the emergence of heroes, principally because their inmates are engulfed in moods of uncertainty and doubt.

An odd thing to say, perhaps, but the most thoughtful authors I've read on the subject of why heroism is distorted or muted or *dead* in the twentieth century stress the *lack* of the uncertainty factor in modern industrial states. Winston Churchill, in his book of essays entitled *Thoughts and Adventures*, deplores the evaporating of the basic survival quandaries that hovered over generations a hundred and two hundred years ago. "Can modern communities do without great men? Can they dispense with hero-worship? Can the common sense of the masses provide a larger wisdom, a nobler sentiment, more vigorous actions than were ever got from the Titans?" Aleksandr Solzhenitsyn in *A World Split Apart* makes a case for those inward-looking "self-contained cultures" that thrived in dangerous worlds, where "mystery and doubt and valor and spiritualism" enriched a life.

That's where we were, in Hanoi, being closed in on by dangerous, erratic, and unpredictable forces over which no means of gaining leverage was immediately obvious. In those conditions, hardly a person exists who does not in his heart of hearts secretly beseech the gods to grant one or more around him the instinctive grasp of where leverage lies and the personality to demand and receive the acquiesence of the group to let him come forward and do his stuff.

I don't want to labor subjects with which you are generally familiar, such as prison stories from North Vietnam in that long ago war. I just want to give you some facts that will sharpen your perception of how the naval service nurtures leaders and how in particular this academy's graduate naval flying officers stacked up in the comparative sense. Although navy pilots and their back seat weaponeers poured into Hoa Lo prison for eight and a half years, the really *telling* years were only four: November 1965 through November 1969, "four years of darkness." It was during this period that there was plenty of acquiesence to let the standouts *of any rank* come forward and do their stuff.

When it came to passing out punishment, the Vietnamese were anything *but* inefficient. They were expert at identifying and nailing the people who were leading the resistance against them. So a study of the solitary confinement and torture records of that American prisoner population, which swelled from 50 to 331 over those four years of darkness, can be seen as a graphic distribution of American leadership effectiveness over the period. How did that distribution check with rank order? with service affiliation? Let me give you one example: In the summer of 1967, the Vietnamese began announcing that they were going to exile those "who most severely incited others to oppose the Camp Authority" and spent three months torturing, cross-checking stories, working up *their* list of our most effective leaders (*their* most effective troublemakers). Who made that cut to two years in exile in solitary and leg irons? (Bear in mind that we're talking about a population of officers only, American officers, and a population in which no more than one in three, one in three in all ranks, were naval officers.)

Eleven American officers were singled out as leaders too dangerous to keep in areas where they could in any way communicate with others. And I want to tell you that, from my vantage point as leader of the underground in that summer of 1967, that they picked the first team. Five were navy full commanders. The other six split out as two lieutenant commanders, one air force major, two air force captains, and one navy lieutenant (junior grade). The navy should be proud of that array. We called ourselves the Alcatraz Gang.

These overall solitary confinement totals for the four years of darkness should make the navy and particularly this Naval Academy proud. Average per capita months solo: non-navy average (field of 221): 6.5 months per prisoner; all-navy average (field of 110): 11.7 months per prisoner; U.S. Naval Academy average (field of 28): 15.5 months per prisoner.

To be locked up for *three years* in solitary, you really had to be a resistance problem to the Vietnamese. Only 8 prisoners of the 331 were in solo that long. Six of those 8 were navy. Five of the 331 were in solitary all four years. Four of the five were navy. Two of these four were U.S. Naval Academy graduates. U.S. Naval Academy grads represented only 8 percent of the total prison population.

Four of that Naval Academy twenty-eight who weathered all or part of that four years of darkness are here with me tonight: Denver Key, Jack Fellowes, Ned Shuman, and Bill Lawrence. In Hanoi, the tough, the intelligent, and the imaginative were the best performers; the experience was anything *but* a by-the-numbers routine. Each of these four had plenty of all three of those qualities *and* the moxie to bring his very best to bear; each proved himself to be a gold star resister when the going was tough. Some day you midshipmen will know what a comfort it is to be flanked in times of crisis by people of known reputation and backgrounds that evoke your total trust. And I needn't remind you that Naval Academy graduates were among those who gave their lives in prison.

That brings up the subject of an action that epitomizes the highest virtue to some of us and the worst sin to others: the willful giving of one's life for a cause, that is to say, human self-sacrifice. Philosopher Glenn Gray spent his youth as a soldier on the World War II battlefields of Europe and in his book *The Warriors* tells us that many humanists attack the impulse to self-sacrifice as the very core of moral evil, and some express their abhorrence of Christian saints like Paul and Augustine for their mystical conviction that without sacrifice no purgation from sin is possible. By contrast, after seeing men throw away their lives in battle when caught up in communal passion and expose themselves recklessly and carelessly to mortal danger, Gray admits that he was "cured forever of any easy interpretation of human motivation."

Gray the philosopher concludes: "Nothing is clearer than that man can act contrary to the alleged basic instinct of self-preservation and against all motives of self-interest and egoism. Were this not so, the history of our civilization would be completely different from what it has been."

Now a scientist, Edward O. Wilson of Harvard, geneticist, entomologist, and founder of sociobiology, from his book *On Human Nature*, chapter 7, "Altruism": "Generosity without hope of reciprocation is the rarest and most cherished of human behaviors, subtle and difficult to determine, distributed in a *highly selective pattern.* . . . In modern wars, a large percentage of Congressional Medals of Honor were awarded to men who threw themselves on top of grenades to shield comrades, aided the rescue of others from battle sites at the cost of certain death to themselves, or made other extraordinary decisions that led to the same fatal end."

I think the above quotations, from philosopher Gray and biologist Wilson, both professional scholars who are also personal friends of mine, are appropriate background for my final set of heroic examples. When Sybil and I are about to depart for the annual Congressional Medal of Honor Society get-together, people will say to us things like "I'll bet it's really a thrill to be with leaders like that" or "military thinkers like that" or "religious patriots" like that. Almost any gratuitous bestowal of specific virtues will do; we've heard most all of them. And many complimentary adjectives *do* apply to many of the members (there are about 185 Congressional Medal of Honor wearers now alive).

In sociological terms, the society is a diverse group. There are a few generals and admirals and privates and chief petty officers, men with advanced degrees, others who never finished the eighth grade, millionaires, postal letter carriers, chaplains, and bartenders. All these men mix on solid common ground—not only on a first-name basis but as true friends who take care of one another.

But to categorize them in what I might call "fitness report" language gets you off on a completely wrong track. These guys all have but *one big thing* in common: they will not accept the status quo if it does not meet their standards. They all have a short fuse when predicaments, as they see them, are not tolerable. For an instant or an hour or a month, each of them has stood up and turned his world around. "It's not *right* that that ticking hand grenade should kill everybody in this foxhole." "It's not *right* that this company of marines surrounded on this mountain top by the Chosin Reservoir should wither and freeze and surrender! We're going to break out of here!" "It's not *right* that I should bring harm to my fellow prisoners by letting myself be forced to inform on them."

Nobody gets this medal for his words or his attitude or his consistent high-quality judgment or reliability. It can't be given like an honorary degree after a superb campaign. He gets it for a specific *act*. (And it's not something he can try to get.) It all centers on this one impulse: "No, by God," "Not me," "Over my dead body."

I'm not drawing pictures of one-dimensional people. Guile, intelligence, cunning, subtlety, wizardry, stealth are all often part of what goes into the heroic act, in conjunction with the usual courage, willpower, and commitment. But the important thing is we're not talking about clever foxes; we're talking about hedgehogs. (I'm making the ancient Greek Archilochus's distinction, from his poem: "The clever fox knows many things, but the hedgehog knows one *big* thing.") And the one big thing these hedgehogs know is "Blast out; go for the jugular, never hesitate to lay down your life for your friends."

By way of your professional education I'll throw in the fact that the phrase "above and beyond the call of duty," which must be included in the citation, must be *literally* true, not just as we hear it in a manner of speaking. Literally, the phrase means that the act for which the medal is awarded must be beyond the concept of "duty," an act the recipient could not be properly ordered to perform. There are some very prestigious medals for heroic performance of duty out there—but this one is reserved only for acts that a person, often without conscious forethought, finds himself doing outside the law, outside the rules of procedure, outside what a decent person would ever feel justified in ordering him to do.

There *is* historical precedent for such criteria, starting with Napoleon's initiation of the highest class of his Legion of Honor in 1802 (it has been the European tradition ever since to have various *classes* of high awards, with only the highest being "above and beyond"—the German Iron Cross and others are examples). Only Britain and the United States have one "above and beyond"—the Victoria Cross, begun by Queen Victoria during the Crimean War, 1854, and the Congressional Medal of Honor, begun by Abraham Lincoln during the Civil War, 1862.

What I might call the post-1862 criterion of military heroism is given further legitimacy by those few modern philosophers who dare to address heroism. The old Spaniard Ortega y Gasset has an interesting chapter on heroism in his book *Meditations on Quixote*, which he wrote in 1914 while a professor of metaphysics at the University of Madrid. In specific terms, he goes even further than my remark about a hero being a person who once stood up and turned his world around. "The heroes of Homer," writes

Ortega, "belong to the same world as their desires. In Don Quixote, we have, on the other hand, a man who wishes to reform reality. Such men aim at altering the course of things; they refuse to repeat the gestures that custom, tradition, or even biological instinct try to force them to make."

Ortega's hero is so idealistic that he will not even tolerate reality. I like this thought, as you can tell, maybe because Don Quixote, hero, came out of the mind of a man who had been where I've been. Miguel Cervantes, author of that book by the same name, a best-seller in the West, second only to the Bible, had been a warrior captured by his enemies and restrained in a sixteenth-century prison not much different than mine. He was there, in an Algerian prison, for six years, was tortured, attempted six escapes, took six months in the hole with cuffs and irons, then was chained in his cell.

As I wind this up, I want to reiterate to you members of the brigade of midshipmen, you soon-to-be fellow alums of this beloved alma mater of mine, that my idea has not been to give a pep talk but to give you heads-up information that every military leader should have filed away about the depth and power and mystery that pervade that precious few that are always here and there in this great naval service of ours and just might wind up under your command. I don't think I have to labor the obvious. You know from common sense that what you have to say to the ordinary bloke to get him to charge will put these people into orbit. In times of peril their understandable impulsiveness and extraordinary conscientiousness require your best and special counsel and your protection against their squandering themselves on efforts that are not worthy of them.

To where have I come? My heroes, from Mad Jack to Jack Broughton to the Alcatraz Gang to the Congressional Medal of Honor Society to Don Quixote, all took action to try to make the world meet their standards. They all took on the status quo. Seldom, seldom, were they organization men—by that I mean acting a part that would normally be expected of a person, the best sort of person, performing the functions of his slot as listed on the organization chart. Hardly any of them performed their heroic acts in behalf of their organization as such. The organization was only incidental. What they did they did in behalf of their consciences. They were outside the organization game. Many came onto the stage from the wings, performed briefly, albeit brilliantly, and then disappeared into the wings. They performed their best outside the law and in the realm of stark individuality. I don't mean illegally, I mean extralegally, beyond the law. Maybe not too far from Aristotle's ideal: somewhere between the gods and the humans. Thank you.

HANOI REVISITED

*Address to the student body of the U.S. Naval
Postgraduate School, Monterey, California,
March 15, 1994.*

I'M GOING TO SHOW some slides and then a five-minute video clip. When I
called for the video setup, I thought that I would have a little movie of the
Stanford Travel Study trip to Hanoi to show you—complete with narration,
dialogue, music, the works.* It's about three days late because the studio of
our camera man, Ron Wyman, is in Portsmouth, New Hampshire, and he's
had mail and FedEx troubles due to snow. But for this presentation, I had
some of the regular photos we shot blown up for slides—fifteen quick
shots—and then a five-minute segment of the movie, a copy of which we
kept at Stanford.

This Stanford Travel Study trip emanated in Singapore, where we em-
barked on a brand-new shallow-draft ocean-going deluxe cruise ship. We
went up the Mekong to Phnom Penh, Cambodia, and then on up to Angkor
Wat in a beat-up Soviet turboprop, then back to Phnom Penh the same way,
and down to Saigon on the Mekong. Then it was the open sea, up to Da
Nang, with side trips to Hue and other cities, then up to Haiphong and into
Hanoi, then back to Haiphong and up to Hong Kong. We went north on
this trip as lecturers for Stanford University alums and south, back to Singapore, as lecturers for a mixture of Cornell University and Stanford University alums.

Half the slides are at the Hoa Lo prison north wall, in Hanoi. I did not
want to go through the North Vietnamese government to get permission to
go into the prisons. Former prisoners I know who have gone through the
government for photo coverage inside the prison have wound up on film in
conversations with people the likes of Hanoi Hannah. *Not for us!* But this
did not disturb the Stanford Alumni organizers, even though part of the big
draw they got for this trip centered on the *hope* we could tour inside. They
relied on their connections in the international tourism business, and the
Hanoi office got what they announced as an okay to go inside. But, typical
of my old captors, at lunch before we were to have prison access at 2 P.M.,

---

*Copies of the video are available for $29.95 each from the Stanford Alumni Association,
1-800-786-3738.

a man came rushing in to tell us the government had rescinded the agreement. So the buses just drove up and parked, and I gave a talk there beside the north wall and walked them all around the four-plus-block perimeter.

The little film clip is about my getting rid of some frustration by trying to storm the Citadel, the military headquarters area of the country, to see the little "bottom of the barrel" prison, a place we named "Alcatraz," where I and my ten henchmen spent a year and a half in exile located in the compound, right in front of the Ministry of National Defense. Then I'll talk no longer than twenty minutes, and we'll have the rest of the period for questions from you.

Now for the film, we went first to a place we called "the plantation," which I knew to be near Alcatraz; I had seen it only once but had never been locked up there; it was where the Vietnamese would take Jane Fonda to see the very few prisoners who would (1) be civil and (2) converse with her. From there, I go on instincts delved up from the night of October 25, 1967, twenty-seven years before, when I was taken from Hoa Lo, blindfolded in a jeep, to a parking place near the road, near this place we called the plantation, and walked into Alcatraz.

The commentator on this film—Clark Neher, professor of political science at Northern Illinois University, and widely studied and traveled in Southeast Asia—was one of the six lecturers (including me) on this Stanford Travel Study trip. Another speaker was George Shultz's former chief of staff, Charlie Hill, a career diplomat and now with the secretary general of the United Nations. All three of our wives also gave talks—both the other women are college professors, and as you know, Sybil knows Vietnam inside out.

Everybody wants to know what was the emotional/psychological impact on you and Sybil of having made this trip? this return, twenty-one years later, to a locale that has had such an impact on your lives? The *Stanford Magazine*, for one, wanted us to do a story about how we felt "way down here" while in Hanoi. I said, "Wait till it's over; there may not be any story there." And I'm glad I did say that because now that we're back, though Sybil and I have scratched our heads, we can think of no "surprising lessons learned," no "rebirths of perspective," no "inspirational revelations."

I think it's fact, and not sour grapes, when I say that Vietnam is the same place I left in 1973—a run-down country controlled by an authoritarian government, which the people fear. In the movie clip, a young, English-speaking representative of the Vietnam Tourist Bureau shook and almost cried when, after the last scene, I told the van driver to stop at the big yellow and red main gate of Vietnam's National Military Headquarters—their so-called Citadel of several square blocks in which Alcatraz is located. I asked him, our tourist guide, to come with me up to the big gate and interpret for me as I tried to get in to see a general officer to ask him if Sybil and I could be escorted on the *inside* of the wall, back a block and a half, to see Alcatraz proper.

He shook and wouldn't move. As I pleaded with him, a rinky-dink little soldier with a rifle almost as tall as he was wandered out of the gate and stared at us in the van. This terrified my tourist guide friend, and he pleaded, "No, no, no, we'll be in *trouble*; you don't *do* that here." I yelled at him, "You are scared to death, you are afraid of your own government!" The scene was on the film, with my words on the sound track, but for some reason the Stanford people cut it out. Throughout the visit, in matters that touched on my life there as a prisoner, I was listening to the same words I had heard from the Hanoi regime of the 1960s.

This "new openness" that the American business community is so thrilled with is mighty selective and mighty shallow. While we were in town—it was during that week when five U.S. senators and several senior American military officers were there, greasing the skids for the Clinton move to drop the embargo—the Hanoi government's English-language handout news sheet featured an article stressing the fact that their new economic ideas had *nothing* to do with internal political control of the people.

Friday, January 21, 1994. Headline! Communist Party Says "Doi Moi" Correct. Text: "In a political report to the Communist Party's midterm congress, the central committee confirmed the maintenance of its leadership and its categoric rejection of any pluralism or multiparty system." On page 2 was a story making fun of our attempts to maintain the embargo in the face of their black market: Headline! U.S. Products Sidestep Embargo. Text: "Marlboro cigarettes, 7-Up, Kodak film, Cummings engines, Carrier air-conditioners, and Hewlett-Packard computers are available *throughout* a country against which the U.S. government imposed an economic blockade when South Vietnam fell to the communist north nineteen years ago."

In a word, as I walked the streets of downtown Hanoi I felt right at home. Rebuffed by the government, the air hot, rich with bad smells, everybody running scared. As for what is to be *seen* in the city of Hanoi, except for a very "Soviet" square where Ho Chi Minh lies in state, the landscape is straight Tijuana, sprinkled with some majestic but mildewed old French buildings dating back to the nineteenth century.

After completing the downtown circuit it was Sybil who remarked, incredulously, that there was absolute *no sign* of bomb damage anywhere—the old French ministries of this and that, the old French Opera House, were all run-down and crumbling, but there had not been one chink of mortar disturbed by any bomb blast in the last hundred years.

During eleven days in late December 1972, however, the American press was full of horror stories about our B-52s over Hanoi. CBS gave six times more space to critical comment than to favorable comment. The *New York Times* had a ratio of nineteen to one, and the *Washington Post*, twenty-five to one. Samples:

> *New York Times* editorial, December 22, 1972: "terrorism on an unprecedented scale. . . . in the name of conscience, Americans must speak out for sanity in Washington and peace in Indochina."

> *Washington Post* article: Terror Bombing in the Name of Peace: "To pretend that we are doing otherwise, that we are making 'enduring peace' by carpet bombing our way across downtown Hanoi with B-52s—is to practice one more cruel deception."

> Front-page headline, *Washington Post*, December 30, 1972: Nixon's Christmas Deluge of Death

> Anthony Lewis: "a policy that many must know, history will judge, as a crime against humanity."

> Tom Wicker: "It is *we* who have loosed the holocaust."

> George McGovern, NBC interview, December 29: "In the last ten or eleven days, we've seen the *most murderous aerial bombardment in the history of the world.*"

U.S. bombing comparisons:

Tokyo, March 9, 1945—83,793 dead
Hamburg, July 27, 1945—44,600 dead

I was an eyewitness to the B-52 bombings of Hanoi and verify the following:

> Hanoi official claim: daily average for eleven days—119 dead (about the same as the daily stroke-death figure for that city of one million in those days).

Where were the bombs going? As the U.S. government said, out on the rail yards, out on the power plants. So much for George McGovern!
The backlash starts:

> Mal Browne, *New York Times*, March 31, 1973: "The damage caused by American bombing was grossly overstated by North Vietnamese propaganda."

Baltimore Sun: "Evidence on the ground disproves charges of indiscriminate bombing."

Washington Star: "In fact, the *city* of Hanoi was hardly touched."

But there are never any apologies from any of the offending papers or their journalists.

It is this kind of hypocrisy, and this sort of lying about the Vietnam War, which so many of the American people swallowed whole, that is upsetting for people like me to review, to relive. If there was an emotional undercurrent to our visit, it was this. And then on the ship I gave lectures about the war, not only the Tonkin Gulf affair but the overall way the war was waffled and screwed up by doves in hawks' clothing. McNamara, the chameleon, was doing LBJ's bidding blindly, flouting rule after rule that you and I as military officers hold sacred—all to get the war started, the Tonkin Gulf Resolution through Congress while the confusion factor was still blocking out the truth. Then, after nine months of waiting for LBJ to get reelected and settled in, *finally* Rolling Thunder started, a Rolling Thunder that was *designed* to destroy the North Vietnamese infrastructure à la Desert Storm—with rapid-fire timing, not allowing the enemy to recover between large-scale attacks, forcing them to withdraw from the war before they had any Russian equipment to speak of. McNamara then started backing off, pausing, playing the kind of mind games that were all the vogue in the "game theory" cult with whom he was at home. And then, waffling more seriously, McNamara chose the "middle course," which, as Winston Churchill said in his World War II memoirs, always leads "direct to the bull's-eye of disaster."

What I'm talking about was McNamara's throwing his weight behind a "cautious land war," to the disgust of not only General LeMay, chief of staff of the air force, but Harold Johnson, chief of staff of the army. And then, in November 1965, McNamara became a *dove dove dove* after seeing the results of the first battle in which DRV regulars faced off with helicopter-borne U.S. Army first-line regulars at the battle of Ia Drang. Within three months after I was shot down, all the decisions had been made that shaped the Vietnam War in the LBJ period.

Depressing as it was to go over all that with those Stanford grads, at least there was the compensation of their goodwill, many saying that they understood the Vietnam War and all the emotional undercurrents that went with being a participant for the first time.

Flashing back, I can't resist quoting myself from *In Love and War*, when this revelation suddenly struck me in prison. It was at the very low point of my imprisonment. I was at my wit's end, having been blindfolded and cuffed behind for a month, hunching around naked on the cement floor of Riviera cell number one, with a freshly rebroken left leg, caused by a goof of my regular torture guard. (He got nervous and put tension on my broken rather than my good leg as he was "giving me the ropes" at my "trial"—hemmed in between a semicircle of seated senior officer "judges" ahead of us and three ranks of soldiers with fixed beyonets behind us.)

In Love and War, page 276:

> My uncertainty extended to America's national resolve. As October [1967] wore on, it was clear, even to one whose only contact with the world was aural, that the bombing raids that were finally doing the job late that summer had dropped off. No longer did the siren scream all day. No longer were the Riviera doors being blown open by concussion. Just when America had finally gotten the idea of how to get this war over with, it was clear that we were being *betrayed* by the very men who couldn't wait for the right justification to start it. For the last three years or so, ever since those three days in August 1964 [Tonkin Gulf affair], I had had premonitions about getting left stranded high and dry on this LBJ Vietnam venture. And now the bottom was dropping out. Those conscience-stricken pissants who ran our government had suddenly "got religion." And my life was about to turn inward, away from all matters international.

Well, thank God I didn't know how screwed up we were before I put together and got the orders out for this underground organization that was now running things. I might not have had the drive, the heart to do it. And thank God I had been to postgraduate school, which in hindsight I think gave me the confidence to throw out a good portion of "the book" on how to run a prisoner-of-war civilization and to start over. The situation required it, and there was no other way to go. Survival training missed the Vietnam predicament by a mile (not a word about the tap code), and the Code of Conduct, though good in most aspects, became an executioner's block for the guillotine of *guilt* in a torture system in which no human being could stick to name, rank, serial number, and date of birth. We brought no psychotics back, and I take my share of credit for that. I was brought up short on that score when, at a West Point Society dinner, I had my ear bent considerably by a man who served his prisoner-of-war time in another place in another war, still a shaken man, haunted by guilt. We went the hard route and came home feeling good about ourselves.

One of my more traditional colleagues in prison was obviously feeling uncomfortable about the casualness with which I was transcending conventional thought, if not the Constitution itself: I mean, for instance, forbidding anybody to take amnesty. After I got home, I got a long letter from William Bundy about that; he was horrified. My prison friend used to say, "If we just knew what the people back in Washington would have us do!" And I said then and say now, "Thank God we had no communication with them; that was our number one asset." If I had had a secret telephone line with Washington and told them we were ordering people into torture, extending their prison time beyond what the benevolent Vietnamese thought appropriate, and so on, it would have blown their minds—at least the mind of William Bundy, assistant secretary of state for Far Eastern affairs.

No, any officer worth his salt, on detached duty and out of communication, has to have the right to sensibly modify the law, issue rules that fit the conditions, and be prepared to defend himself in court. Throughout those years, I figured that that was my most important function.

But I'm not here to sell the idea of "letting it all hang out." On the contrary, I intend that my message this afternoon makes it clear that even in the oddest circumstances of detached duty, we as warriors must keep foremost in our minds that there *are* boundaries to the prerogatives of leadership: *moral* boundaries.

Napoleon said, "In war, the moral is to the physical as three is to one." To focus a little closer on what *moral* meant to those early-nineteenth-century military thinkers who framed modern warfare, I go to Clausewitz: "It is not only in the loss of men, horses, and guns but *in order, courage, confidence, cohesion* and *plan* which come into consideration whether the engagement can still be continued or not. It is principally the *moral* forces which decide here." What he was saying was that failures of technique and management are tactical shortcomings that can be fixed but that failures of leadership's *nerve* and *character* are terminal, catastrophic. The moral forces are order, courage, confidence, and cohesion, forces that assure the troops' *faith* in the *integrity* of leadership, its *dependability* to keep consistent standards of right and wrong.

Integrity is a powerful word that derives from a specific concept. It describes a person who is *integrated*, blended into a *whole*, as opposed to a person of many parts, many faces, many disconnects. The word relates to the ancients' distinction between *living* and *living well*. Contrary to popular thought, a person of integrity is typically easygoing with a sense of humor. He knows himself, reflects a definite and thoughtful set of preferences and aspirations, and is thus reliable. Knowing he is whole, he is not preoccupied with riding the crest of continual anxiety but is free to ride the crest of *delight with life!*

Clausewitz again: "If we take a comprehensive view of the four components of the atmosphere in which war moves: danger, physical effort, uncertainty, and chance, it is easy to understand that a great *moral* force is needed to advance with safety and success in this baffling element, a force described as *energy, firmness, staunchness, strength of mind and character!*"

(Isn't it comforting that in the language of these old warriors, *morality* is something *manly* and not some drivel about its absence being circumscribed by only sexual abandon or fiscal irresponsibility, the only two applications I've ever seen the Pentagon make of the word.)

Morality *shadows war* and the preparation for it. Its echoes were always quietly vibrating even in the corridors of the North Vietnamese prisons. In the ordinary sense, what was moral to our jailers was immoral to us, but the *subject* lurked, always. I am not saying they honored our moral positions; but even as they waved them aside, if they detected conviction, consistency, and a sense of personal honor in us, their eyes sometimes betrayed the fact that they were inwardly moved. They winced when you stood your ground and made them send you through the ropes one more time. The commissar later muttered, "You are nothing like the French; we could always count on them to be *reasonable*." Aha!!

My patron saint, the first-century philosopher Epictetus, used to tell his students—aristocrats in their twenties, sent to him to learn what life is all about before they entered public service—"The judge will do some things to you which are thought to be terrifying, but how can he stop you from taking the punishment he threatened?" That became *our* kind of Stoicism in that pressure-packed microcosm of all human conflict. *Pain* was tactical and repairable, but *shame* was strategic and made you eternally vulnerable to those who would manipulate you to your downfall. Even the peasant soldier—and maybe *particularly* the peasant soldier—seemed to sense that, in the end, prolonged struggle is a *spiritual* battle and that the leak in the dike always starts from within.

That is human nature in the raw—in all its strengths, in all its pride and bullheadedness. Now it is sometimes thought "cool" to try to take the edge off that, to make allowances for every congenital defect, every wimpish inclination, to, as they say, "rise above human nature." But as Sir Arthur Conan Doyle had Sherlock Holmes say to Watson: "When one tries to rise above nature, one is liable to fall below it. The highest type of man may revert to *the animal* if he leaves the straight road of destiny. Consider, Watson, that the materialists, the sensualists, the worldly would all prolong their worthless lives. The *spiritual* would now avoid the call to something higher. It would be the survival of the least fit. What sort of cesspool may not our poor world become?"

That is what I learned in prison and what I believe. Thank you.

ANDERSONVILLE
MEMORIAL DAY SPEECH _____

1994

LADIES AND GENTLEMEN and *particularly* my fellow prisoners of war: May I welcome you to Andersonville, Georgia, the ceremonial home of all American prisoners of war—past and future. As most of you know, an organization named Friends of Andersonville, under its president, Carl Runge of Atlanta, a former prisoner of war himself, is supporting us in a fund drive to create here a fitting place for our remembrance of our former comrades behind bars and a place where loved ones and descendants of all American prisoners of war of all times may visit, reflect, and remember the sacrifices of their forebears.

This is the right place for such a memorial, for the National American Prisoner of War Museum we plan to complete here. It's right for symbolic reasons, for historic reasons. First, because by a tremendous margin, our Civil War produced many times more prisoners of war than any other war in America's history. More than fifty thousand of them *died* in prisoner-of-war camps, North and South. If their names were on a memorial it would be as big as the Vietnam Wall, where Americans who gave their lives *for all causes* in that late lamented war are listed. And such numbers would of course exceed American deaths *for all causes* in both World War I and the Korean War.

And in what *camp* have more American prisoners of war spent time than *in any other* in our history? You guessed it, Andersonville, right here. Forty-five thousand of them, at one time or another, in the just less than fourteen months it was an active prisoner-of-war camp for Union soldiers.

So this Andersonville place is our "center of gravity." This is a national historic site, the only prison ground in America to be so designated, and for our support here we have the National Park Service, with Fred Boyles, our local superintendent. The law providing for this national historic site prescribes that it be a place "to interpret the role of prisoner-of-war camps in America's history." And there will be plenty of scholars doing just that when our National Prisoner of War Museum is completed and stocked with archival documents—yours and mine.

People out west ask me, "Why so many prisoners, and why so many prisoner deaths in places like Andersonville in the Civil War?" For fourteen years, I have been working in an office surrounded by books, and *they* tell me it goes something like this: Almost nobody on either the South or the North side predicted the length or ferocity of the maelstrom that was precipitated by actions at Fort Sumter in mid-April 1861. The *firepower* of both sides grew to be *tremendous* as compared with previous wars, *the will to win* of both sides grew to be *furious*, and the combat generals *became* skilled, determined, and (naturally) *destructive*, particularly in the last year of that four-year war. It got the world's attention; the woods were full of authorized neutral military observers from Europe, frantically following every maneuver on the battlefields, taking notes. What we now think of as modern warfare was being born. In the first year, casualty and prisoner capture rates on both sides registered record levels, and by the fourth year, they exceeded what would have been *anybody's* estimate beforehand.

At the time of Fort Sumter, the United States Army was made up of fewer than sixteen thousand officers and men. A year later, they found themselves *in custody* of more than sixteen thousand *prisoners!* And in those years, prisoners were nothing but a drain on the captive power; you had to feed them and guard them, and when you were short of material, you had to use it on the war first and on them second. In February 1862, just ten months after Fort Sumter, U. S. Grant himself took fourteen thousand prisoners in a single day when General Buckner surrendered Fort Donelson in the woods of Tennessee. At the time, that fourteen thousand was the largest number of prisoners ever captured in any American war. (In the months ahead, either side's taking fourteen thousand prisoners grew to be routine.) Unconditional surrender was the order of the day on both sides! Many of you probably remember Grant's famous reply, scratched on a scrap of paper at three in the morning by torchlight, to Buckner's request for terms: "No terms but unconditional surrender; I propose to move immediately upon your works."

Three years and three months later, in May and June 1864, the same General Grant with about 115,000 men locked horns with General Robert E. Lee and his about 75,000 men for a month of fighting near Richmond. These were pitched battles in the Wilderness, at Spotsylvania, at Cold Harbor, and other spots. Grant *lost* fifty-five thousand men in a month, many of them taken prisoner, and he probably captured two-thirds as many from Lee.

Robert E. Lee's anticipation of those late-war battles in the Richmond area brought about the commissioning of this prison at Andersonville. By the end of 1863, a cluster of Yankee prisoner-of-war holding sites had grown up around Richmond. General Lee had ordered their dispersal to a location farther from the action, farther from the threat of northern cavalry recovery parties. This spot here in southwest Georgia filled that requirement, and early in 1864, this ground was hurriedly cleared and wheels set in motion to accommodate about ten thousand prisoners from the Richmond area. The first drafts started to arrive in late February 1864, only two and a half months before the heavy confrontations between Grant and Lee in the Wilderness.

I've read extensively from the writings of two Union sergeants who were early arrivers here: John McElroy of the Illinois Cavalry, who came with a draft from Libby Prison, Richmond, on February 26, and two weeks later, John Ransom, Michigan Cavalry, who had been in several prisons in the Richmond area, including Bell Isle and the third floor of the Pemberton Building, a large tobacco warehouse. They were *only here for six months* before being taken to another prison, which was typical of the times. (Some say the average time in the stockade here overall was only four months per prisoner.) Both my sergeants left Andersonville on the same night, September 7, 1864, one week after Sherman took Atlanta. Only a month before their departure, on August 8, Andersonville had hit its high watermark of prison population: 33,200 prisoners sharing only twenty-one acres of ground (I subtracted the areas of the creek, the swamp, and the deadline space), in the stockade, out there in that Georgia summer sun.

I think the compressed nature of the story helps us understand the rush-rush immediacy, the lack of logistic warning and preparation, and the over-crowding that nobody anticipated, that framed the sagas of the camps activated late in the war, both North and South, which wound up with the highest death rates.

Consider this just a modern-day Yankee's quick study if you like, but I think I've got it right. Andersonville was born of Lee's anticipation of trouble with Grant in the prison backyards of Richmond. Then the unprogrammed escalation of battlefield activity in the Richmond area started a flood of prisoners, which overfilled the prison to twice its design capacity *within three months* after it opened and then to more than *three times* its capacity during the *next* three months. Meanwhile, what had been peace of mind, a haven safe from enemy action down here in southwest Georgia, when the prison opened, changed to a feeling of insecurity, brought about by Union cavalry sorties into places like nearby Macon as a part of Sherman's preparation to envelop Atlanta. (I'm thinking particularly of the Stoneman raid in July 1864, which had Sherman's permission to come on down here and open up the prison gates after they destroyed their assigned targets in Macon, fifty-plus miles up the road. Thing was, Stoneman was stopped cold in his tracks at Macon, and only those of his men who were taken prisoner ever actually got down here.)

On July 11, General Johnston, then in charge of Atlanta's defense, sent a telegram to President Jefferson Davis strongly recommending immediate "redistribution" of the prisoners then in Andersonville. By late July, slaves and such guards as remained (the experts, the Confederate regulars, having been called to the battlefronts) were frantically building defensive earthworks around the stockade. Ransom and McElroy's departure on September 7 was part of the first "redistribution" draft (eighteen detachments, sixty-five hundred prisoners) headed for Savannah, where they would build their own prison. By the end of November, only 1,350 (mostly ill) prisoners remained, and they dribbled off until Andersonville was finally closed at the end of the war, at the time of Appomattox.

Andersonville's mortality rate was high; forty-five thousand captives and thirteen thousand deaths comes to 29 percent. But that rate was less than the 32.5 percent at the Union prison at Elmira, New York, another "late in the war" improvised prison that did not open until four months after Andersonville and was at *twice* its designed capacity within a month. And although the Union prison in Chicago, named Camp Douglas, had a mortality rate of only 17 percent of the 22,301 prisoners they processed, they lost 10 percent of their prisoner population in the period of a single month, mostly to smallpox.

After reading just five books on Civil War prisons, as a seasoned, nearly eight-year prisoner of war myself, I want to give you my gut feelings about the camp conditions North and South. The deaths were tied almost exclusively to poor sanitation and contagious diseases. I sensed nothing like the purges I and some of you have been through, where they isolated one prisoner after another and tortured him, choked him, shut off his blood circulation, sometimes broke his bones to get him to spill his guts about who authorized the escape attempt or whatever. In a book about the trial of Andersonville's stockade commandant, Captain Henry Wirz, I saw incompetence, I saw neglect, but I didn't see conspiracy, the crime he was executed for. My two rough-cut sergeants give me a real feel for what he was like. On March 25, two days before Wirz took over the stockade, Ransom had a first look at him and reported it like this: "Not a very prepossessing looking chap. Is about 35 or 40 years old rather tall, and a little stoop shouldered. Skin has a pale, white livered look, with thin lips. Has a sneering sort of cast of countenance. Makes a fellow feel as if he would like to go up and boot him." Ransom, in the same diary a month later, April 26: "On the 21st of April, the tunnel was opened and two fellows belonging to a Massachusetts regiment escaped to the outside. Hendryx and myself next went out. The night was very dark. Came up out of the ground way on the outside of the guards. [They were found by dogs and recaptured.] Captain Wirz interviewed us. After cussing us a few minutes we were put in the chain gang, where we remained for two days. . . . Not so bad after all." In fourteen months, 329 prisoners successfully escaped from Andersonville, by that I mean, made it back to their own people. McElroy said a very telling thing about Wirz: "He has no concept of governing." But later he says, "I never saw him kill anybody, and I never talked to anybody who did." Sounds to me like just the regular dumbbell misfit we've all seen running prisoner-of-war prisons.

There is a myth that prisoners of war don't like to talk about their experiences. I love to talk about mine, and when I run into somebody who clams up, I want to ask, "What are you ashamed of?" *No two wars have the same kind of prison regime.* My prison experience was *entirely* different from McElroy's and Ransom's. As I said earlier, prisoners in the Civil War were a sheer bother, period, to both sides. And they were a logistic drain: guards for them meant a loss of combat manpower, the camp a deadweight millstone around the detaining power's neck, definitely not worth sacrificing an ounce of war effort on. Neglect of prisoners and indifference toward them grew to be standard operating procedure in such places.

God, how I wish I could have had a little of that neglect and indifference. During the cold war, the Communists took a look at the worldwide, almost universal participation in newspaper reading and radio listening and made their prisoners of war prime targets for propaganda extortion. "World approval" was the master chip every tinhorn power coveted; a soulful plea for peace and seemingly heartfelt disapproval of his country's so-called aggression from a sincere-looking hangdog prisoner of war were thought to be *dynamite!* "Political officers," commissars of propaganda, ran the prisons, and their every effort was bent on producing sufficiently intimidated prisoners to deliver the lines prescribed by their masters on schedule, at press conferences with fellow-traveling newsmen who would see that the transcriptions or television newsclips got on world news. Coercion and torture were used to intimidate, and the highest crime was "inciting the other criminals to oppose the camp authority," exerting American leadership, in other words. To the die-hard leaders went years of solitary confinement and isolation. (I myself had more than four years totally alone.) Food and medicine were Third World and bland but seldom the crucial things. Any amount of coarse commodities or manpower was worth sacrificing to keep the propaganda mill rolling. After the regulars went to the front, Andersonville got down to about one guard to thirty or forty prisoners; I spent two years in a compound with thirteen tiny cells, in leg irons and solitary throughout, and the eleven of us prisoners there were watched by two officers and thirty-three guards.

But things got so bad we staged another riot there anyway. (We got in that tiny prison pesthole by staging a riot, and this was a second.) As a result, I got kicked out of even this place we called Alcatraz and for a year was not allowed in *any* compound; special handlers kept me in dark cubbyholes.

Sergeant Ransom had one thing wrong. He said the Civil War took the spunk and fire out of prison life. What about spunk and fire in this stockade in July 1864 when you had the gang wars, North versus North, the Raiders versus the Regulators! God, I would have loved to have been there—a real drama, in which the prisoners set up control of their own lives with their own police force!

At a later time, I shared a set of leg stocks on a single slab bed with a fellow prisoner who, as a shot-down fighter pilot in 1944 and 1945, had served time in a Nazi prison in Germany. I asked him to compare the two predicaments. "Very different," he said. "The Nazis wanted nothing from us, no military secrets (they knew all that), no propaganda; we were just a bother to keep alive. All I had to worry about was wear and tear on my body; I was cold and I was hungry. But here, it's wear and tear on your nervous system."

Different, different, different. Who knows what's next?

But as there have been and will be differing challenges to different generations of American prisoners of war, there are also commonalities of virtue that we all try to live up to: Being loyal to our fellow American prison mate, making sacrifices in his behalf if he is down; if tempted, being strong to resist; if missing the mark, having the courage to try again; and so living that you can stand unashamed and unafraid before your prison mates, your loved ones, and the Almighty.

This is the message our National Prisoner of War Museum must resonate!

Perhaps you will share the meaning of this closing poem, which I'm told was found, unsigned, in a Civil War prison:

> We asked for strength that we might achieve;
> God made us weak that we might obey.
> We asked for health that we might do great things;
> He gave us infirmity that we might do better things.
> We asked for riches that we might be happy;
> We were given poverty that we might be wise.
> We asked for power that we might have the praise of men;
> We were given weakness that we might feel the need of God.
> We asked for all things that we might enjoy life;
> We were given life that we might enjoy all things.
> We received nothing that we *asked* for
> But all that we *hoped* for.
> And our prayers were answered. We were most blessed.

Thank you.

MY KIND OF GUYS

LAUNCHING OF THE NAVY FRIGATE
AUBREY WRAY FITCH ⸻

Remarks made in Bath, Maine, October 16, 1981.

IT HAS BEEN CLEAR to me ever since I arrived in Maine that the people of this great shipyard and the people of Sagadahoc and Lincoln Counties see the launching of this U.S. Navy frigate *Aubrey Fitch* not only as an event that bodes well for the defense of our country, a clear and important manifestation of our president's commitment to rebuild the fleet, not only as yet another time to take pride in Bath Iron Works' craftsmanship and efficiency, but as a genuine old-fashioned community celebration, a celebration of tribute to that hero of this state, in fact of this very neighborhood, for whom this ship is named.

It is a celebration of tribute to Grandfather Fitch for me and my family, too. You see, his grandson David, whose wife, Cindy, is our matron of honor, was both a college and a prep school classmate and best friend of my son Sid. So it was also with his brother Bill Fitch and my son Stan. Moreover, my wife, Sybil, and the boys figured out, while I was away as a prisoner of war, that Grandfather Fitch was my Naval Academy superintendent during my last year as a midshipman. He commissioned me more than thirty-five years ago.

The coincidences continue. I'm now at Stanford University, in California, a senior research fellow at the Hoover Institution, whose archives include the official and personal papers of Admiral Aubrey Fitch. I've read them all, and I want to use most of the few minutes I'll be before you to tell you people from this shipyard and nearby countryside more about the early service life of my old boss and your old neighbor than appears in his many inspiring official biographies of the sort that is in our programs today. I hope I can give you a picture of the magnificently spirited, impish, resilient, case-hardened, compassionate husband, father, and warrior that comes through to me.

They called him Jakey, or sometimes Polecat, during his days at Annapolis. He came from a small town in Michigan where he generated an intense ambition to see the world as a service officer. By the time the Spanish-American War started, he was in a military prep school in Wisconsin. It took him two tries to get into the Naval Academy from there, but that didn't worry him. He knew he was going to make it. He knew he would fit. And he was right in both cases. Only five feet seven inches but the toughest scrapper in the class of 1906—varsity football, boxing champ, oarsman, top gymnast. Then off to the China Station on his destroyer, via the Suez Canal and the Red Sea. Junior officer hijinks in Manila in the old Army-Navy Club with his pals "Spuds" Ellyson and Ken Whiting. Jakey and Ken had been perennial opponents in the boxing finals at the academy, and when their ships visited the same port and they came face to face in the better bars of the Far East, like the British Club in Shanghai, for instance, they would sometimes enjoy confusing the patrons with a mock fist fight before strolling off arm in arm for a drink. "Seventy years ago barflies half way around the world were disappointed in the sudden ending of what started like a good grudge fight," writes Admiral George van Deurs, a later shipmate of them all in their flying days.

Spuds and Ken were destined to be among our navy's first aviators. Spuds, our very first, got himself into flight training in 1911; that is to say, he learned to fly under the personal instruction of Glen Curtiss. And there's hardly a naval aviator alive who didn't learn to fly at the field in Pensacola named after early aviator Ken Whiting. Jakey Fitch would get into flying in due course; in fact it would be he who would *first* execute in battles at sea the tactics that those old pals of his were to develop in open cockpits over a dozen dirt airstrips in the 1920s. But Jakey had a lot of other important things to do first—like coming back to the East Coast and getting married to Dennie (in 1912), having a family of three boys, fighting World War I as gunnery officer of a battleship, and working his way up to command a couple of ships not too much different in size from the one behind me. It was sheer providence that he took the time to develop a reputation as a seaman that would put him in a senior position of command at sea at a crucial time.

Jakey sprung himself loose and went to Pensacola in 1929. He got his wings on February 4, 1930. He was forty-six years old, and yet he could fly like a man twenty years younger.

There's not time for me to go through the life story in chronological order. There is no surprise ending. You probably know that Aubrey served for seventeen more years, the last five of which included not only the Naval Academy but high-level wartime service as commander of all aircraft in his close friend William Halsey's South Pacific Fleet and as deputy chief of naval operations for air. I'm sure you know he retired with four stars in 1947 at the age of sixty-four and *still* saved another thirty years to enjoy living on his beloved coast of Maine with you folks. (In his papers I came across a letter he wrote on August 20, 1946, just a couple of months after I graduated. It was to the First National Bank of Damariscotta, asking them to keep an eye open for waterfront property for him and Mrs. Fitch.)

What I want to get on to, what I want to remember about him, what should go forward as legend and example to the future crews of this ship that bears his name, is that essence of vigor, of spirit, of bravery, of practiced resilience under stress that he himself had nurtured through self-discipline and ultimately crystallized into action and judgment in the service of his country when the chips were down. I'm talking about those special six months in his life when it all came together. I'm talking about the spring of 1942.

(We all wind up with long life stories, but I think that in our heart of hearts most of us can see it as all uphill to one well-defined pinnacle, or at least one plateau, then all downhill, often in a pleasant glide to be sure, but downhill from that decisive time when all of our being was called for and used.)

Jakey had made rear admiral about a year and a half before Pearl Harbor and by the time of that attack was well into his first flag job as commander, Carrier Division One, in the aircraft carrier USS *Saratoga*. He knew ships, he knew aircraft carriers (he had commanded both the *Langley* and the *Lexington*), and he knew aviation (he had been actively at the stick and throttle for ten years, had commanded two major air stations and the major patrol wing at Ford Island). The U.S. Navy's communication system was choked up with superpriority emergency traffic just after Pearl Harbor. Never preoccupied with details, after Admiral Fitch got his planes aboard the *Saratoga* and his two destroyer escorts ready to go, he just sent a commercial telegram to Washington saying that he was heading for points west to look for Japanese naval units and left San Diego with his little task force on December 8. At that time there was a total of five aircraft carriers in our Pacific Fleet. During the next six months Aubrey Fitch would at one crucial time or another control three of them.

By the time the *Saratoga* approached Hawaii, it was clear that the Japanese attacking force that launched the Pearl Harbor assault had retired to the west. Fitch, one of the few tactical aviators qualified for task force command, found himself the man of the hour at Pacific Fleet headquarters. He and his staff were transferred immediately to the *Lexington*, where he was to command the air task force of that ship and the *Yorktown* as they sped southwest to head off the obvious Japanese thrust to the south. Singapore fell in February, and the Philippines were under seige in March when Admiral Fitch launched one of the first telling counterblows of the war: On March 10, more than a hundred of his airplanes from the *Lexington* and *Yorktown* interdicted an ongoing Japanese amphibious landing at Rabaul; two cruisers were sunk. The Doolittle raiders took the next shot as they left the *Hornet* on April 18. Corregidor fell on May 6 as Fitch's carriers took positions in the Coral Sea to confront the major Japanese fleet closing toward Australia.

Reading of these times, and comparing them with the recent past, drives home what a different frame of reference, what a different breed of leader, was in the driver's seat then. Robert Strange McNamara, who ran the Vietnam War, couldn't have stood to have Aubrey Fitches on the line, Chester Nimitzes at Pearl Harbor, and Ernie Kings in Washington. And I don't think they would have hung around to play games with him. In that spring of 1942, the press asked Admiral King, chief of naval operations, what his strategy was. "Calculated risk," he laconically replied. "We just put the bulk of what we have where the Japanese are most likely to strike, where the U. S. stands to lose or win the most." Not exactly McNamara's schoolboy "keeping one's options open" philosophy.

In Aubrey Fitch, King had exactly the right man on the spot to carry out his "calculated risk" strategy. On May 7 the scout aircraft landed back aboard *Lexington* at 8:45 in the morning with Japanese fleet sighting reports. By 11 A.M. both the *Lexington* and the *Yorktown* air groups were airborne with bombs and torpedoes en route to intercept those units sighted, some two hundred miles to the northwest. At 11:30 Jakey Fitch broke into a smile as Lieutenant Commander Bob Dixon's radio message to him was relayed back: "Scratch one flat top."

The next day, May 8, was more exciting. Early in the morning, our scouts located a Japanese task force with two more carriers. Fitch launched his planes as before. Reconstruction of the battle shows that ours and the Japanese air armadas crossed out of sight of each other. (Armada is a good word: this was as historic a sea battle as the English victory over the Spanish Armada in 1588; it was the first ever in which opposing ships were never close enough to fire their guns at one another.) As our planes were in the midst of their attack of the Japanese fleet, 108 Japanese aircraft rolled in on the *Lexington* and the *Yorktown*. At one point in the sixteen-minute attack, Admiral Fitch's lookouts were reporting to him eleven torpedo wakes in sight. He evaded all but two of them. Also, two bombs went through the deck, but, through it all, his white head and grinning face could be seen high above as he looked over his bridge rail holding up fingers to keep the damage control crews on the flight deck up to date on how many Japanese planes were shot into the water. He ran out of fingers five times. Stanley Johnson of the *Chicago Tribune* was aboard, watching the admiral in disbelief. "Throughout, he remained easy going, relaxed, never ruffled," he wrote. Maybe some of those bouts with Ken Whiting nearly forty years before had taught him not to panic. At that point in time, Aubrey Fitch was a month away from his fifty-ninth birthday. I checked his logbook, and he had flown two back seat SBD-3 hops off the *Lexington* two days before.

Well, by the time the remaining Japanese planes staggered away and our planes got back home, the *Lexington* fires appeared to be under control. The damage control gangs had righted the ship to only about a six-degree list, the engineers had built up power for about twenty-four knots, and our planes were landed aboard. All over the ship people were elated as reports circulated about our air groups' having severely damaged another Japanese carrier and sunk a bunch of ships. But then Jakey's sixth sense, a sense of caution that he seldom called on, came into play. There were too many ruptured gas lines on that ship, too many fumes, too many unsolved damage control puzzles down below. He gassed the planes and sent 'em to the beach as a precaution. Sure enough, within an hour, gigantic explosions started to rock his old *Lexington*, a ship he had commanded six years before. His experienced leader's mind was clear of anxiety, frustration, or self-doubt as he strolled up behind Captain Sherman, the current skipper, tapped him on the shoulder, and said in what I think must have been a calm, almost fatherly voice: "Fred, it's time to get the men off this thing." That call alone saved twenty-seven hundred lives. The *Lexington*, listing more and more, without steering power or radios, went down soon after a casualty-free evacuation.

Oh, yes. Like everybody else, the admiral abandoned ship and was recovered safely. He helped a few sailors out of the water himself. He got back in touch with Admiral Nimitz and was aboard the *Saratoga* as soon as possible, racing toward the other major battle of that tide-turning spring, the Battle of Midway. But he was just too far away to get there in time.

Then he started getting promoted into what conventional wisdom would label as bigger and better things. But I doubt that he thought of them that way. After all, the Battle of Coral Sea epitomized the spirit of his generation, "calculated risk." And he got to be the very guy who brought it off! It was close, but it worked. The ship losses were about even; we had fewer air losses, but we were a smaller force and intentionally took a disadvantageous position in harm's way at the crucial time and turned the trend of the whole war around. Aubrey Fitch's whole life had prepared him to fill that unique gap in a way that no one could have exactly anticipated. He fit, just like he did when he got to Annapolis. And he knew he would, just like he did there. Not many are so fortunate in their lifetimes. Maybe that's one reason why he reflected a happiness in the autumn of his years here in Maine with you.

He would like this sleek frigate behind me. Like him, there is something so open, so "no-nonsense" about it. Straight integrity, no frills. It's not gold-plated, just iron, cold iron. And that's what we need.

> Gold is for the mistress
> Silver for the maid
> And copper for the craftsman

Cunning in his trade.

"Good!" said the Baron,
Sitting in his hall,
"But iron—cold iron
Shall be master of them all."
—Rudyard Kipling

THE FATE OF A
GOOD DOCTOR

A review of A. B. Feuer, ed., Bilibid Diary:
The Secret Notebooks of Commander Thomas Hayes
(Hamden, Conn.: Archon Press, 1987).

THOMAS HAYES WAS BORN on February 8, 1898, became a physician, and was commissioned in the Medical Corps of the U.S. Navy in 1924. A reflective dreamer and thinker, he was later to write in these prison camp memoirs that he sensed his life taking an irreversible turn in the summer of 1940 when, as a senior lieutenant commander, he received orders to sea aboard the cruiser USS *Milwaukee.* "I had known happiness—real happiness. I had found the life I always wanted. But I knew when I left on this cruise that I was done, washed up as a happy wanderer." He was never again to see the wife and son he left in Tidewater Virginia.

After a year aboard ship (during which he "never did adjust," he later wrote), he made the promotion list for commander and was transferred to the staff of the Sixteenth Naval District, Philippine Islands. Pearl Harbor came four months later. Bombed out of Cavite on December 10, he made his way to the Fourth Marine Regiment, where he became its chief medical officer, and on New Year's Day 1942, his date of rank as a three-striper, his new command became a part of the American holdout garrison on Corregidor. Captured by the Japanese on May 6, 1942, he was put in the old Spanish Bilibid penitentiary in downtown Manila on July 2. He remained there for nearly two and a half years, until, at the age of forty-six, he was swept up in the frantic Japanese effort to remove all their prisoners to the Home Islands for service in their factories and mines. But like thirteen hundred other American prisoners, he died a horrible death, under despicable conditions, en route in the hold of a northbound ship.

Hayes's extensive diaries were discovered hidden in Bilibid prison soon after World War II. There are gaps in his chronology (notably a nine-month one from January 2, 1943, to October 1 of that year), but he leaves us a vivid picture of prisoner-of-war (POW) life in Manila during the war. Thanks to his reflective nature and candidness, Hayes also tells us much

Reprinted from the *Naval War College Review*, Spring 1990.

about the captives' frame of mind during those years. In comparing POW concerns under Japanese Imperialists with those under Vietnamese Communists, more is different than the same. But contrary to popular lore about the difference between soldiers' attitudes in "popular" versus "unpopular" wars, Hayes's reminiscences and skepticisms could just as well have come from a similarly cynical and strong-willed American POW in Vietnam.

For a veteran of Hanoi's central "clearinghouse" prison (the French-built Hoa Lo) to review these precious, unspoiled first-person accounts of life in Manila's central "clearinghouse" prison (the Spanish-built Bilibid), and not digress on the differences of captors' style and philosophy, would seem to me to be a waste of knowledge. In a nutshell, while to Japanese Imperialists a POW prison was a bother, to Vietnamese Communists it was a propaganda farm.

The purpose of a modern communist prison is the breaking of prisoners' wills in an effort to squeeze secrets and propaganda performances out of them. The purpose of a World War II Japanese prison seemed to be just keeping people locked up and feeding them as little as possible. Stories of these Japanese prisons are chronicles of dietary deprivation, dysentery, fever, recreational prisoner bashing, and high death rates. Communists aren't "good feeders," but their wear and tear is not so much on the prisoner's physical plant as on his nervous system. Every prisoner is considered to be in "workup" for propaganda exploitation; the commissar has deadlines to meet, and that means he must discipline his guards to *never* engage in personal conversations with prisoners, to demand strict obedience of a myriad of "tripwire" laws, and to engage in "prisoner bashing" only as scripted by the boss. His prisoners must be prevented from communicating with one another, and his political cadres are schooled to bear down on them with solitary confinement, one-on-one intimidation sessions, and repeated, emphatic, controlled, and purposeful physical torture sufficient to gain total submission. Prisoners are valuable assets, and their deaths are practically limited to natural causes and torture overshoots.

So it is with surprise, knowing in advance of the horrible death rates, that a prisoner from a communist "pressure cooker" reads of hundreds of American POWs almost totally without threat of solitary or torture and in direct contact with English-speaking Japanese and Filipino nationals (military and civilian) who had the run of the city. The result is a relatively disciplinless prison, open to smuggled notes from the outside, newspapers, espionage contacts, intrigue—a place where senior prisoners like Hayes (chief of surgery and later senior medical officer of the prison) are in semi-social contact with their jailer counterparts, taking meals and drinks in their quarters on occasion and sometimes at Manila restaurants.

To be sure, these jailer (Japanese medical officer) counterparts were seldom the vicious caricatures we used to see in war films of the 1940s, but as the story unfolds it becomes clear that their second- and third-level functionaries were capable of heinous terrors (like ordering the murder of the fifteen sickest Americans on their way to the hell ships bound for Japan). But to a person used to the total silence and solitude of a "clamp-down" prison, day-to-day life as a captive of the Japanese in Manila reads more like being caught in a treacherous web of intrigue in a semicivilian atmosphere.

This "civilian atmosphere" has roots. The Japanese professed great interest in the "Geneva treaty" with regard to the treatment of prisoners. That, of course, was the Geneva Convention of July 27, 1929—the last one of that series to have been ratified before World War II. Since their inception, Geneva Conventions on the treatment of prisoners of war have been phrased in terms that take the prisoner out of the military context to the maximum extent possible and put him in a category of "benevolent quarantine," with minimal residual national ("home country") obligations, "answerable only to himself and humanity." They don't speak of the senior prisoner being commanding officer of his countrymen incarcerated with him. They refer to "prisoners' representatives," subject to a prisoners' vote where possible and, in the case of the 1929 convention, also "subject to the approval of the military authority"—which the Japanese obviously presumed to be Japanese military authority.

Accordingly, the Japanese selected the American prisoners' representative of their choice ("camp warden," they called him), who, so far as they were concerned, commanded the American contingent in prison. In the case of Bilibid, that designated commander was an alcoholic chief warrant officer (machinist) who had his own private liquor supply and mess, played favorites, worked deals, had a free gangway to and from town, ruled like a despotic potentate, buttered up the Japanese, and throughout his term of office told American commanders and colonels, such as Hayes, what to do. This camp warden (the "field marshal," as many Americans called him) was given real power by the Japanese. If an American prisoner wanted a few hours alone out in town, he, and only he, could set it up with the gate guards. Hayes would not trust the "field marshal" with sensitive material like escape plans and had reason to believe that to make his muster lists come out right, he had forged at least two American death certificates. "[He is] crooked, untrustworthy, characterless, and dumb," wrote Hayes. "The most disgusting and unforgettable fact [which typified his regime] . . . is the toadying, backslapping, handshaking, and condoning of his acts which has marked the conduct of so many of our officers. They feared him and hoped to feather their nests by playing up to the bastard."

It wasn't until after the Korean War that President Eisenhower issued the American military man's Code of Conduct, which clearly and specifically overrode all Geneva Convention biases against Americans' national obligations behind bars. His Code of Conduct established the position that the regular American chain of command holds in or out of captivity and that for the American POW the war continues behind bars. Under this code and the instruction now attendant to it, American prisoners would have known in advance never to obey the orders of an American set up as a puppet governor by the captor power.

This bogus chain of command, which the American prisoners let stand, played no small part in generating the "me-first" mood Hayes's commentaries repeatedly complain about. He describes a prison population who grew to let personal interests override the greater good of the community: "It is a constant fight against personal selfishness, a continual battle against individuals who would sacrifice their comrades for personal gain." Another catalyst for this self-centered attitude, also triggered by the Geneva Convention, were the provisions for a more or less independent economic life for each of these "obligation-free, citizens of the world" prisoners. Prisoners, said the Geneva rules, are supposed to be able to buy things in stores, and they are supposed to be paid by the captor power. The Japanese allowed a store to be run by a U.S. Army clerk, who bought items of food out in town, first with collections from prisoners who arrived with pocket money and eventually from the "pay" the Japanese started printing up.This led to endless squabbles, which came to dominate much of prison life, and eventually put the American prisoners in the position of being partially responsible for their own starvation.

Neither the flavor of the times in Manila nor of the mind of Hayes can be had without a few last quotes from his diaries:

On the run-down physical condition of Americans. June 9, 1942— "Conspiracies are at work" (under the food distribution system worked out by the "field marshal"). July 22, 1942—"The Japanese couldn't understand why we were in such a state of starvation and malnutrition at the time of our surrender, and yet there were tons of food stored on Corregidor. That's something we would all like to have explained to us."

On the plight of prisoners taken at Corregidor. July 30, 1942—"We have every reason to belive that our country has scratched us off their list as a lost cause. Certainly, if they made no attempt to help us while we were fighting, they surely won't consider it worthwhile now." August 23, 1942— "It was one year ago that I arrived in the Philippines. . . . It was expected of me to come out here and be captured. . . . Great going, F.D.R."

Insights into Bilibid life. August 10, 1942—"The observation of all who pass through this camp is that we are the poorest fed prisoners in the

Philippines." September 25, 1942—"The Japanese are now offering us two bottles of beer for every can of dead flies."

On home. May 13, 1944—"It's a hot sultry night and walking back from the upper compound, I paused for a moment under the mango tree and looked up at the stars. My eyes fixed upon an old familiar constellation that always seemed to free the night over Williamsburg and Yorktown."

Hayes's body was incinerated on Formosa in January 1945.

MY KIND OF GUYS _____

Address to the Citizens Crime Commission of
Delaware Valley on Law Enforcement Appreciation Day,
May 2, 1988, Philadelphia, Pennsylvania.

COMMISSIONER KEVIN TUCKER, Chairman William Grala, honored guests, ladies and gentlemen: Today we honor outstanding members of a uniformed service who risk their lives for our citizens' rights in the municipal arena. I spent my life in a uniformed service, not infrequently risking it for our country's rights in the international arena. There is, beyond a doubt, a kindredship here. A kindredship of selfless, and frequently dangerous, service to the American people. But after doing some reading in preparation for this talk, I've come to believe that there is a *special* kindredship between today's big-city municipal law enforcement officers and people who have undergone experiences of the sort that I had as a political prisoner—the kindredship of knowing what it's like to live in what I call a pressure cooker. And by pressure cooker I mean an environment where one's maintenance of self-esteem and personal honor is an ongoing day-in-day-out battle, at center stage in his life, his main concern, and not just a "given," an assumed fallout of competent performance of workday chores, as I've come to believe it is in most American lives, including the one I now enjoy.

Now having said that—and I mean it and will presently explain it—I want to say that as I sat down to prepare this talk, I was overcome by a sense of the ironic. Isn't it odd that a man whose best insights into human nature were formed behind bars should have the honor of addressing these heroic law enforcement officers on this special occasion? Now it's true that while behind those bars I was performing my duty as a commissioned officer of the United States, albeit, without contact with the front office for nearly eight years—a sort of head of government, you might say, of an autonomous colony of American prisoners of war in Hanoi.

But there is the viewpoint problem. I mean that if some outside hiring agency were to ask me to list my *proven* skills, of course, I could include the conventional ones of naval officer or teacher or fighter pilot or test pilot or author. But in all honesty, I would have to add that my only proven skill in which I might claim world-class status lies in organizing and running prison underground organizations. I think I know that business inside out. For instance, a few years ago I gave the convocation address at a state college in a little town in northern California called Susanville. The other significant institution in town was a federal prison, and I was introduced to its warden. He said his number one problem was overcrowding. (Come to think of it, I think that was eight years ago. Did any of you see *60 Minutes* last night? It seems that our federal prison population has *doubled* in these past eight years.) I said to the Susanville warden: "Why don't you just concentrate on keeping the troublemakers locked up in the prison itself and put the harmless ones out in work farms?"

"My God," he replied, "who is going to decide which is which?" Then I mentioned that I had just been released from a hoosegow where being able to make that call was the principal occupation of the prison commissar. "Well, let me tell you," the warden replied, "in my case I would have to get verification of my judgment from a whole battery of psychologists, lawyers, anthropologists, you name it, before I would dare do anything like that— even if I were fool enough to try to guess just exactly who among these convicted criminals had so-called troublemaking instincts—and who didn't."

Too bad, I thought, but how could I tell an American governing body, national, state, or municipal, that I had seen it done, and done accurately, by a man who wouldn't know what a psychologist or anthropologist or our kind of lawyer was? He did it with intense powers of observation, a high-volume feedback from an elaborate spy system, a retentive memory, infinite patience, an in-depth commonsense understanding of human nature, and, oh yes, unlimited powers to torture and isolate. He needed those powers because he was running a political prison.

A political prison is not a place where people serve terms or pay their debts to society or sit out wars. They are there to be used, and once the juice has been squeezed out of them, they are free to go. Political prisons have been around since time immemorial, and will be around forever, because in the battle for people's minds, influential enemies are a problem. Getting these influential enemies to discredit their own *causes* is an attractive solution, and some political systems permit going about this by forcing these enemies of the state to disavow all their previously held positions and render public confessions of evil aims, fraud, and guilt.

Please bear in mind that these are not tales of a distant past like the Stalinist trials of the 1930s in Koestler's *Darkness at Noon*. This procedure is gaining popularity as worldwide communication (radio and television) reaches higher and higher percentages of the world's population. My fellow shot-down pilots (totaling over four hundred by the end of the war) and I spent the best years of our lives trying to fight off attempts to force us to make public confessions of so-called evil aims, fraud, and our personal guilt surrounding the Vietnam War.

The North Vietnamese aims grew to match the protest marches in America they so enjoyed hearing about, with a giant, worldwide, televised "protest march of American pilots against the war." Our defense? United resistance. Organization. Elaborate covert communications. Rules made on the spot. A "take torture" list. "Refuse to do a, b, c, d, or e." "Make them hurt you. Force them to inflict significant pain before you budge. They don't like to do that. Also, the commissar has to meet his quotas of intimidated prisoners to meet taping and press conference commitments. He can't afford to go to war with all of us at once." "Unity over self."

North Vietnam's enticements? "Go home." "Accept our amnesty." "Repent your crimes, truly repent and make convincing statements and home you go, before the war is over. Make a tape of convincing remorse, be the unabashed star of a press conference or two, and you go home right now. And, oh yes, you must also make a tape convincing the comrades you leave behind in prison that you have chosen the right way and that they must follow your example." Talk about temptations! Talk about betraying comrades!

We had to prevent a run on that amnesty business or we would become animals—or like the demented bluefish former Police Officer Henry Winter loved to meet in running schools when he was out in his boat with his casting rod. He's the major character in a book, *Buddy Boys*, about a police precinct in New York City going wild. These Buddy Boys, like bluefish, were crazed with temptation. Going after any bait. Taking bites out of each other in their frantic rush of self-indulgence. Not acting like comrades in arms but like crazed gluttons: "What's in it for me?"

In Hanoi, our instincts, like those of you here today, told us we *had* to have public virtue and comradeship. This required that we first build a culture. And because most of us were in solitary confinement this culture had to be spread by faint but rhythmic tapping signals picked up by ears pressed to the bottom of drinking cups, open ends strategically placed at listening posts along prison walls. We came to live by these taps and responses, transmitting orders, encouragement, and solidarity in paragraph after paragraph. Without tools or paper or pencil, nothing but brains, stealth, knuckles, and drinking-cup listening devices, our society took root and grew—a society of our own making with our own laws, customs, traditions, heroes, folklore, and *citizens*. And in practicing public virtue— the concept from which our native United States grew, borrowed by our Founding Fathers from an ancient Roman Republic—each *citizen* of the cell blocks of Hoa Lo prison in Hanoi grew to proceed from the assumption that his society's fate was his fate and that he was therefore responsible for its fate and its honor. "Death before dishonor." "Unity over self." It was phrases like these that we came to live by.

Little wonder that the commissar was pretty mad when he found out that I was running this thing. He left me in solitary for over four years (he didn't know I could run the underground from there). But before that he had me taken back into the torture mill, this time for a couple of months, my leg broken a second time, and finally, "Yes, I will give you a list of my organization's members." (He called them my troublemakers, I thought of them as my leaders—don't ever forget that one man's troublemaker is another man's leader and vice versa.)

Well, I got my real surprise when he brought back my list with several names scratched off! "They are harmless," he casually said. It took all my acting ability to not show the depth of my shock. Because he was dead right. Those he excised were on the leadership team by virtue of their military rank *alone*. (Rank alone is too coarse a screen for this type of work.) These particular guys he had scratched off did what they were told but were not mischief makers *by nature*. All those endless interrogations, demands, pressures, so-called punishments (tortures), and isolations this commissar had ordered served not only to meet his propaganda quotas but to have him "know his enemy" and to know exactly what sort of acts each and every prisoner was constitutionally capable of. He had *everybody* exactly pegged.

This was my "pressure cooker": a minefield of tripwire, moral and physical booby traps, temptations, and merciless reprisals. But, of course, physical torture has limits. (After you get accustomed to taking it, being slugged, having the blood flow in your upper arms shut off by rope bindings, and getting smothered in claustrophobia, you eventually come to the realization that they can get out of you only what they know you know.) Isolation is more effective in unhinging a person, but it takes time—two years at least. Blackmail is probably better than either if a person can be caught in (more likely maneuvered into) deep shame. Then, after what seems like a lifetime in such a snakepit and you finally come home, people rush forward and ask questions like "How was the food?" "Did you get any fresh air?" "Were you warm enough?" "How was the mail service?" You guys out there know what I mean.

But when you get old political prisoners alone, you don't hear a word about food, ventilation, warmth, and such trivia. They exchange tales of quite a different nature—of nervous exhaustion, uncontrollable sobbing in solitude, the wages of fear, the horror of brooding guilt, alone for months, bearing wear and tear on nervous systems while being stalked, booby-trapped, blindsided, and all the while knowing that once you lose your precious grip on your self-esteem and personal honor, you are lost.

So what about the police world? I believe that pressures being what they are on today's streets, particularly in drug-ridden districts, that you seasoned police veterans must also have your "tales of a different nature" when you find yourselves in private conversation. What I'm saying is that both you honorees here today and old political prisoners like myself have worked in predicaments fully understandable only by those who really know the territory, those who have actually been there. But I can't leave it at that without stressing an additional, very important dimension in *your* lives. That is the dimension in public responsibility you law enforcement officers must *also* handle simultaneously with all of the above. You see we prisoners, in organizing, wrote our own rules of conduct. (Yes, there is an armed forces Code of Conduct, but it is so general as to be a sort of constitution around which those on the spot are well advised to complement with their *own*, usually *tougher*, laws, applicable to the situation at hand.) And the *rules* that we improvised were totally functional and designed *only* to optimize our chances of sticking together and getting out of our straits with honor. We were addressing a simple "they versus us" case.

Today's police officer can't enjoy the luxury of thinking like that. If in the fell swoop of circumstances he finds himself in frustration, letting slide his responsibility to observe his lawful limits of action imposed by regulations and the Constitution as he presses forward to prevent crime and apprehend offenders at any cost, he is on a slippery slide to personal defeat and the loss of that honor and self-esteem his badge stands for. He can't simply design his strategy on a "they versus us" basis and ignore his responsibilities to that public he is sworn to protect and that does not deserve to get caught in the cross fire.

As that friend of mine and of this audience Dr. Ed Delattre has said, the job of the men we honor today is more complex and demanding than that of Saint George, who had only to go out and slay the dragon. Saint George did not have to work in a chain of command or deal with the public and abide by policies and regulations. He did not have to work with the press or the media or with informants. He did not have to cooperate with, or work in, internal affairs or be guided by legislation or accept the decisions of the courts. All he had to do was put on his uniform, in his case made of metal; mount his vehicle, in his case an armored horse; draw his weapon, in his case a sword; find the dragon and slay it. Whereas you gentlemen in blue have to enforce the law in all its aspects while at the same time capturing dragons. And according to me, you do so today in a complex and gut-wrenching environment that few outsiders can fully appreciate.

But you and we—you cops and we political prisoners—*can* understand what Napoleon meant when he said that in war the moral is to the physical as three is to one—risking bullets is sometimes the easy part. And finally, I think we both, in our heart of hearts, are proud of the lives we chose to lead, if only to escape the near-fate of Joseph Conrad's Captain McWhir, that character in his great book *Typhoon*. After all, who wants to go—

> skimming over the years his years of existence—
> to sink gently into a placid grave—
> ignorant of life to the last—
> without ever having been made to see
> all it may contain—
> of perfidy, of violence, and of terror.

You're my kind of guys.

MIKE THORNTON'S RETIREMENT ⎯⎯⎯⎯⎯⎯⎯⎯⎯⎯⎯⎯⎯⎯

Talk given at Little Creek Amphibious Base,
Friday, May 1, 1992.

⎯⎯⎯

TODAY I'M ENCIRCLED by warriors I admire greatly. They are those who are wearing this Congressional Medal of Honor around their necks like I am, and they are all close personal friends. Also in the audience I have a close friend who was in my high school class back in Illinois when he joined the navy after our football season sophomore year (1939). Jeb Lambaiso was a boat cockswain aboard a submarine tender in Manila when the Japanese struck right after Pearl Harbor; he was on Corregidor with MacArthur, survived a death-defying ride in the hold of a Japanese ship to the Home Islands, and was a prisoner there for the rest of World War II. He finished a thirty-year career here at Little Creek as a chief petty officer and is now in business in Virginia Beach. Two other very close friends, both Virginia Beach residents, are Captain Jim Mulligan and Commander George Coker. We, together, are of nine now living who, with two others now deceased, were the principal leaders of the prison underground in Hanoi. In 1967 we were found out, purged in torture, and exiled to two years in leg irons and solitary in a tiny dungeon we dubbed Alcatraz. This Alcatraz Gang has been the subject of several stories and books.

The man we honor today, Mike Thornton, grew up in Spartanburg, South Carolina, and joined the U.S. Navy in that same 1967 when we were exiled. He was immediately selected for sea, air, land (SEAL) training and spent the last four years of the Vietnam War in, successively, a SEAL platoon in the IV Corps area, a billet as military adviser to Thailand, and two final tours as a military adviser to the South Vietnamese SEALs. His last tour was spent in the northern I Corps area, rescuing American pilots shot down behind enemy lines and conducting intelligence operations.

In a crowd of heroes, Mike is a special hero today as he retires after twenty-five fighting years in our navy. After Vietnam he was a leading instructor of the Basic Underwater Demolition School at the Coronado SEAL school, then assigned to SEAL Team Two here in Little Creek, and then two years (1978 to 1980) in the United Kingdom serving in the British Special Boat Squadron and as sergeant major of their Mountaineering Winter Warfare Team—in other words, as leader of their ski troops. Officer candidate school came in 1982, fifteen years after he joined the navy. In his ten years as an officer, he has been in deep-sea diving (officer in charge of the school here at Little Creek), in the ship's company of the USS *Edenton* as first lieutenant and diving and salvage officer, and the salvage officer for Combat Support Squadron Eight. His present assignment is as Bravo Company commander with Amphibious Construction Battalion Two. In Operation Desert Shield/Storm he headed up a 122-man contingent based with the amphibious task force.

And oh, yes, along the way, he was in our first hostage recovery and antiterrorist unit, SEAL Team Six, and a senior chief petty officer and expert parachutist for both low- and high-altitude chute openings—tactics tailored to particular kinds of assaults. Mike had just come back to Washington, D.C., when I hailed him to come and join our table at a luncheon for our Congressional Medal of Honor Society. (The Joint Chiefs of Staff host this event as part of the festivities of a presidential inauguration; this was 1980 and President Reagan was starting his first term.) I asked Mike to sit between me and our then chief of naval operations (CNO), Admiral Tom Hayward. Mike had just returned that morning from a Middle East operational air base, where he had been sitting alert with Team Six to be part of a vertical envelopment of the prison in Tehran, Iran, should our hostages not be released before President Reagan was sworn in. Iran had folded, and in his rush to make our luncheon on time, Mike was still in his operational costume, full hippy attire, hair down to his shoulders and kinky civilian clothes. I said, "Chief Thornton, I would like to have you meet our CNO, Admiral Hayward." Tom Hayward, affable as always, smiled and said, "How long have you been out of the navy, Chief?" Mike replied, "Sir, I'm on active duty." Tom's jaw dropped and his eyes popped out of his head while Mike began silently and frantically mouthing the words "SEAL Team Six," "SEAL Team Six." It took them a minute, but they finally came to a silent understanding between them.

Stories are boundless about this one-of-a-kind individual. Unselfconscious, funny—while walking in a patriotic parade with him, he'll suddenly be missing, and then you'll see him, way up ahead, over on the sidewalk, in uniform and medals, in front of a candy store with a couple of kids in his arms, laughing with their parents. And can he dance! You should see him and Sybil dancing the night away in some dixieland place. He is so quick, so intuitive, so powerful, like a giant graceful leopard, that it's almost scary. He is not a modern man; he is the reincarnation of one of Alexander the Great's unit commanders. When he shows up, you just know that *something* is going to happen. And throughout, he's lightning fast in thought, highly intelligent, and possessed of an *innate sense of propriety*. What he does is always different but somehow appropriate to the circumstance. You can tell I like him very much. We have a deal. He will be a pallbearer at my funeral or I at his.

It's time to talk about heroism and what I think it is. This may sound strange, but to me a hero is a man who will not accept the status quo if it does not meet his standards. For an instant or for an hour or for a month or in the case of prisoners, maybe longer, he will stand up and turn his world around. "It's not *right* that that ticking hand grenade should kill everybody in this foxhole. I'm going to fall on it." "It's not *right* that this company of marines surrounded on this mountain top by the Chosin Reservoir should wither and freeze and surrender! We're going to break out of here!" "It's not *right* that I should bring harm to my fellow prisoners by letting myself be forced to inform on them. I'm going to break a window and cut myself up!"

Let's set the stage for Mike Thornton on this: late 1972, northern South Vietnam. During the previous Easter time of 1972, the Americans, in their preoccupation with gradual withdrawal, had been caught flat-footed as North Vietnam regulars marched across the demilitarized zone and established themselves in South Vietnam as far south as Dong Ha, maybe one hundred miles in. (There is very interesting literature on this period: How a marine reserve colonel on an area checkout found himself in charge of the whole of northern South Vietnam while nobody would answer the phone in Saigon. How a marine captain singlehandedly blew up the bridge at Dong Ha and contained a North Vietnamese outfit marching south.) This was *not* a time when mass movements stopped the flood; what stopped it were spires of excellence among the few, spires of excellence from those formerly thought of as ordinary blokes.

By the early fall of 1972, Mike Thornton, petty officer 2d class, was an old hand, conducting "downed pilot" missions and making insertions to collect intelligence behind enemy lines. He often teamed up with a short, slight, very smart navy lieutenant team leader named Tom Norris. (They fit together; Mike was big, quick, and strong, and Tom was by that time famous within SEAL circles for being a genius at rescue missions. In April 1972 Tom had been recommended for a Congressional Medal of Honor for a four-day, very hairy operation in which his team had persisted and brought out the two guys they were sent to get.)

In late October, Tom and Mike were teamed up to do a special "behind enemy lines" dawn reconnaissance up near the demilitarized zone and report back about the feasibility of a surprise U.S. Marine Corps amphibious operation to encircle the many ensconced North Vietnamese troops that owned the territory up there. It was the night before Halloween when Tom, Mike, and three South Vietnamese SEALs boarded a South Vietnamese junk and, in blacked-out conditions, chugged up the coast north to be inserted at

4 A.M. at a point about 2,000 meters south of the former U.S. boat base at the mouth of the Qua Viet River—a base now under the command of the North Vietnamese.

Once ashore, Mike knew they were in deep trouble as soon as he got his night-viewing lens up and looked north to the old boat base and realized that he was looking at objects he remembered seeing in the demilitarized zone; sure enough the junk had been given a bad vector to the drop point, and Tom and Mike were about six miles north of where they were supposed to be! Nothing to do but cut across country and try to get the data, and then, when it was light, get on the radio and try to arrange for a pickup point up near where they were. As they sneaked along in the early mist Tom and Mike started seeing Soviet tanks with red stars on them parked here and there—they were right in the middle of the North Vietnamese army!

After a couple of hours up there sneaking around, they were satisfied that they had their data, and they had started back out when at about 8:30 A.M., still 500 meters from that northern beach, they were discovered by two North Vietnamese soldiers. Mike grabbed one, but the other escaped, firing his weapon. Then the enemy started closing in on them. Tom was on the radio, now sure of where he was, calling the U.S. cruiser *Newport News* offshore for gunfire support. Mike was killing their attackers right and left with his trusty AK-47. Both Mike and Tom were reconciled to the fact that they were going to have to swim out of this mess by sea—no hope for a pickup. They were in this state, firing and falling back, gunfire support coming in, for about an hour, when, in a lull, Tom told Mike he would cover him and two South Vietnamese SEALs while they made for the beach and then they would cover while he followed. In the earlier melee Mike had been hit badly in the legs by grenade fragments, but he could still run. When he got almost to the beach, the third South Vietnamese SEAL came running up alone and said, "Lieutenant Norris dead."

Here's the turning point. Mike would not have it; he bolted inland alone, 150 yards through North Vietnamese fire, to where Tom lay. He found him bloody, his head caved in and an eye gone, but breathing. Mike slung Tom over his shoulder and commenced a 200-yard dash through open terrain under constant enemy fire, holding fast and lugging his unconscious commanding officer. Mike took hits in the legs but kept going. The cruiser's gunfire knocked Mike sprawling, but he recovered Tom and plunged on, into the sea, diving through a four-foot surf while being chased and fired at by twenty or so North Vietnamese.

In the water, Mike was in his natural element. After swimming out of the range of gunfire, fully clothed with field gear, unconscious Tom dressed the same on his back, he put an underwater demolition team life jacket on Norris and performed such first aid as was possible. Then Mike swam seaward for two full hours, at which time the understandably confused pickup junk finally sighted them and transported the team to the USS *Newport News*. Mike carried Lieutenant Norris to sick bay and left only when he was sure the doctors had the picture; he was then told to report to the ship's captain in his cabin.

Typical of good sailor Mike, when I first knew him, he told me in all seriousness: "You know, that captain of the *Newport News* was a fine fellow. He just wanted to hear my story; he didn't seem to give a damn about my dripping Tom's blood, vomit, and everything else that had run out of his body, all over his rug."

So there you have it: "above and beyond the call of duty." With this retirement, for the first time since 1914, the U.S. Navy is left without an active-duty Congressional Medal of Honor wearer. At least, we're pausing on a *very high note*. Mike, you were the prototype for whom that navy chaplain prayed at our luncheon in Honolulu: "You have struggled through the winds and the rains and the sleet; you have stared at the sun—and have *not* been overwhelmed by it." Have a happy "rest of your life," and God bless you.

PEROT-STOCKDALE ELECTION NIGHT GALA

Events at the Kempinski Hotel, Dallas Texas, Tuesday, November 3, 1992.

Ross presents the Stockdale family. Jim Stockdale speaks:

THIS IS SYBIL'S AND MY FOUR SONS—all schoolmasters, all husbands of wonderful women, all fathers of our grandchildren, five so far, with another to be born in a few months.

We have all watched and supported Ross Perot as he changed forever presidential politics in America. No more will candidates pay homage to political gurus, political pundits—those supposedly learned *filters* who read or listen to your stuff and then grade you on the appropriateness of your being taken seriously by the American people.

No more! You don't have to talk to Sam Donaldson to get on TV. Ross has shown the world that candidates can *bypass* these filters and get directly to the public. And scholars of the presidency that I know say its a *good thing, about time.* (I'm quoting Dr. Tom Cronin of Colorado College where three of our four sons over there took their undergraduate degrees.)

Senator John McCain, my fellow prisoner in Vietnam, said in the morning paper that campaigns like the two that got Ronald Reagan elected are now and *forever* pageants of the *past.*

Ross saw that, thus the demise of Ed Rollins.

What underpins this change beside Ross Perot's spirit and spunk? This is also a matter under discussion by political scientists. Many think it is yet another sign that the two major political parties are in *decay.* Professor Ted Lowi, professor of American institutions at Cornell and *president* of the American Political Science Association, thinks that the Republican and Democratic Parties have been brain dead for twenty years, that they could not exist without American government subsidies for campaigns and conventions and without the prejudice of the states against those who petition to get on their ballots. And we here know a lot about that.

We're overdue for a three-party country, says Professor Lowi. More on this later. Keep your eye on United We Stand, America.

HERB BROWNE RELIEVES
JOE PRUEHER

*Speech given November 5, 1993, aboard the
USS* Kitty Hawk *in Coronado, California.*

ADMIRALS PRUEHER AND BROWNE, distinguished guests, ladies and gentlemen:

Today's *event* seems to have a forward tilt to it—no permanent farewells, no regrets—a momentary pause at the intersection of the careers of two extremely bright and talented flag officers, each thundering forward into *unpredictable* circumstances. Somalia, Bosnia, North Korea—the times are a-changin' all over the world, and though we may all be assured that each of you have studied his play book, I can't forget my friend Bill Walsh's (former coach of the San Francisco 49ers) warning to me as I studied *his* play books. "Remember," he said, "spontaneity and instinct in the clutch are going to have a lot more to do with the outcome of the football game than rote memory and petrified plans."

Of course I knew that, as do our principals today and all of you elders out there in the crowd. It was Ralph Waldo Emerson who popularized the expression "spontaneity and instinct." He considered them the tools of genius, with some justification. It was "spontaneity and instinct" that set up my first visit to the *Kitty Hawk*.

This morning, nostalgia prompts me to begin with a brief account of some little-known *Kitty Hawk* history. It was on its second deployment, thirty years ago, June 1964, when I came aboard by helicopter from the *Constellation*. These two *then* biggest carriers in the world were side by side a mile apart, lying off the desolate coast of Vietnam, just south of the demilitarized zone.

You middle-aged guys out there knew that location as Yankee Station, but it was several months after my visit before anybody thought of naming it that. I showed up late on the afternoon of June 7 as commanding officer, Fighter Squadron (VF) 51, supposedly deployed in the USS *Ticonderoga* but *here* under secret orders. In fact I had slept on the *Ticonderoga* the night before as it steamed south toward the Philippines from Sasebo.

I'll make this quick: A year before, on a 1963 cruise—when Da Nang was just a dumpy little derelict strip called Lorainne—we of VF 51 were at times ordered to orbit our Crusaders over South Vietnam, as a precaution against what seemed to me to be the *extremely remote chance* that aircraft would come sweeping down from the north. And as I watched the small but pitched battles in progress on the ground below, it became clear to me that if VF 51 was going to get into the war on my commanding officer cruise the following year, it had to be in the air-to-ground mode. We had to shake loose the fighter purists' stonewalling of the installation of Crusader rocket tubes and bomb racks that were just coming out.

And so later, back stateside in early 1964, without any particular person's permission, we drew the gear and put ourselves through air-to-ground training over on the Chocolate Mountain ranges, there being no Replacement Air Group (RAG) syllabus or interest in the project. At the operational readiness inspection in Hawaii going west again that spring, we provided the novelty of Crusaders entering the air-to-ground derbies, got *good* scores and notice in the debriefing report that was shotgunned to all senior commands.

As we pushed on west in early May, the big world news was *not* about Vietnam but about the Pathet Lao moving into the Plain of Jars in Laos, in violation of a 1962 agreement President Kennedy had engineered. Unknown to us (everything seemed to be top secret in 1964) this *Kitty Hawk* was tasked to hover offshore and daily send unescorted photo Crusaders up into the Plain of Jars, on the deck at 600 knots, to bring back evidence of Pathet Lao intrusion. On Saturday, June 6, a lieutenant named Chuck Klusman was shot down. High-level Washington decision: "Continue photo overflights with air-to-ground-capable escorts." VF 51 was the only squadron in the U.S. Navy that could perform that mission—keep up with photo Crusaders at 600 knots at treetop level and shoot Zuni rockets at the same time. (At that point, the F4s had *zero* air-to-ground capability.) So late that night of June 6, Vice Admiral Tom Moorer, 7th Fleet, sent a message to the *Tico* ordering VF 51 to fly to the *Constellation*, which was relieving *Kitty Hawk* of the photo duty, at latitude and longitude such and such, *in all haste*. Our mail address was not to change; mum was the word, a destroyer was to pick up our sailors and ground pounders for the trip to the *Connie* at noon that Sunday.

When we flew into radio range of the *Connie* and *Kitty Hawk* early that afternoon of Sunday, June 7, the *Kitty Hawk* traffic pattern was filled with screaming pilots in various airplane types, most low state, some shot up. Earlier that Sunday, a *fighter* Crusader had been bagged as he tried to locate Klusman, and the *Kitty Hawk* had sent in a gaggle of airplanes to see that the helicopter got to the pilot on the ground—Bud Lynn. The *Kitty Hawk* was having its own little two-day war over there months before formal hostilities started; few knew about it then and not many today. They got Bud Lynn back and, luckily, everybody aboard. (In the midst of that melee in the traffic pattern, a Crusader without a radio and a wing that would not raise because of battle damage came straight in on a 190-knot approach. The pilot popped the stick forward at just the right instant to dip his nose down and let his dragging tail clear the ramp. He made a wing-down, damage-free trap, the only one I ever heard of, and I had more time in the Crusader than anybody in the world in those days. Who was he? An air force captain just out of the RAG. I never knew his name, but he's my candidate for the Carrier Aviation Hall of Fame.)

VF 51 trapped aboard *Connie*, and good Captain Fred Bardshar, who died only weeks ago here in San Diego, sent me right over to the *Kitty Hawk* to get the dope on how to be boss of what was soon to be called "Yankee Team Ops." It was from *this* code name for the secret Laos operation in the spring of 1964 that Yankee Station got its name.

Back on *Tico* two months later, I led the first-ever bombing raid into North Vietnam, all because of that stateside unsupported "spontaneity and instinct" of getting the gear to do what had to be done. But it was in prison, a year and a half later, that I really became my own boss, freely using those urges so dear to philosopher Emerson. The situation required it, and there was no other way to go. Any officer worth his salt, on detached duty and out of communication, has to have the right to sensibly modify the law, issue rules that fit the conditions, and be prepared to defend himself in court. Throughout those years, I figured that that was my most important function.

But I'm not here to sell the idea of "letting it all hang out." On the contrary, I intend that my brief message this morning will make it clear that even in the oddest circumstances of detached duty, we as warriors must keep foremost in our minds that there *are* boundaries to the prerogatives of leadership: *Moral* boundaries.

Napoleon said, "In war, the moral is to the physical as three is to one." To focus a little closer on what "moral" meant to those early-nineteenth-century military thinkers who framed modern warfare, I go to Clausewitz: "If we take a comprehensive view of the four components of the atmosphere in which war moves: danger, physical effort, uncertainty, and chance, it is easy to understand that a great *moral* force is needed to advance with safety and success in this baffling element, a force described as *energy, firmness, staunchness, strength of mind and character*!

Morality shadows *war and* the preparation for it. Its echoes were always quietly vibrating even in the corridors of the North Vietnamese prisons.

My patron saint, the first-century philosopher Epictetus, said: "The judge will do some things to you which are thought to be terrifying, but how can he stop you from taking the punishment he threatened?" That became *our* kind of Stoicism in that pressure-packed microcosm of all human conflict. *Pain* was tactical and repairable, but *shame* was strategic and made you eternally vulnerable to those who would manipulate you to your downfall. Even the peasant soldier—and maybe *particularly* the peasant soldier—seemed to sense that, in the end, prolonged struggle is a *spiritual* battle and that the leak in the dike always starts from within.

That is human nature in the raw—in all its strengths, in all its pride and bullheadedness, and now it is "cool" to try to take the edge off that, to make allowances for every congenital defect, every wimpish inclination, to, as they say, "rise above human nature."

But as Sir Arthur Conan Doyle had Sherlock Holmes say to Watson: "When one tries to rise above nature, one is liable to fall below it. The highest type of man may revert to *the animal* if he leaves the straight road of destiny. Consider, Watson, that the materialists, the sensualists, the worldly would all prolong their worthless lives. The *spiritual* would now avoid the call to something higher. It would be the survival of the least fit. What sort of cesspool may not our poor world become?"

I can tell you that being "cool," trying to rise above human nature, is *not* impressive to the Third World, where much of our work in the coming decades might well have to be done. And being "cool," as we have seen, is not conducive to supporting the professional *constancy of purpose*, which we have inherited from our forefathers in naval air.

I spent last weekend with many of our forefathers in naval air. I was aboard the *Yorktown* to be inducted into *that* Carrier Aviation Hall of Fame. There were five of us, three posthumous: Admiral Mike Michaelis, well known here, for whom our departing Admiral Joe Prueher served as aide some seventeen years ago; Commander Don Runyon, who got his wings in 1938 as an enlisted aviation pilot (AP) and early in World War II became the first AP ace and eventually the top navy F-4 Wildcat ace; and marine Colonel Arnold Lund. Lund and I were the first inductees whose main flying activities were *not* in World War II. He spent most of the Korean War flying from the CVE 116, nicknamed the "Bing Ding" Strait; he was a squadron commander who sort of "wrote the book" on U.S. Marine Corps close air support.

The one living guy besides me was eighty-three-year-old Dick Best, Naval Academy class of 1932. A finer man than Dick, I never met—he is, for sure, a man of *integrity*. He was commanding officer of Bombing 6 aboard the *Enterprise* at the Battle of Midway—flew two hops on June 4, 1942, the day we wrecked the Japanese carrier force. The first was the big gaggle launched at 7:00 in the morning, in which the flight leader, Dick's air group commander, Wade McClusky, providentially sighted the Japanese fleet just before reaching "bingo" state; and Dick Best was again on the 3:30 in the afternoon launch, leading twenty-four dive bombers to destroy the fourth and last Japanese carrier. Dick Best had a good day on June 4, 1942: two flights, two direct bomb hits, each dead center on a carrier deck of two of the Japanese ships that were part of the Pearl Harbor strike force. Dick was described repeatedly by those old-timers as "one of the top four performers at the Battle of Midway." The other three were already in the Hall of Fame.

I asked him about improvisations he had to make on that most famous day in the history of naval air. He laughed and said that in the morning, as soon as everybody could see the carriers down through the breaks in the clouds, he was astounded when Wade McClusky assigned his squadron the farthest-out carrier when he was behind McClusky in column. "Wade came up in fighters and didn't know the first thing about bombing doctrine." (I was a fighter pilot air group commander flying lots of attack hops in Vietnam—got shot down on one in fact—and I'm sure they said the same thing about me.) Dick added, "It might have mixed up the Japanese, too, because nobody shot at me all the way down."

What was left of the Japanese fleet was in flight in succeeding days. Dick said there was lots of scurrying around trying to improvise some bomb load that could penetrate the decks of the Japanese battleships. "The bombs we had could never have penetrated a battleship deck and maybe not even a cruiser deck." He said, "Halsey's ordnance officer found some 16-inch battleship rounds in the *Enterprise* magazines and was after me to figure out a way to fuse them and hang them on our planes, but I was getting sick fast and couldn't help him."

It turned out that, on Dick's second flight on that busy day of June 4, his oxygen system was polluted with caustic soda, which triggered an immediate and serious case of tuberculosis. He was immediately hospitalized and in 1944 physically retired from the navy as a lieutenant commander. He now looks good. "Why shouldn't I?" he said, "I spent my middle years in bed."

Joe Prueher, I am honored to have been invited to do this, and I know you will shed honor on your country as a vice admiral in command of our Sixth Fleet in the Mediterranean.

Herb Browne, we know you showed the right stuff as a carrier skipper in the Red Sea throughout the gulf war and will do us proud here in the Pacific.

Thank you one and all.

STOCKDALE'S FINAL SCRIPT FOR THE LANCE SIJAN DOCUMENTARY FILM

This entire script was recorded at the multimedia laboratory at the U.S. Air Force Academy, September 16, 1994, and is on file there.

LANCE PETER SIJAN, United States Air Force Academy class of 1965, was posthumously awarded the Congressional Medal of Honor for extraordinary heroism and intrepidity above and beyond the call of duty, at the cost of his life, by President Gerald Ford, at the White House, on March 4, 1976. Sijan Hall, here on the academy grounds, was dedicated three months later, as a tribute to the fighting heart and love of country of this first Air Force Academy graduate to receive the highest military award for bravery that can be given to any individual in the United States of America.

I was there in the East Room of the White House when Secretary of the Air Force Thomas Reed commenced his reading of the citation. (Its form dates back to Abraham Lincoln, who originated the Congressional Medal of Honor award during the Civil War.) "The President of the United States, authorized by Act of Congress, March 3, 1863, has awarded in the name of the Congress the Medal of Honor posthumously to Captain Lance P. Sijan, United States Air Force." Then came the terse paragraph outlining Lance's composure and straight thinking from the start as he regained consciousness from a low-altitude, high-speed ejection and how, despite broken bones, lacerations, brain concussion, lack of food and drink, he did it all: evasion, escape, stoic resistance to torture. How he gave his country the last full measure of himself.

I stood at the side of Lance's loving parents, Jane and Sylvester Sijan of Milwaukee, Wisconsin, when President Ford with heartfelt remarks, presented them with Lance's medal—like this medal I am wearing. I, like Lance, had just become the only graduate of *my* service academy, Annapolis, to be awarded the congressional medal in the course of that longest war in U.S. history, Vietnam. And like Lance, I was shot down in a fighter plane, was a prisoner of war, and had other life experiences similar to his, which I'll mention in the course of this narration.

I'm very proud to be the narrator of this documentary, and I hope to bring it to you in a way that will make you understand how the story of the last two and a half months of Lance Sijan's life—of his ordeal *alone* in the wilds of Laos, of his commitment to our Code of Conduct, of his tough-mindedness and resistance to his eventual captors, even as he was dying, made him a hero to every prisoner of war in Vietnam. To us, he was the real article. He inspired us, as he is inspiring cadets here at his great alma mater.

Like me, he was a middle American from the Midwest. The oldest child of three of Jane and Sylvester Sijan, he had a younger brother and a still younger sister. It was a tightly knit family; the parents cared about their children, and the children cared about their parents and one another.

Lance grew to be a big, husky kid—six feet, three inches, two hundred pounds. He went to the public schools of Milwaukee. At Bay View High, he was cocaptain of the football team and the *Milwaukee Journal*'s choice for all-city end. Bay View won the city championship his senior year, something they had not done since Lance's father, "Syl" played end there.

But athletics was only one side of Lance Sijan's competencies. He got the leading role in the class play *The King and I* and got permission to let his beloved three-and-a-half-year-old sister play the part of the little princess. He got good marks and was president of the student government. His well-roundedness was epitomized on graduation day 1960, when he was presented with *both* the scholastic and the extracurricular gold medals for his achievements over his four years at Bay View.

Lance had lived those schoolboy years with an urge to fly. He was artistic and, even as a grade-schooler, would draw airplanes and then make flying models of what he had drawn. Going to the Air Force Academy became his life's ambition.

In 1960, the young Air Force Academy was in the process of establishing a prep school for prospective cadets who needed an extra year of course work after high school. The army and navy had long had such schools for their academies and thus at that time were directed to meet the needs of the air force. In the fall of 1960, then, Lance was assigned to the Naval Academy prep school at Bainbridge, Maryland. He had a good year there and was well liked. The then-all boys' school had traditionally dedicated their yearbook to some student's girl friend, who was then known as the "queen of the yearbook." For Lance, as a tribute to his embodiment of the virtues of his time, his class broke precedent and elected him the "king of the yearbook." A famous painting of Lance by artist Maxine McCaffry, featuring his Congressional Medal of Honor, which now hangs in Sijan Hall at the Air Force Academy, is duplicated in the lobby of the Naval Academy prep school, now located at Newport, Rhode Island.

Lance found the Air Force Academy to be both physically and mentally demanding. During basic cadet training, a young man by the name of Bart

Holaday was assigned to Lance's squadron. His memories of Cadet Sijan were clear. He wrote: "I first met Lance during our basic cadet training. Because I was a half-inch shorter, I always had to march and run behind him. I quickly grew to respect his strength and determination. The runs became increasingly exhausting. I felt I could go no farther. But by focusing on Lance right in front of me, with his quest for victory in every stride he made, I was able to go on. Without Lance as an example, I would have surely quit. In the following years, our friendship became a powerful force in my life."

Grim determination, the "come from behind" spirit—studies show that people who can hold onto *that* through the hard knocks of life are disproportionately represented in the Legion of Valor, people with Air Force Crosses and Congressional Medals. Academy life requires some of that from most of us. Except for a few, successes come nowhere as easily at the academy as they did back in our comfortable high schools. With total dedication, never missing a practice, never breaking training, never ducking a heavy hit, Lance found himself in his third year still on the junior varsity football team. That was like me in my academy days—scrimmaging the varsity two or three afternoons a week, going to the showers afterward with bruises all over my body and blood on my face, and then feeling that resentment on Thursday night when the travel list came out and I was not on it. Experiences like that plant seeds in your breast.

Lance was primed to do his very best to make the varsity his last year. His coach encouraged him to think he would make it. Winter term, junior year, he could taste the zeal he would put into spring practice. Just about then he was felled by his academic nemesis, electromagnetic physics. He just couldn't keep up that across-the-board pace he had set for himself and not run out of energy for that extra study time he was finding he needed in advanced science courses. (At that time, he was also the photo editor of *Talon* magazine, an officer in the skydiving club, and singing in the glee club.)

Lance was called before the Academic Review Board and wrote home, telling his family how he was hoping he would not let them down. The review board gave him some hard choices, either retake and pass the physics course the next summer (missing the overseas program the rest of his class would get) or face that fact that football was eating up too much of him and that it was in his long-range best interest to give it up.

This was an ice-water bath for Lance, and, as he would show the world later, he bit the bullet and took it like a man. He told a sympathetic coach that he was quitting football, that flying fighter planes for his country required it.

Later that winter, Lance's father made a visit to the academy. They discussed their mutual respect and affection for each other, as well as their hopes and dreams for the future. The love bonding that father and son was to be manifested in future events.

During the graduation ceremony a year later, June 1965, Lance's parents noticed that his hair was wet. It was then traditional at the academy to find the toughest individual in the graduating class and throw him into the fountains in the Air Garden. For this honor, the class of 1965 chose Lance P. Sijan.

After the Air Force Academy, Lance attended pilot training at Laredo Air Force Base, Texas. He obtained his *pilot's* wings after completing both T-37 and T-38 training. He was then assigned to George Air Force Base, California, for upgrade training in the F-4 Phantom, the plane that he would eventually fly in Southeast Asia.

The air force had *pilots*, men with pilot's wings, flying in the back seat of the F-4C in Vietnam. The navy was different; it had nonrated officers working the gear back there. I just want to make it clear that Lance also flew combat hops in the front seat; it was just the fate of the newly minted F-4 aviators to fly most of their first combat tour in the back seat and their second in front.

On the night of November 9, 1967, First Lieutenant Lance Sijan stood before his bachelor officers' quarters dresser at his base in Da Nang. He gazed quietly at the pictures of his family. Before each mission, Lance would mentally spend time with them at their red-brick Tudor house overlooking Lake Michigan. It was his premission ritual. Lance looked into the faces of his mother, Jane, father, Syl, Marc, his younger brother, and Janine, his little sister. He would often write letters or record tapes for his family before his flights.

On his 8 P.M. mission over Laos, Lance would be flying back seat to his squadron commander, Lieutenant Colonel John Armstrong, a West Point graduate and F-86 pilot of the Korean War. Lance, who always wore a confident smile, was unusually subdued. Earlier that day, after returning from rest and recreation in Bangkok, he was informed that his best friend had been shot down the previous afternoon. A dark cloud hung over Lance the entire day.

Dressed in his G suit, the survival vest bulging with emergency supplies and equipment, Lance Sijan walked onto the tarmac. The tropical heat made its presence immediately known as he climbed up the ladder into his F-4C. After completing the preflight checklist, Lance and Lieutenant Colonel Armstrong took off for their target, the Ban Loboy ford near the Ho Chi Minh Trail. This would be Lance's fifty-third mission. He once described these night bombing missions to his family as "flying into the mouth of the cat."

Beside them flew another F-4C, voice call AWOL 2. Lance's plane was AWOL 1. Beneath each airplane were six 750-pound bombs with a new fusing apparatus set to explode six seconds after they were pickled off in a screaming dive, passing 8,000 feet of altitude. A forward air controller (FAC) in an O-2 out of Udorn, Thailand, dropped his flares over the target, lighting it up, along with the limestone ravines and mountain slopes below, so the pilot could aim his bombs. The planned fusing delay of six seconds was calculated to get the bombs just into the ground before they exploded.

The first run was to be made by AWOL 1, and, on signal from the FAC, Colonel Armstrong rolled in for an attack but abruptly pulled off after losing sight of his target down in the flare glare below. Lance checked his watch. It was 8:35. Airborne only thirty-five minutes and in the thick of things already. On Armstrong's second run, just as the bombs were released, a blinding flash engulfed the cockpit. No fusing delay whatsoever! Over two tons of high explosive had instantly blown up less than 50 feet from the plane! They were out of control, and the airplane was in the process of ripping itself apart.

Instinctively, Lance pulled his ejection curtain. Even so, his ejection from the steeply diving plane was too low to be seen by AWOL 2 or the FAC. He remembered hanging silently in the chute for a few seconds but probably lost consciousness just before he went into the black roof of the forest.

As he fell through the jungle's canopy, his helmet, parachute, and auxiliary survival pack were torn away. Anybody less muscular than Lance would probably have been killed on the way through those hardwood trees.

Lieutenant Colonel Armstrong was never seen again. On November 11, two F-4Ds from the 8th Fighter Wing were heading for their targets north of Hanoi when they heard a May Day beeper coming from the jungle below. The airborne command center was immediately notified. When the F-4Ds had a decent fix on the source of the beeper transmissions, the command center ordered them to contact the survivor on "guard" channel.

"AWOL 1 Bravo," answered a calm voice. "I'm hurt kind of bad, compound fracture. My head's hurt pretty bad too. I was unconscious all day yesterday." Lance noticed that his wristwatch was stopped at 8:39 the night before last. That was when he ejected through the fireball of the exploding bombs. It was now nearly thirty-five hours later, and he had spent most of those hours unconscious on the steep forest floor.

A formal search and rescue went into effect while the survivor was asked for further identification. "Sijan. Lance Peter, first lieutenant, U.S. Air Force," came the reply. Reassured that the voice coming from the ravines was actually American and not a North Vietnamese English-speaking booby trap baiter, the rescue mission went into full swing. Sikorsky HH-3 "Jolly Green

Giants" would be used for the actual pickup. In the meantime, the voice rising from the jungle had to be positively identified by using prearranged questions.

"Who is the greatest football team in the world?"

"The Green Bay Packers," Sijan answered, lying braced against a gigantic tree root. Bones protruded through his left leg. The three smaller fingers of his right hand were dislocated. The wound behind his left ear throbbed with pain. Lance used the morphine syringe from his first aid kit to dull the pain in his head.

North Vietnamese ground fire began against the air armada that was gathering around that high limestone karst mound on which Lance was "somewhere" lying. The pilots kept talking to Sijan to keep his morale up. Lance's voice remained professional. He stated he was OK. A radio direction-finder fix of his position with the precise accuracy the helicopter needed was finally made. The process took hours, and several of the planes were hit and damaged in the process. Sijan was linked to civilization only by his precious handheld emergency radio.

"AWOL 1, this is Gunfighter Lead, Glen Nordin. Lance, how you doing, boy?" He recognized that voice. It was his flight commander from Da Nang. Lance had always impressed Major Nordin as being a quality officer, respected by everyone.

"There's a lot of us here, and by God, we're going to stay here until we get you out. Copy?"

"Gunfighter Lead, AWOL 1 Bravo. Thank you, sir. I'm OK. Hanging in there. Standing by for the Jolly Greens."

As shadows crept into the valleys, the major became frustrated. The North Vietnamese were taking a beating from the bombing runs of our planes but knew their gunfire had hit several of them. Both men and machines had been wounded.

Finally, as the sun was getting low in the west, the Jolly Green Giant, which had never gotten near enough to Lance's position to make the high branches sway above his head, succeeded in doing just that. "Drop your penetrator," radioed the lieutenant.

The chopper pilot was set on sending the rescue specialist in his crew down with the penetrator to get Sijan correctly connected to the cable for his "lift out." "Negative," replied Lance. "There's bad guys down here." (He had heard whistles in the distance.) "Drop your penetrator. I'll crawl to you."

The penetrator at the end of the cable came through the greenery above and rested on the ground maybe forty feet away from Lance. With a burst of adrenaline, he hunched on his back across jagged stones as he hacked away at thorny vines over his shoulder with his knife. Rescue lay a mere twenty feet away as the North Vietnamese became more persistent in their firing. Having to avoid enemy fire, the rescue chopper pulled away, taking Lance's chance for freedom with it. The remainder of the planes were recalled.

Major Nordin and his wingman roared back across the valley. In a few minutes he would be safe at base. Lance, on the other hand, would spend another night in desolation, with the North Vietnamese scouting parties coming up the hill and getting closer. The flight commander could hear Lance on the radio trying to contact the helicopters. The young lieutenant sounded grim.

"Lance," Nordin stated, "We're coming back tomorrow."

"Roger, Gunfighter, copy. Please advise mission status. Over," came the reply from the jungle below.

Glenn Nordin hit the transmit button: "We will definitely be back at dawn."

Lance, exhausted and in pain, dragged his crippled body backward toward the tree where he had hidden his pistol. He never saw the sinkhole beneath the underbrush directly behind him. The ground swallowed him up; he was falling backward, headfirst. Then his lights went out; his head bashed again, he was to be in and out of consciousness for another couple of days.

The search and rescue team started early on November 12, but, unable to make any contact at all with Lance, after two hours the mission commander canceled the rescue. Nordin was dismayed, and stayed with his six F-4s until it was time to refuel.

Lance gained partial consciousness that afternoon. Every inch of his body ached. And he was *very* thirsty. Looking around the sinkhole he found it full of pieces of broken sewer pipe. Then he realized he had fallen into one of the abandoned old French latrines he'd been told about at jungle survival school.

He passed out and awoke again in the dark. The jungle was alive with the sounds of monkeys, insects, and lizards. He withdrew the radio from his vest pocket. He would try to contact his rescuers. Something was wrong, though. He had either left the beeper on, running down the battery, or it had been damaged.

Without the radio, a helicopter rescue was almost out of the question unless he could get himself out in the open where he could signal an American overflight with his strobe light or mirror. Things were going wrong, and Lance intuitively knew he had to move and change the status quo, for water if nothing else. Thirst was becoming his most urgent and alarming problem.

Sure, if he could get back to his pistol under the leaves over there where he came to rest after shootdown, he could fire signal shots to call in the North Vietnamese and surrender.

But that was not part of him. It was his duty under the American fighting man's Code of Conduct to evade and escape. Also, the displays of American prisoners of war in Hanoi he had seen on television back in the states had horrified him. "I will never be taken prisoner," he had vowed to his friends.

Lance was blessed with an uncommon tough-mindedness. He never kidded himself. He was getting terribly run down, drifting in and out of consciousness and in and out of rationality except when he was rested. (Maybe he remembered that line from the cadet's prayer: "I ask true humility, that, knowing self, I may rise above human frailty.")

He needed to go east and get down off that karst plateau and into the areas of creeks below. And then he had to look for an open spot where he could illuminate himself by flashing to American aircraft. He remembered from jungle survival school that, in the thick underbrush of these areas, small animals made "game trails," tunnels through the thicket to get around to water and to food. He couldn't hope to stand on his bad leg, but he could splint it for horizontal if not vertical rigidity with G suit parts and life jacket binding.

He struggled and finally made it out of the French latrine, recovered his pistol where he had hid it, and then behold! There on the ledge where he had spent those first days were crisscrossed fresh tracks of human feet—the North Vietnamese had swept the area while he was passed out in the invisible hole a few feet away. "Blessings come in many forms," he thought to himself.

It's about here in the story that I start to talk about performance "above and beyond the call of duty." What Abraham Lincoln's Congressional Medal of Honor phrase "above and beyond the call of duty" *means* is doing something that no decent superior officer would have the temerity to order a human being to do. Please keep that in mind as we follow Lance down that game trail going east—the trail he finally found after an agonizing search.

He got in the tube and learned to progress, maybe one hundred yards a day, sometimes more, squirming on his back, his nose just below the thorn bushes that were the "roof" of the tube. He *willed* himself to ignore his thirst. He *willed* his body to press on.

And so Lance Sijan got down the hill, found water, chewed leeches, bugs, and leaves when he couldn't find berries, tore the vines with the crooked-finger hook blade of his parachute knife, slept only when totally exhausted, capitalizing on the self-knowledge that he could "think straight" for only an hour or two after awakening.

Thus, he struggled through the underbrush of Laos, having the thick muscles of his thighs cut raw by sharp-edged chunks of limestone. There Lance suffered setbacks that would have crushed a lesser human being: such as, after a couple of weeks of steady plodding, when he had the presence of mind to check his gear and found that his gun, strobe light, and radio had all fallen out of his tattered clothing along the way. But nevertheless, he struggled on east with mirror and compass intact, in fact, remembering that he was in an area with 4 degrees of west variation, he steadfastly held a course of 086 degrees magnetic. Right out of the academy's fourth-class knowledge manual, *Contrails*, he was showing "self-discipline, adaptability, stamina, and courage to perform responsibly in extreme and prolonged conditions of risk and stress."

Although Lance had long since lost the ability to keep accurate track of time, he felt it must be December when the rains started. Water was plentiful, and, as if by a miracle, he lost his hunger completely. He could hear American bombing to the south and east; he was getting near the target of his and Colonel Armstrong's final run. Then he started seeing truck lights at night—North Vietnamese convoys moving south on the Ho Chi Minh Trail up ahead. "The Vietnamese normally lie low in the daytime. Maybe I could get out there on that trail and mirror flash an American plane," he might have told himself. At any rate, at dawn Christmas morning, 1967, Lance Sijan, almost spent, slithered out on that desolate Ho Chi Minh Trail and passed out. In forty-plus days, he had come almost three miles in enemy territory, undetected.

Captain Guy Gruters, bound in leg irons and cuffs, sat bent over on the straw and mud floor of his cell at the Bamboo prison north of the town of Vinh, North Vietnam. He was screaming at his captors to stop. The North Vietnamese were pounding the hell out of the new guy in a cell nine feet away. Clubs struck flesh and bone. There were piercing screams. Gruters and Major Bob Craner, both shot down in their forward air control F-100, had also been clubbed, then trussed with their arms tightly tied behind them, elbows touching, the pain unbelievable. Whoever this poor devil was, the North Vietnamese were not getting any information.

"Name of base commander?" Gruters recognized the voice of the North Vietnamese officer in charge of this satellite "holding point" prison about three days' truck ride south of Hanoi. Unable to obtain the names of any Vietnamese prison officials, the Americans there had nicknamed him "Rodent."

"I'm not going to tell you anything," a weak but defiant voice replied. "It's against the code."

"Your leg very bad. Your head very bad. We hurt you if you do not answer all questions."

Terrible blows followed. Screams filled the air. "You bastard," the prisoner shouted, "I'll break your neck."

The interrogation went on and on. Gruters went to his knees in prayer.

Later, when Gruters was being taken for interrogation himself, he laid back, trailing behind the guard, so he could swing open the new prisoner's door and have a momentary glimpse of him. What he saw was an emaciated figure with an outsized cast of dirty plaster where his left leg should have been. He quickly gave the prisoner a thumbs-up, shut the door, and moved on.

The next morning, Gruters and Craner were ordered to take the prisoner to the latrine and clean him up. Nothing either man had seen in battle prepared them for the horrifying sight. The prisoner's skull was battered, hip bones projected through the skin. What shocked Gruters the most were the numerous open sores and the expanse of raw flesh. It was as if the poor man had been flayed. Regaining their composure, the two men stooped down to lift the prisoner. "Big guy, huh?" Gruters said to Craner, amazed at the incongruity of the man's height and perhaps only one hundred pounds of body weight.

"Aren't you Guy Gruters?" the skeleton asked.

"Yeah, who are you?" Gruters said, staring questioningly at the individual.

"Lance," the friendly voice answered.

"Lance who?"

"Lance Sijan."

Gruters burst into tears. He and Lance Sijan were both in the 21st Squadron at the academy. They had jumped together as members of the skydiving team.

Lance groaned as they gently carried him into the yard. "How secure is this place?" he asked Gruters. "What are the chances of getting out of here?"

Gruters and Craner were astonished. Inside a badly beaten body, Sijan's spirit was undaunted. Gruters was interrogated by Rodent the next day. He pleaded with the North Vietnamese officer, saying that if Sijan received medical treatment, he would become well enough to answer questions.

"Sijan criminal," Rodent stated. Then he told of the happenings over in Laos down by the Ho Chi Minh Trail. On that Christmas morning, a truck slammed on its brakes to avoid running over a slouched figure collapsed on the roadway. (The North Vietnamese were not "lying low" in the daytime. They were making a full court press, day and night, to get as much war matériel into South Vietnam as they could while America had tied its hands by honoring a "Christmas holiday cease-fire.")

Rodent explained that, after capture, Lance was given food and put under observation. Alone with the guard, Lance lured him close to his bed, bashed him with his left hand, knocking him firmly and completely unconscious, and escaped by crawling, under cover of a rainstorm, into the jungle. It took the North Vietnamese most of a day to find him. The crude heavy leg cast he was wearing was put on as an impediment to preclude further

Sijan escapes. He was then put on a truck for this holding point prison near the city of Vinh.

Rodent resumed the torture of Lance. Gruters and Craner yelled for him to stop. Lance's voice had been reduced to a whisper. Yet name, rank, and serial number were all he offered.

With the monsoon rains came disease. Lance became ill during the transfer of the three of them to the big Hoa Lo prison in downtown Hanoi. Craner and Gruters cradled Lance for three nights as the truck lurched over rutty roads.

The Vietnamese took care to have the truck arrive at the prison in the dead of night. An officer we called Bug met the truck. The guard brought a pallet out of the main gate. Lance was covered and lifted inside; the Vietnamese didn't want anybody to see his condition. They even forwent putting Craner and Gruters through their institutionalized "welcome aboard" torture sessions until after they had served as cell mates and caretakers of this man who was obviously not going to live very long. "Wash him down," was their first order after they got out of the truck at 2 A.M. on a Sunday morning.

Within three or four days of working out of solitary cells, having interrogations with Bug, and helping with Lance, Gruters and Craner were moved to a three-man cell we Americans knew in Hoa Lo as "Thunderbird 5 West." Lance was there to greet them, lying on a wet canvas cot against the dripping wall of the cell, having trouble breathing with what had to be pneumonia. They immediately called for a doctor. An old man showed up in due course. He spoke French and gave Lance what looked like a massive dose of antibiotics. He also removed the grotesque plaster cast from Lance's leg and gave him a blanket.

In the few days left, Gruters and Craner took turns staying awake throughout the night hours, fearing that Lance might choke with his now very serious respiratory problems. He awoke one night, looked at Craner, and said, "Do you know Bart Holaday?" Craner said, "I remember that name, wasn't he a football player?" Lance said, "I was just talking to Bart." And then his head fell back and he was unconscious again.

In his last hour, Lance could barely form words with his mouth, using signals to say that he was OK. Incredibly, he never complained. "I'll make it up to you two when I'm better." Then his eyes flashed with comprehension as the guards came in about 10 P.M. and lifted him onto a pallet. They were taking him away to die.

"Oh my God," he yelled as he was carried away down the gloomy passageway. "It's over, Dad. Dad, help me. Dad, I need you!" Driving home from work on a chilly January night in 1968, Syl Sijan was seized with a feeling of pain and remorse. His son had been shot down two and a half months before. "Lance!" he found himself shouting. "Where are you?"

Captain Lance P. Sijan died on January 22, 1968. His body was exhumed and returned to American custody in Hawaii six years later. He was then brought home to Milwaukee, to Jane and Syl, brother Marc, and sister Janine, in a coffin draped with the American flag he loved.

Lance was and *is* in the minds of all who knew him a mountain of a man. It is indeed appropriate that the new dormitory here at this academy, set against the horizon of the jagged and unyielding Rockies, should be named for him. He and these mountains share many similar invincible qualities.

finis

EDUCATION
FOR LEADERSHIP
AND SURVIVAL

THE STOCKDALE COURSE _____

By Joseph Gerard Brennan

WHEN COMMANDER JAMES BOND STOCKDALE lay in prison in North Vietnam, he told himself that if he ever got out alive he would teach a course in
moral philosophy. After seven and a half years in captivity, much of that
time in solitary confinement and under torture, he was released at last and
returned to the United States. Promoted rapidly to vice admiral and appointed president of the Naval War College at Newport, Rhode Island, he
introduced and taught just such a course. I helped him organize the course
and served as his tutor and team-teacher staying on to teach the course at
the War College after Stockdale retired from the navy in 1979.

MORAL PHILOSOPHY AT THE NAVAL WAR COLLEGE

[Our association, after some initial correspondence, began when] in
late 1977, Stockdale asked me to come up to visit him at the War College in
Newport. In a sunlit office overlooking Narragansett Bay, I found myself
stared at by a man who looked a little like James Cagney in his prime but
more handsome. Piercing blue eyes bored into me from under a shock of
thick, prematurely white hair. Stockdale wore the blue- and white-starred
ribbon of the Congressional Medal of Honor on his uniform. Intense, feisty,
and impatient with anything but directness, Stockdale moved about rest-
lessly, stumping back and forth on his leg that had been broken and rebroken
by beatings from his captors. He asked me if I would help him put together
a course in moral philosophy and team-teach it with him. I had just retired
as professor emeritus of philosophy at Barnard College of Columbia University and was on the point of accepting a State Department offer of a

Joseph Gerard Brennan, professor emeritus of philosophy at Barnard College of Columbia
University, until 1992 was electives professor and academic adviser to the Naval Com-
mand College, Naval War College, Newport, Rhode Island. He is the author of six books
and various articles on philosophy and comparative literature. His essay "Alfred North
Whitehead: Plato's Lost Dialogue" appears in *Masters: Portraits of Great Teachers*, ed.
Joseph Epstein (New York: Basic Books, 1981). This selection appeared as a chapter in
M. J. Collins, ed., *Teaching Values and Ethics in College*, New Directions for Teaching
and Learning, no. 13 (San Francisco: Jossey-Bass, 1983).

Fulbright lectureship in India. Stockdale said, "Phone those characters in Washington and tell them to go to hell." I did so, politely, and we set to work at once on organizing the course.

The Naval War College, I found, offered a one-year graduate course of study to military officers in midcareer. The curriculum centered on three core courses—strategy and policy, defense economics and decision making, and naval operations. Upon assuming the War College presidency, Stockdale had expanded the elective course offerings to twenty or thirty, the number depending on the particular trimester in which they were offered. All the elective courses, except the new offering in moral philosophy, were related in some way to the three required core courses. The student body at the Naval War College consisted of about three hundred midgrade military officers ranging in age from thirty-two to forty-two and in rank from lieutenant commander to commander or major to lieutenant colonel. There were a few navy and coast guard captains, as well as a handful of colonels from the other services. About half the student body was in the navy, with the rest split among the other services. A very few civilian officers from various government agencies were also enrolled. Two small groups of foreign officers formed autonomous but integrated colleges within the larger whole—the Naval Command College (senior) and the Naval Staff College (junior). All the officers wore civilian clothes, as did the military faculty, except on days when high-ranking Pentagon officers made official visits.

How were we to organize the Stockdale course for this formidable student audience? The first question was the title. Stockdale did not much like the word *ethics*. He thought the contemporary *ethics explosion* had eroded the older, nobler sense of the word. He knew that ethics courses were spreading rapidly, not only in military institutions but also in business, industry, and the professions. Harvard Business School had become ethics-conscious, IBM and Electronic Data Systems Corporation were working on ethics, and the Cummins Engine Company had taken on a professor of ethics from a major university. Stockdale was uneasy about this trend. He did not want his course to be the military equivalent of what he called "ethics for dentists." He preferred the term *moral philosophy* to *ethics*; the former seemed to suggest the tradition of the humanities, and he believed that, without some background in the humanities and some familiarity with the ancient and modern philosophical classics, it would be hard to teach ethics without boring students, at the very least. Stockdale was convinced that semieducated people (and, in his opinion, that group included many academics) tended to reduce ethics to a branch of psychology. Training in the humanities, Stockdale believed, would show that much of what goes by the name social science serves up ideas expressed earlier and better in classical philosophy and modern literature.

Stockdale was convinced, too, that a course in moral philosophy for military officers did not need to be organized directly around military ideas or writings on military ethics. The study of good philosophy and literature, he held, would benefit human beings; and, since military officers were human, it would be good for them, too, not only as human beings but also as military officers.

FOUNDATIONS OF MORAL OBLIGATION

Foundations of Moral Obligation was the title we finally agreed on. We had only a ten-week trimester to get through the course's readings, lectures, seminar discussions, papers, and examinations. The course opened with the idea of the *hermetic*—the alchemical transformation that may occur when a human being is subjected to intense pressure within a crucible of suffering or confinement. Stockdale's own *Atlantic Monthly* article, "The World of Epictetus" (April 1978), led easily to discussions of the prison experiences and reflections of Socrates, Boethius, Cervantes, Wittgenstein, Sartre, and Anwar Sadat. We went on to readings and discussions of the Book of Job, the Socratic dialogues of Plato, Aristotle's *Nichomachean Ethics*, Kant's *Foundations of the Principles of the Metaphysics of Morals*, and Mill's *On Liberty and Utilitarianism*. These readings were supplemented by selections from the works of Emerson, Sartre, Camus, Conrad, Koestler, Dostoyevsky, and Solzhenitsyn. The course closed, completing a circle, with a reading of Epictetus's *Enchiridion*, the little book that Philip Rhinelander had given to Stockdale and that sustained him in prison—a Stoic work Albert Salomon describes as "a manual for combat officers."

Reflecting on the course years later, Stockdale (1982) said, "We studied moral philosophy by looking at models of human beings under pressure, their portraits drawn from the best materials we could find in philosophy and literature. The professional implications for military men and women followed. We did not have to draw diagrams; the military applications came up naturally in seminar discussions." Stockdale came across a monograph called *The Teaching of Ethics in the Military*, published by the Hastings Institute (Stomberg and Wakin, 1982), an ethics think tank. He exploded at this sentence: "A flight leader threatens American values if he cannot analyze a moral problem." In his review of this monograph, Stockdale wrote, "That's not helpful. A flight leader threatens *human* values—and, by inclusion, American values—if he hasn't the guts ('character') to act like a man."

Stockdale believed that, before one can teach moral philosophy, one must decide whether to emphasize rules or character: both are necessary, of course. As senior officer of the Hanoi "Alcatraz," Stockdale exacted obedience to a stern set of rules. "Our value systems [in Alcatraz] had in common," he wrote in "Back from Hanoi" (*New York Times*, April 1, 1973), "the fact that they were based on rules, that they placed unity above self, and that they precluded self-indulgence." But, for Stockdale, rules were always secondary to character in considerations of moral life. He agreed with Aristotle that the end of a man is to be as human as possible. To achieve this fulfillment is an art that can be learned only by hard habit and stressful training. Acting well and living well follow from character, from what a man is. While he found Sartre's dictum "A man is the sum of his acts" challenging, Stockdale still held that to do something one must be something. He was less enthusiastic about Aristotle's heavy emphasis on the primacy of reason in the moral life. To our class that first year at the War College, he quoted Dostoyevsky's underground man: "You see, gentlemen, reason is an excellent thing, there's no disputing that, but reason is nothing but reason and satisfies only the rational side of man's nature, while will is a manifestation of the whole life, that is, of the whole human life, including reason and all the impulses."

Stockdale liked the way that, for all their differences, both Dostoyevsky and Aristotle supported the reality of individual freedom and personal responsibility. He endorsed Dostoyevsky's rejection of the Socratic axiom that humans act only in accord with what they think is good for them. He had seen men knowingly choose the bad and consciously rush head down to their own destruction. Like the underground man, Stockdale declined any social system that made men into "piano keys" and believed that any society scientifically organized according to the principles of rational self-interest would end, at best, as a harmonious anthill.

Among Stockdale's favorite pages of Aristotle's *Nichomachean Ethics* were those in which the philosopher distinguishes between voluntary and involuntary action, analyzes the role of choice and intention in human acts, and describes the way free choice and compulsion can coexist. Stockdale denied the existence of brainwashing; one was always responsible. If one broke under torture—and everyone did, at some point—one could always make the torturers start all over again the next day. His captors did not like to do that, Stockdale remarked; it made things so much easier for both sides if the victim "cooperated." When his comrades, racked by twisted ropes, had "spilled their guts" and returned to their cells weeping from shame, Stockdale would comfort them via the tap code on the wall: "We've all done it. Just make them work for it. Don't give anything away free." And so, to our Naval War College class, he read from the *Nichomachean Ethics*: "There are some instances in which such actions elicit forgiveness rather than praise, for example, when a man acts improperly under a strain greater than human nature can bear, and which no one could endure. Yet there are, perhaps, also acts which no man can possibly be compelled to do, but rather than do them he should accept the most terrible sufferings and death." Stockdale himself had risked death when he beat himself into bleeding insensibility with a wooden stool to prevent himself from being filmed for North Vietnamese propaganda purposes.

STUDENT REACTION TO STOCKDALE'S COURSE

The Naval War College has a detailed course evaluation system, and the student officers are frank in their estimates. How did they react to the Stockdale course? Most of them admired Stockdale just short of idolatry and gave the course very high ratings. A few found the admiral ill at ease in the more intimate seminar discussion sessions. All applauded the chance the course had given them to read the works that were discussed. For the greater part of their military careers, these military officers had concentrated on highly technological material. The writings and thoughts of Aristotle, Kant, Sartre, and the others were mostly a new experience for them, but they were quickly at home with these writers. Woody Hayes came one day to visit the class and was delighted to hear that Wittgenstein's *Was kommt leicht hat keine Wert* was no more than his own charge to his old Ohio State football teams: "If it comes easy, it ain't worth a damn."

The first midterm examination was formidable; Stockdale and I were determined (it was a mistake, of course) to throw everything in. Senator John Glenn was visiting that day, and Stockdale brought his old classmate to my office. Clutching a copy of the midterm Stockdale had proudly thrust upon him, John Glenn stood shaking his head in bewilderment, saying, "Pretty heavy test, Professor!" Meanwhile, screams of anguish from officers taking the test down the hall were painfully audible.

What the officers liked best of all about the Stockdale course was the opportunity to reflect on questions they felt had always been in their own minds, but just below the surface. This course, they agreed, provided them their first chance to raise those questions to the level of mature consciousness. At the close of the school day, the carpools back to the officers' homes and families at Fort Adams and Coddington Cove resounded with arguments on what they had heard that day, what they had read the night before, and how they saw it in the context of their own lives and work. A conversation repeated to me disclosed that one carpooler had said, "Kant's ethics is all right in theory, but in practice, it won't work," to which his comrade had replied, "But Kant's not telling how people do act or what does work, but how they ought to act and what should work." That officer had done his homework for the course.

During the year we taught together, I passed on to Stockdale a number of passages from my own reading. These he carefully copied onto his note cards, of which he kept a voluminous file. One of his favorites was a remark Sartre made in 1940 to a Catholic priest, when both were prisoners of war in a German camp at Trier. In his *Avec Sartre au Stalag 12D*, Fr. Marius Perrin recalls the remark "L'Important n'est pas ce quon a fait de vous, mais ce que vous faites de ce quon a fait de vous"—"The important thing is not what they've made of you, but what you made of what they've made of you." Stockdale had good reason to endorse that belief; he had lived it.

READING LIST

These were the reading assignments for Foundations of Moral Obligation. This list, except for minor revisions, is the same one offered when the Stockdale-Brennan team taught the course for the first time in the fall of 1978.

Week One: *From 20th-Century Technology to the World of Epictetus. The Meaning of Moral Philosophy.*
J. B. Stockdale, "The World of Epictetus." *Atlantic Monthly*, April 1978.
A. Koestler, *Darkness at Noon.*
R. A. Gabriel, "The Nature of Military Ethics."
M. Walzer, "Prisoners of War."

Week Two: *The Book of Job. Life Is Not Fair. The Problem of Evil.*
The Book of Job. Old Testament.
A. Solzhenitsyn, *One Day in the Life of Ivan Denisovich.*

Week Three: *Socrates. Doctrine and Example. Civil Disobedience. Can Virtue be Taught? Soul and Body.*
Plato, *Euthyphro, Apology, Crito,* and *Phaedo.*

Week Four: *Aristotle. Happiness as Living Well and Faring Well. The Moral and Intellectual Virtues. Courage as Balance and Endurance.*
Aristotle, *Nichomachean Ethics.*
J. Conrad, *Typhoon.*

Week Five: *Kant and Hart. Ethics of Moral Duty and Civic Law.*
Motives and Consequences. "Ought" and "Right." The
Meaning of Natural Law.
I. Kant, *Foundations of the Metaphysics of Morals.*
H. L. A. Hart, *The Concept of Law*, chapters 8 and 9.

Week Six: *Mill. Morality as Social Utility. Justice and the Greatest*
Happiness Principle.
J. S. Mill, *Utilitarianism* and *On Liberty.*
F. Dostoyevsky, *Notes from the Underground*, part I.

Week Seven: *Individualism and the Collective, I.*
R. W. Emerson, "Self-Reliance."
J. P. Sartre, "Existentialism Is a Humanism."
A. Camus, *The Plague.*

Week Eight: *Individualism and the Collective, II.*
K. Marx and F. Engels, *The Communist Manifesto.*
V. I. Lenin, *What Is to Be Done?*
F. Dostoyevsky, "The Grand Inquisitor" from *The Brothers*
Karamazov.

Week Nine: *Science and Values. Does the Universe Have Meaning or*
Purpose?
J. Monod, *Chance and Necessity.*
H. Smith, *Kamongo.*

Week Ten: *Return to the Beginning. Epictetus. The Stoic Ideal and the*
Ethics of the Military Officer. Philosophy as Technical
Analysis and Way of Life. Wittgenstein and the Ethics of
Silence.
Epictetus, *The Enchiridion.*
L. Wittgenstein, *Tractatus* (selections).
N. Malcolm. *Ludwig Wittgenstein: A Memoir.*
Plato, *Phaedo* (rereading of opening and death scene).
J. B. Stockdale, "Freedom," *Parade*, June 29, 1980.

REFERENCES

Stockdale, J. B. Untitled review of *The Teaching of Ethics in the Military. Naval War College Review* 35, no. 5 (1982): 97–99.

Stomberg, P. L., and Wakin, M. *The Teaching of Ethics in the Military.* Hastings, N.Y.: The Hastings Institute, 1982.

THE TOUGH MIND
OF EPICTETUS _____

Talk given at the Institute of Classical Studies,
University of London, November 15, 1993.

_____

I AM HERE AT THE INVITATION of Professor Sorabji to talk about my understanding of Stoicism, about the chance acquaintance I made with Epictetus
and how he has affected my life. Most of what I say today comes from
where my interest lies, in what might be called the modes of thought and
conduct set down by Epictetus to mold others to a Stoic life that they might
reap its benefits. And if I were asked, "What are the benefits of a Stoic life?"
I would probably say, "It is an ancient and honorable package of advice on
how to stay out of the clutches of those who are trying to get you on the
hook, trying to give you a feeling of obligation, trying to get moral leverage
on you, to force you to bend to their will." Because I first reaped its benefits
in an extortionist prison of torture, I could go on and say, "It's a formula
for maintaining self-respect and dignity in defiance of those who would
break your spirit for their own ends."

I know of no book that delineates, as a code breaker would delineate,
Epictetus's rules and tactics and the logic behind them. Books about the
practical application of Stoicism don't seem to get written. Most everything
I have to say, I've had to dig out myself, by deduction, after repeated readings
and note takings of *The Discourses* and *The Enchiridion*. But I do this work
with enthusiasm because, once I've nailed down a logic pattern, I have never
found an inconsistency in all of the thousands of words of Epictetus that
Arrian set down in print.

I am fairly well read in the broad descriptive literature about Stoicism;
there's certainly *more* than enough books about that. But as I think you can
tell, I am not going to retrace the steps of the strengths and weaknesses of
its materialism or its so-called conflicts of free will and necessity or its
coherence as Cicero saw it or its incoherence in others' eyes. No, I've been
through all of that, still like Stoicism, and seek not to fight old battles to yet
another draw. No, I am hooked. I have taken up the cudgel as directed by
Epictetus (4, 5, 33). Control over my moral purpose has become *my true*
business.

My interest in philosophy did not emerge until I was thirty-eight years
old. By that time I had been in the navy for twenty years and was living a

happy life with my wife, Sybil, and our three sons, with another on the way. I had been a fighter pilot most of that navy time—and had gotten into high technology as an experimental test pilot at our Naval Air Test Center at Patuxent River, Maryland. (Later I was an academic and flight instructor at our navy's Test Pilot School; I am now an honorary fellow in the International Society of Experimental Test Pilots. Sybil and I travel to their meetings, including one in England at Bath and air shows at the experimental test station on the Salisbury Plain at Boscome Downs.)

My undergraduate education had been straight engineering at Annapolis, graduating in 1946. By 1960, after a series of western Pacific cruises flying off aircraft carriers, the navy offered me a "sabbatical" from flying: two years of humanities at Stanford University. Our family moved to nearby Los Altos Hills with delight. I got a master of arts degree, but because the navy favored me with two full years on the campus, I also took courses in fields not associated with my degree. Being older and thinking of myself as worldly-wise, I found myself nagging professors after class with questions that tested their patience. A typical reply was, "You're getting into philosophy; that's beyond the scope of this course." After several such encounters, my curiosity was piqued about this philosophy thing. And after pleading with my adviser, he said, "Okay, go on over there to Philosophy Corner, but you're wasting your time; you'll have to take three courses before you'll understand the terminology."

It might have wound up that way, except for a great stroke of luck. As I wandered through philosophy's halls, in civilian clothes, of course, I heard a friendly voice call out from an office I was passing: "Can I help you?" I entered and saw a pleasantly smiling gentleman, maybe ten years older than I. My hair was already streaked with gray, and he thought I was a professor. I told him, "No, I'm a naval officer, a graduate student." "Sit down," he said, "I used to be in the navy during World War II." Thus began my friendship with Philip Rhinelander, professor of philosophy and dean of the university's humanities and sciences. Within fifteen minutes, we had agreed that I would enter his two-term course in the middle and that, to make up for my lack of background, I would meet with him for an hour a week for a private tutorial in the study of his campus home.

Phil Rhinelander opened my eyes. In that study it all happened for me— my inspiration, my dedication to the philosophic life. We went from Socrates to Aristotle to Descartes. And then on to Kant, Hume, Dostoyevsky, Camus. All the while, as we spent this hour alone each week, I could tell Phil was trying to psych me out, trying to figure out what I was seeking. He thought my interest in Hume's *Dialogues Concerning Natural Religion* was quite interesting. On my last session, he reached high in his wall of books and brought down a copy of *The Enchiridion*. He said, "I think you'll be interested in this."

There is a similarity of religious orientation between Epictetus and Hume. But years later I thought of a contradiction that I doubt occurred to Phil as he handed me that little book. His course was one he originated when he taught at Harvard soon after World War II. There, he was a favorite of Harvard president Conant, a chemist who was big on getting engineers acquainted with the humanities and vice versa. Conant improvised and taught a course in engineering for humanities majors and asked Phil to do likewise, "humanities for engineers." It was then that Phil started his two-term survey course that I took, which he called "The Problems of Good and Evil." I remember being swept off my feet with his first explanation of the underlying theme of the course. The idea of it was, in his words, that "there is no moral economy in the universe," that though people seem to have a *need* to believe that virtue is rewarded and evil punished on this earth, the evidence is overwhelming that there is no such connection. Martyrs frequently die poor, and swindlers die rich. The innocent get carried away by natural disasters or die in gas chambers in concentration camps. Phil started his course with the theme that "life is not fair," reading the Book of Job and citing examples in other readings, such as *King Lear*, where people reacted erratically when it dawned on them this "moral economy of the universe" that they had counted on was not there. In *King Lear*, of course, we have a good father whose solution to his children's betrayal of him was to go insane. "A good education," said Phil, "is one that includes the pointing out of the lack of a moral economy in the universe."

The contradiction is (and it was months before it occurred to me) that the invaluable prize that Phil Rhinelander gave me after completing his course and absorbing its lesson was a book, *The Enchiridion*, by a man, Epictetus, who was committed to the principle that there *is* a moral economy in the universe. Look at these pronouncements in his *Discourses*:

No man can do wrong with impunity. (4, 1, 120)

No one is evil without loss and damage. (2, 10, 18)

No evil befalls a good man in life or death. (3, 26, 28)

No one comes to a fall by another's deed. (1, 28, 23)

For it is impossible that the man who has gone astray is one person, while the man who suffers is another. (1, 28, 10)

W. A. Oldfather's footnote to the latter passage: "Not merely does suffering always follow error, but it is also morally unthinkable that one man's error can cause another's 'suffering,' in the Stoic sense; or in other words, no man can be injured or be made to suffer except by his own act."

I've taken this route to zero in on what I think as the *heart* of the Stoic viewpoint. Uniquely to the Stoic, the only good things of absolute value are those that lie within the control of his will. "If you can't make it happen or not happen, forget it." For the Stoic, the state of his *inner self*—and by that I mean the working of his conscience, his tranquility, his inner fearlessness, his inner freedom, and so on—is all that is important. Epictetus believed that conscience could be counted on to punish the evildoer, which was the key to his moral economy of the universe.

In Rhinelander's universe (the universe of most everybody but Stoics), men good and bad can be seen faring well and ill, almost at random, but *faring* in terms of things like their wealth, their health, their living, their dying, their pleasure, and their pain—*none* of which lie within the control of their wills. To the Stoic, the *greatest* injury that can be inflicted on a person is administered by *himself* when he destroys the good man within him. For the non-Stoics, almost all great injuries are based on deprivations of "things" controlled by external persons or forces. To a Stoic, there is no such thing as being a "victim"; you can only be a "victim" of yourself.

Moreover, Epictetus says a person must choose to live either for the "inner man" or for "things outside." You can't have it both ways. "You must be one person, either good or bad; you must labour to improve either your own governing principle or externals; you must work hard either on the *inner man*, or on *things outside*; that is, play the role of a philosopher, or else that of a layman." (3, 15, 13) (And, of course, in the Roman Empire at the time of Epictetus, almost all philosophers were Stoics.)

Most of what Epictetus has to say to me is "right on" for modern times. Will Durant says that human nature changes, if at all, with "geological leisureliness." According to me, not much has happened to it since the days of Homer. Epictetus lived a tough life: born a slave, crippled by a cruel master, went from boy to man in the murderous violence of the household of a totally indulgent Emperor Nero. And he read human nature across a spectrum like this, and by the standards of my spectrum, it rings with authenticity. Who but a man who had seen life as he had could drop in lines to his students like this?: "A man is responsible for his *judgements*, even in dreams, in drunkeness, and in melancholy madness."

Epictetus makes the points (1) that significant shame is *not* generated by the life-and-death goings-on in wars but by betrayal of self, destroying the good man within you, and (2) that that shame is heavy, a heavier burden than any physical wounds. It's been my observation that when a person emerges from prisoner-of-war captivity, the man in the street bombards him with all the wrong questions. These questions sound like movie scenarios that portray ultimate hardships as hunger and broken bones. In a prison like mine, the major wear and tear was not on the body but on the nervous system. Let me tell you that *facing your own fragility*, after mere minutes in a flurry of action while being bound with tourniquet-tight ropes, with care, by a professional, hands behind, jackknifed forward and down toward your ankles held secure in lugs attached to an iron bar, that with the onrush of anxiety, knowing your upper body's circulation has been stopped, and feeling the ever-growing induced pain, and the ever-closing in of claustrophobia, you can be made to blurt out answers, sometimes correct answers, to questions about anything your interrogator knows you know, *is a very humiliating experience*. But it doesn't grab you right then, so much as it does in the ensuing month or more, while you are locked in place in irons, in isolation, in a dark cell.

Even our interrogators were ignorant of the fact that feelings of guilt cannot be generated in the absence of memory connections to your own experiences. They would tell us, "Contemplate your crimes, of bombing churches, schools, and pagodas and killing innocent civilians." Our experiences were devoid of consciousness of any such actions; even if we had known *somebody else* did it, collective guilt is a loser. But we had *much more serious* guilt problems that they, thank God, seemed to have no feel for and thus were unable to capitalize on. Ours was the Epictetus guilt of self-betrayal: We had not anticipated our fragility, did not know that the cultivated gentleman of confidence could be, with the right techniques and the right violence, reduced to a self-loathing wreck in a period of minutes. In the darkness of our isolation we repeated to ourselves endlessly: "I could have hung on longer before I submitted; I could have kept silent if I had just had more courage." "I can never face my friends again."

And when you do get returned to a solitary cell in a block and get whispered to by the guy next door, what was the first thing 95 percent of us replied? "You don't want to talk to me; I'm a traitor." Only when your unseen friend replied, "There are no virgins in here; you should have heard what I told them" did the mending process start. Broken bones, and many people had them in those instances, were, in comparison to shame, totally insignificant.

Achilles was ashamed and grieved *because he wanted to grieve*. Behind that statement lies a whole group of concepts that are considerably *empowering* to a person in tight straits. They are empowering not because they somehow mysteriously increase your courage, but because they clear your head and rid you of the myths that the fate of your inner self is in hands other than your own. The Stoic thinks of emotions as acts of will. Fear is not something that darts out from behind a bush and settles itself on you in the dark. You fear because you decided to fear, you fear because you want to fear. The same with grief, pity, affection, and so on.

> We ought not to look for the *motive* for an act anywhere outside ourselves. In *all* cases it is one and the same thing, and that is that the cause of our doing a thing or of our not doing it, of our saying things, or of our not saying them, of our being elated, or of our being cast down, or our avoiding things, or of our pursuing them. Is it anything else than that we *wanted* to do them?—Nothing.—From this day forward, let us agree that your actions or frames of mind shall be ascribed to no other causes than the *decisions of your will*, that is to say, that you *wanted* to do them. And this applies to what you do good as well as what you do evil. (1, 11, 33)
>
> But if a person subjects me to the fear of death, he compels me. (1, 17, 25)

No, it is not what you are subjected to that compels you, but the fact that you *decide* it is better for you to do something of the sort than to die. It is the decision of your own will that compelled you, that is, moral purpose compelled moral purpose.

Tough-mindedness. Epictetus doesn't say, "ignore threats of death." He just says, "don't deceive yourself; it's habit forming."

Professor Sorabji indicated some interest in what I have deduced about the Stoic's treatment of feelings of grief, pity, and affection. All three, being emotions, are acts of will. Epictetus thought grief and pity and, to a lesser extent, affection tended to be emotionally destabilizing states of mind. They could be impediments to the dispassionate judging of phantasia, impressions, a chore of the highest importance to right living. In varying degrees, they could disturb the soul—give it "vertigo" (Oldfather's translation) or "fits of dizziness" (Percy Matheson).

Of the three, grief was the worst, pity was a form of grief and next in ill repute. Affection was the least blighted of the three yet still of the same family. Although affection never gets this charge, indulging grief and pity is frequently described in the *Discourses* as evil. But Epictetus never condemns any of these emotions across the board—each were worthy of specific exceptions in proportion to their overall tendencies toward troublesomeness.

Involving oneself in ameliorating another's *grief* could result in one's thwarting God in his administration of the universe:

> Now another's grief is no concern of mine, but my own grief is. Therefore, I will put an end at all costs to what is my own concern, for it is under my control; and that which is another's concern I will endeavor to check to the best of my ability, but my effort to do so will not be made at all costs. Otherwise, I shall be fighting against God [in his administration of

the universe]. And the wages of this fighting against God and this disobedience will *not* be paid by my "children's children," but by me myself in my own person, by day and by night, as I start up out of dreams and am disturbed, trembling at every message." (3, 24, 24)

But, the exception: "When you see anyone weeping for grief . . . do not disdain to accommodate yourself to him, and if need be, to groan with him. Take heed, however, not to groan inwardly, too." (*Ench.* 16)

Pity was thought to be an embarrassing, condescending emotion to have directed toward you and a disturbing emotion to serve up. Like grief, it makes all the "bad" lists in *Discourses*:

> Let him who disobeys divine governance be abject, be a slave, suffer *grief*, envy, *pity*, in a word, be miserable and lament. (3, 24, 45)

> I wanted your help but not your pity; my plight is *not* an *evil* one. (1, 9, 28)

But there is a prominent exception to the general rule of not serving up pity. It is that it is okay, even *desirable*, to pity a person who has inflicted *himself* with the venom of evil, destroying the good man within him: "The greatest thing in each man is right moral purpose, and if a man is deprived of this very thing, what ground is left for you to be angry at him? . . . Pity him, rather, but do not hate him." (1, 18, 9)

Because Medea deluded herself, Epictetus suggests that she deserves pity. And in a particularly humorous story he invents, where a man comes forward to complain to him about being pitied by some high-society, rich non-Stoics whose social circle he is clearly intent on joining, Epictetus comments as follows:

> Since, therefore there is so great a difference between the things which men desire, their deeds, and their prayers, do you still wish to be on equal footing with them in matters to which you have not devoted yourself, but they have? And after all that, are your surprised if they pity you, and are you indignant? But they are convinced that they are getting good things, *while you are not so convinced in your own case.* That is why you are not satisfied with what you have, but reach out for what they have. Because if you had been truly convinced that, in the case of things which are good, *you* are the one who is attaining them, while they have gone astray, you would not even have taken account of what they say about you. (4, 6, 36)

The dialogue closes as follows:

Epictetus: Are you concerned whether the rest of mankind pity you?

Mr. Fidget: Yes, but I do not deserve to be pitied.

Epictetus: And so you are pained at that? And is a man pained worthy of pity?

Mr. Fidget: Yes.

Epictetus: How, then, do you fail to deserve pity after all? By the very emotion which you feel concerning pity you make yourself worthy of pity.

A single paragraph of Epictetus will explain his view on affection:

How, then, shall I become affectionate?—As a man of noble spirit, as one who is fortunate; for it is against all reason to be abject, or broken in spirit, or to depend on something other than yourself, or even to blame either God or man. I would have you be affectionate in such a way as to maintain at the same time all these rules; if, however, by virtue of this natural affection, whatever it is you call by that name, you are going to be a slave and miserable, it does not profit you to be affectionate. (3, 24, 58)

COURAGE UNDER FIRE: TESTING EPICTETUS'S DOCTRINES IN A LABORATORY OF HUMAN BEHAVIOR

Speech delivered at the Great Hall, King's College, London, November 15, 1993.

I CAME TO THE PHILOSOPHIC LIFE as a thirty-eight-year-old naval pilot in grad school at Stanford University. I had been in the navy for twenty years and scarcely ever out of a cockpit. In 1962, I began my second year of studying international relations so I could become a strategic planner in the Pentagon. But my heart wasn't in it. I had yet to be inspired at Stanford and saw myself as just processing tedious material about how nations organized and governed themselves. I was too old for that. I knew how political systems operated; I had been beating systems for years.

Then, in what we call a "feel out pass" in stunt flying, I cruised into Stanford's philosophy corner one winter morning. I was gray-haired and in civilian clothes. A voice boomed out of an office, "Can I help you?" The speaker was Philip Rhinelander, dean of humanities and sciences, who taught Philosophy 6: The Problems of Good and Evil.

At first he thought I was a professor, but we soon found common ground in the navy because he'd served in World War II. Within fifteen minutes we'd agreed that I would enter his two-term course in the middle, and to make up for my lack of background, I would meet him for an hour a week for a private tutorial in the study of his campus home.

Phil Rhinelander opened my eyes. In that study it all happened for me— my inspiration, my dedication to the philosophic life. From then on, I was out of international relations—I already had enough credits for the master's—and into philosophy. We went from Job to Socrates to Aristotle to Descartes. And then on to Kant, Hume, Dostoyevsky, Camus. All the while, Rhinelander was psyching me out, trying to figure out what I was seeking. He thought my interest in Hume's *Dialogues Concerning Natural Religion* was quite interesting. On my last session, he reached high in his wall of books and brought down a copy of *The Enchiridion*. He said, "I think you'll be interested in this."

Enchiridion means "ready at hand." In other words, it's a handbook.

Rhinelander explained that its author, Epictetus, was a very unusual man of intelligence and sensitivity, who gleaned wisdom rather than bitterness from his early firsthand exposure to extreme cruelty and firsthand observations of the abuse of power and self-indulgent debauchery.

Epictetus was born a slave in about A.D. 50 and grew up in Asia Minor speaking the Greek language of his slave mother. At the age of fifteen or so, he was loaded off to Rome in chains in a slave caravan. He was treated savagely for months while en route. He went on the Rome auction block as a permanent cripple, his knee having been shattered and left untreated. He was "bought cheap" by a freedman named Epaphroditus, a secretary to Emperor Nero. He was taken to live at the Nero White House at a time when the emperor was neglecting the empire while he toured Greece as actor, musician, and chariot race driver. When home in Rome in his personal quarters, Nero was busy having his half-brother killed, his wife killed, his mother killed, his second wife killed. Finally, it was Epictetus's master Epaphroditus who cut Nero's throat when he fumbled his own suicide as the soldiers were breaking down his door to arrest him.

That put Epaphroditus under a cloud, and, fortuitously, the now cagey slave Epictetus realized he had the run of Rome. And being a serious and doubtless disgusted young man, he gravitated to the high-minded public lectures of the Stoic teachers who *were* the philosophers of Rome in those days. Epictetus eventually became apprenticed to the very best Stoic teacher in the empire, Musonius Rufus, and, after ten or more years of study, achieved the status of philosopher in his own right. With that came true freedom in Rome, and the preciousness of that was duly celebrated by the former slave. Scholars have calculated that in his works individual freedom is praised six times more frequently than it is in the New Testament. The Stoics held that all human beings were equal in the eyes of God: male/female, black/white, slave and free.

I read every one of Epictetus's extant writings twice, through two translators. Even with the most conservative translators, Epictetus comes across speaking like a modern person. It is "living speech," not the *literary* Attic Greek we're used to in men of that tongue. *The Enchiridion* was actually penned not by Epictetus, who was above all else a determined teacher and man of modesty who would never take the time to transcribe his own lectures, but by one of his most meticulous and determined students. The student's name was Arrian, a very smart, aristocratic Greek in his twenties. After hearing his first few lectures, he is reported to have exclaimed something like, "Son of a gun! We've got to get this guy down on papyrus!"

With Epictetus's consent, Arrian took down his words verbatim in some kind of frantic shorthand he devised. He bound the lectures into books; in the two years he was enrolled in Epictetus's school, he filled eight books.

Four of them disappeared sometime before the Middle Ages. It was then that the remaining four got bound together under the title *Discourses of Epictetus*. Arrian put *The Enchiridion* together after he had finished the eight. It is just highlights from them "for the busy man." Rhinelander told me that last morning, "As a military man, I think you'll have a special interest in this. Frederick the Great never went on a campaign without a copy of this handbook in his kit."

I'll never forget that day, and the essence of what that great man had to say as we said good-bye was burned into my brain. It went very much like this: The Stoic viewpoint is often misunderstood because the casual reader misses the point that all talk is in reference to the "inner life" of man. Stoics belittle physical harm, but this is not braggadocio. They are speaking of it in comparison to the devastating agony of shame they fancied good men generating when they knew in their hearts that they had *failed* to do their duty vis-à-vis their fellow men or God. Although pagan, the Stoics had a monotheistic, *natural* religion and were great contributors to Christian thought. The fatherhood of God and the brotherhood of man were Stoic concepts before Christianity. In fact, one of their early theoreticians, named Chrysippus, made the analogy of what might be called the *soul* of the universe to the *breath* of a human, *pneuma* in Greek. This Stoic conception of a celestial pneuma is said to be the great-grandfather of the Christian Holy Ghost. Saint Paul, a Hellenized Jew brought up in Tarsus, a Stoic town in Asia Minor, always used the Greek word *pneuma*, or breath, for "soul."

Rhinelander told me that Marcus Aurelius took the Roman Empire to the pinnacle of its power and influence. And Epictetus, the great teacher, played his part in changing the leadership of Rome from the swill he had known in the Nero White House to the power and decency it knew under Marcus Aurelius.

Marcus Aurelius was the last of the five emperors (all with Stoic connections) who successively ruled throughout that period Edward Gibbon described in his *Decline and Fall of the Roman Empire* as follows: "If a man were called upon to fix the period in the history of the world during which the condition of the human race was most happy and prosperous, he would without hesitation name that which elapsed from the accession of Nerva (A.D. 96) to the death of Marcus Aurelius (A.D. 180). The united reigns of the five emperors of the era are possibly the only period of history in which the happiness of a great people was the sole object of government."

Epictetus drew the same sort of audience Socrates had drawn five hundred years earlier—young aristocrats destined for careers in finance, the arts, public service. The best families sent him their best sons in their middle twenties—to be told what the good life consisted of, to be disabused of the idea that they deserved to become playboys, the point made clear that their job was to serve their fellow men.

In his inimitable, frank language, Epictetus explained that his curriculum was *not* about "revenues or income, or peace or war, but about happiness and unhappiness, success and failure, slavery and freedom." His model graduate was not a person "able to speak fluently about philosophic principles as an idle babbler, but about things that will do you good if your child dies, or your brother dies, or if you must die or be tortured." "Let others practice lawsuits, others study problems, others syllogisms; here you practice how to die, how to be enchained, how to be racked, how to be exiled." A man is responsible for his own "judgments, even in dreams, in drunkenness, and in melancholy madness." Each individual brings about his own good and his own evil, his good fortune, his ill fortune, his happiness, and his wretchedness. And to top all this off, he held that it is *unthinkable* that one man's error could cause another's suffering. Suffering, like everything else in Stoicism, was *all down here*—remorse at destroying *yourself*.

So what Epictetus was telling his students was that there can be no such thing as being the "victim" of another. You can only be a "victim" of *yourself*. It's all how you discipline your mind. Who is your master? "He who has authority over *any* of the things on which you have set your heart." "What is the result at which all virtue aims? *Serenity*." "Show me a man who though sick is happy, who though in danger is happy, who though in prison is happy, and I'll show you a Stoic."

When I got my degree, Sybil and I packed up our four sons and family belongings and headed to Southern California. I was to take command of Fighter Squadron 51, flying supersonic F-8 Crusaders, first at the Miramar Naval Air Station, near San Diego, and later, of course, at sea aboard various aircraft carriers in the western Pacific. Exactly three years after we drove up to our new home near San Diego, I was shot down and captured in North Vietnam.

During those three years, I had launched on three seven-month cruises to the waters off Vietnam. On the first we were occupied with general surveillance of the fighting erupting in the south; on the second I led the first-ever American bombing raid against North Vietnam; and on the third, I was flying in combat almost daily as the air wing commander of the USS *Oriskany*. But on my bedside table, no matter what carrier I was aboard, were my Epictetus books: *Enchiridion, Discourses*, Xenophon's *Memorabilia* of Socrates, and *The Iliad* and *The Odyssey*. (Epictetus expected his students to be familiar with Homer's plots.) I didn't have time to be a bookworm, but I spent several hours each week buried in them.

I think it was obvious to my close friends, and certainly to me, that I was a changed man and, I have to say, a better man for my introduction to philosophy and especially to Epictetus. I was on a different track—certainly not an antimilitary track but to some extent an antiorganization track. Against the backdrop of all the posturing and fumbling around peacetime military organizations seem to have to go through, to accept the need for graceful and unselfconscious improvisation under pressure, to break away from set procedures forces you to be reflective, reflective as you put a new mode of operation together. I had become a man detached—not aloof but detached—able to throw out the book without the slightest hesitation when it no longer matched the external circumstances. I was able to put juniors over seniors without embarrassment when their wartime instincts were more reliable. This new abandon, this new built-in flexibility I had gained, was to pay off later in prison.

But undergirding my new confidence was the realization that I had found the proper philosophy for the military arts as I practiced them. The Roman Stoics coined the formula *Vivere militare!*—"Life is being a soldier." Epictetus in *Discourses*: "Do you not know that life is a soldier's service? One must keep guard, another go out to reconnoitre, another take the field. If you neglect your responsibilities when some severe order is laid upon you, do you not understand to what a pitiful state you bring the army in so far as in you lies?" *Enchiridion*: "Remember, you are an actor in a drama of such sort as the Author chooses—if short, then in a short one; if long, then in a long one. If it be his pleasure that you should enact a poor man, or a cripple, or a ruler, see that you act it well. For this is your business—to act well the given part, but to choose it belongs to Another." "Every one of us, slave or free, has come into this world with *innate* conceptions as to good and bad, noble and shameful, becoming and unbecoming, happiness and unhappiness, *fitting and inappropriate*." "If you regard yourself as a man and as a part of some whole, it is fitting for you now to be sick and now to make a voyage and run risks, and now to be in want, and on occasion to die before your time. Why, then are you vexed? Would you have someone else be sick of a fever now, someone else go on a voyage, someone else die? For it is impossible in such a body as ours, that is, in this universe that envelops us, among these fellow-creatures of ours, that such things should not happen, some to one man, some to another."

On September 9, 1965, I flew at 500 knots right into a flak trap, at treetop level, in a little A-4 airplane—the cockpit walls not even three feet apart—which I couldn't steer after it was on fire, its control system shot out. After ejection I had about thirty seconds to make my last statement in freedom before I landed in the main street of a little village right ahead. And so help me, I whispered to myself: "Five years down there, at least. I'm leaving the world of technology and entering the world of Epictetus."

"Ready at hand" from the *Enchiridion* as I ejected from that airplane was the understanding that a Stoic always kept *separate* files in his mind for (A) those things that are "up to him" and (B) those things that are "not up to him." Another way of saying it is (A) those things that are "within his power" and (B) those things that are "beyond his power." Still another way of saying it is (A) those things that are within the grasp of "his Will, his Free Will" and (B) those things that are beyond it. All in category B are "external," beyond my control, ultimately dooming me to fear and anxiety if I covet them. All in category A are up to me, within my power, within my will, and properly subjects for my total concern and involvement. They include my opinions, my aims, my aversions, my own grief, my own joy, my judgments, my attitude about what is going on, my own good, and my own evil.

To explain why "your own good and your own evil" is on that list, I want to quote Aleksandr Solzhenitsyn from his gulag book. He writes about that point in prison when he realizes the strength of his residual powers, and starts what I called to myself "gaining moral leverage," riding the updrafts of occasional euphoria as you realize you are getting to know yourself and the world for the first time. He calls it "ascending" and names the chapter in which this appears "The Ascent":

> It was only when I lay there on the rotting prison straw that I sensed within myself the first stirrings of *good*. Gradually it was disclosed to me that the line separating good and evil passes not between states nor between classes nor between political parties, but right through every human heart, through all human hearts. And that is why I turn back to the years of my imprisonment and say, sometimes to the astonishment of those about me, "Bless you, prison, for having been a part of my life."

I came to understand that long before I read it. Solzhenitsyn learned, as I and others have learned, that good and evil are not just abstractions you kick around and give lectures about and attribute to this person and that. The only good and evil that means anything is right in your own heart, within your will, within your power, where it's up to you. *Enchiridion 32*: "Things that are not within our own power, not without our Will, can by no means be either good or evil." *Discourses*: "Evil lies in the evil use of moral purpose, and good the opposite. The course of the Will determines good or bad fortune, and one's balance of misery and happiness." In short, what the Stoics say is "Work with what you have control of and you'll have your hands full."

What is not up to you? beyond your power? not subject to your will in the last analysis? For starters, let's take "your station in life." As I glide down toward that little town on my short parachute ride, I'm just about to learn how negligible is my control over my station in life. It's not at all up to me.

I'm going right now from being the leader of a hundred-plus pilots and a thousand men and, goodness knows, all sorts of symbolic status and good-will, to being *an object of contempt*. I'll be known as a "criminal." But that's not *half* the revelation that is the realization of your own *fragility*—that you can be reduced by wind and rain and ice and seawater or *men* to a helpless, sobbing wreck—unable to control even your own bowels—in a matter of *minutes*. And, more than even that, you're going to face fragilities you never before let yourself believe you could have—like after mere minutes, in a flurry of action while being bound with tourniquet-tight ropes, with care, by a professional, hands behind, jackknifed forward and down toward your ankles held secure in lugs attached to an iron bar, that, with the onrush of anxiety, knowing your upper body's circulation has been stopped and feeling the ever-growing induced pain and the ever-closing in of claustrophobia, you can be made to blurt out answers, sometimes correct answers, to questions about anything they know you know. (Hereafter, I'll just call that situation "taking the ropes.")

"Station in life," then, can be changed from that of a dignified and competent gentleman of culture to that of a panic-stricken, sobbing, self-loathing wreck in a matter of minutes. So what? To live under the false pretense that you will forever have control of your station in life is to ride for a fall; you're asking for disappointment. So make sure in your heart of hearts, in your inner self, that you treat your station in life with *indifference*, not with contempt, only with *indifference*.

And so also with a long long list of things that some unreflective people assume they're assured of controlling to the last instance: your body, property, wealth, health, life, death, pleasure, pain, reputation. Consider "reputation," for example. Do what you will, reputation is at least as fickle as your station in life. *Others* decide what your reputation is. Try to make it as good as possible, but don't get hooked on it. Don't be ravenous for it and start chasing it in tighter and tighter circles. As Epictetus says, "For what are tragedies but the portrayal in tragic verse of the sufferings of men who have admired things external?" In your heart of hearts, when you get out the key and open up that old rolltop desk where you really keep your stuff, don't let "reputation" get mixed up with your *moral purpose* or your *will power*; they *are* important. Make sure "reputation" is in that box in the bottom drawer marked "matters of indifference." As Epictetus says, "He who craves or shuns things not under his control can neither be faithful nor free, but must himself be changed and tossed to and fro and must end by subordinating himself to others."

I know the difficulties of gulping this down right away. You keep thinking of practical problems. Everybody has to play the game of life. You can't just walk around saying, "I don't give a damn about health or wealth or whether I'm sent to prison or not." Epictetus took time to explain better what he meant. He says everybody should play the game of life—that the best play it with "skill, form, speed, and grace." But, like most games, you play it with a ball. Your team devotes all its energies to getting the ball across the line. But after the game, what do you do with the ball? Nobody much cares. It's not worth anything. The competition, the game, was the thing. The ball was "used" to make the game possible, but it in itself is not of any value that would justify falling on your sword for it.

Once the game is over, the ball is properly a matter of indifference. Epictetus on another occasion used the example of shooting dice—the dice being matters of indifference, once their numbers had turned up. To exercise *judgment* about whether to accept the numbers or roll again is a *willful* act, and thus *not* a matter of indifference. Epictetus's point is that our *use* of externals is not a matter of indifference because our actions are products of our will and we totally control that, but that the dice themselves, like the ball, are material over which we have no control. They are externals that we cannot afford to covet or be earnest about, else we might set our hearts on them and become slaves of such others as control them.

These explanations of this concept seem so modern, yet I have just given you practically verbatim quotes of Epictetus's remarks to his students in Nicopolis, colonial Greece, two thousand years ago.

So I took those core thoughts into prison; I also remembered a lot of attitude-shaping remarks. Here's Epictetus on how to stay off the hook: "A man's master is he who is able to confer or remove whatever that man seeks or shuns. Whoever then would be free, let him wish nothing, let him decline nothing, which depends on others; else he must necessarily be slave." And here's why never to beg: "For it is better to die of hunger, exempt from fear and guilt, than to live in affluence with perturbation." Begging sets up a demand for quid pro quos, deals, agreements, reprisals, the pits.

If you want to protect yourself from "fear and guilt," and those are the crucial pincers, the real long-term destroyers of will, you have to get rid of all your instincts to compromise, to meet people halfway. You have to learn to stand aloof, never give openings for deals, never level with your adversaries. You have to become what Ivan Denisovich called a "slow movin' cagey prisoner."

All that, over the previous three years, I had *unknowingly* put away for the future. So, to return to my bailing out of my A-4, I can hear the noontime shouting and pistol shots and whining bullets ripping my parachute canopy and see the fists waving in the street below as my chute hooks a tree but deposits me on the ground in good shape. With two quick-release fastener flips, I'm free of the parachute, and immediately gang tackled by the ten or fifteen town roughnecks I had seen in my peripheral vision, pounding up the road from my right.

I don't want to exaggerate this or indicate that I was surprised at my reception. It was just that when the gang tackling and pummeling was all over, and it lasted for two or three minutes before a man with a pith helmet got there to blow his police whistle, I had a very badly broken leg that I felt sure would be with me for life. My hunch turned out to be right. Later, I felt some relief—but only minor—from another Epictetus admonition I remembered: "Lameness is an impediment to the leg, but not to the Will; and say this to yourself with regard to everything that happens. For you will find such things to be an impediment to something else, but not truly to yourself."

But during the time interval between pulling the ejection handle and coming to rest on the street, I had become a man with a mission. I can't explain this without unloading a little emotional baggage that was part of my military generation's legacy in 1965.

In the aftermath of the Korean War, just over ten years before, we all had memories of reading about, and seeing early television news accounts of, U.S. government investigations into the behavior of some American prisoners of war in North Korea and mainland China. There was a famous series of articles in the *New Yorker* magazine that later became a book entitled *In Every War but One*. The gist of it was that in prison camps for Americans, it was every man for himself. Since those days, I've come to know officers who were prisoners of war there, and I now see much of that as selective reporting and as a bum rap. However, there were cases of young soldiers who were confused by the times, scared to death, in cold weather, treating each other like dogs fighting over scraps, throwing each other out in the snow to die, and nobody doing anything about it.

This could not go on, and President Eisenhower commissioned the writing of the American Fighting Man's Code of Conduct. It is written in the form of a personal pledge. Article 4: "If I become a prisoner of war, I will keep faith with my fellow prisoners. I will give no information or take part in any action which might be harmful to my comrades. If I am senior, I will take command. If not, I will obey the lawful orders of those appointed over me and will back them up in every way." In other words, as of the moment Eisenhower signed the document, American prisoners of war were never to escape the chain of command; the war goes on behind bars. As an insider, I knew the whole setup—that the North Vietnamese already held about twenty-five prisoners, probably in Hanoi, that I was the only wing commander to survive an ejection, and that I would be their senior, their commanding officer, and would remain so, very likely, throughout this war that I felt sure would last at least another five years. And here I was starting off crippled and flat on my back.

Epictetus turned out to be right. After a very crude operation, I was on crutches within a couple of months, and the crooked leg, healing itself, was strong enough to hold me up without the crutches in about a year. All told, it was only a temporary setback from things that were important to me, and being cast in the role as the sovereign head of an American expatriate colony that was destined to remain autonomous, out of communication with Washington, for years on end was very important to me. I was forty-two years old—still on crutches, dragging a leg, at considerably less than my normal weight, with hair down near my shoulders, my body unbathed since I had been catapulted from the *Oriskany*, a beard that had not seen a razor since I arrived—when I took command (clandestinely, of course, the North Vietnamese would never acknowledge our rank) of about fifty Americans. That expatriate colony would grow to over four hundred—all officers, all college graduates, all pilots or backseat electronic wizards. I was determined to "play well the given part."

The key word for all of us at first was "fragility." Each of us, before we were ever in shouting distance of another American, was made to "take the ropes." That was a real shock to our systems—and, as with all shocks, its impact on our inner selves was a lot more impressive and lasting and important than to our limbs and torsos. These were the sessions where we were taken down to submission, and made to blurt out distasteful confessions of guilt and American complicity into antique tape recorders, and then to be put in what I call "cold soak," a month or so of total isolation to "contemplate our crimes." What we actually contemplated was what even the most laid-back American saw as his betrayal of himself and everything he stood for. It was there that I learned what "Stoic Harm" meant. A shoulder broken, a bone in my back broken, a leg broken twice were *peanuts* by comparison. Epictetus: "Look not for any greater harm than this: destroying the trustworthy, self-respecting well-behaved man within you."

When put into a regular cell block, hardly an American came out of that experience without responding something like this when first whispered to by a fellow prisoner next door: "You don't want to talk to me; I am a traitor." And because we were equally fragile, it seemed to catch on that we all replied something like this: "Listen, pal, there are no virgins in here. You should have heard the kind of statement I made. Snap out of it. We're all in this together. What's your name? Tell me about yourself." To hear that last was, for most new prisoners just out of initial shakedown and cold soak, a turning point in their lives.

But the new prisoner's learning process was just beginning. Soon enough he would realize that things were not at all like some had told him in survival training—that if you made a good stiff showing of resistance in the opening chapters, the interrogators would lose interest in you and you would find yourself merely relegated to boredom, to "sitting out the war," to "languishing in your cell," as the uninitiated novelists love to describe the predicament. No, the war went on behind bars—there was no such thing as the jailers giving up on you as a hopeless case. Their political beliefs *made* them believe you could be made to see things their way; it was just a matter of time. And so you were marched to the interrogation room endlessly, particularly on the occasions of your being apprehended breaking one of the myriad rules that were posted on your cell wall—"trip wire" rules, which paid dividends for the commissar if his interrogator could get you to fall prey to his wedge of *shame*. The currency at the game table, where you and the interrogator faced one another in a duel of wits, was *shame*, and I learned that unless he could impose shame on me, or unless I imposed it on myself, he had nothing going for him. (Force was available, but that required the commissar's okay.)

For Epictetus, emotions were acts of will. Fear was not something that came out of the shadows of the night and enveloped you; he charged *you* with the total responsibility of starting it, stopping it, controlling it. This was one of Stoicism's biggest demands on a person. Stoics can be made to sound like lazy brutes when they are described merely as people indifferent to most everything but good and evil, people who make stingy use of emotions like pity and sympathy. But add this requirement of total personal responsibility for each and every one of your emotions, and you're talking about a person with his hands full. I whispered a "chant" to myself as I was marched at gunpoint to my daily interrogation: "control fear, control guilt, control fear, control guilt." And I devised methods of deflecting my gaze to obscure such fear or guilt as doubtless emerged in my eyes when I temporarily lost control under questioning. You could be bashed for failure to look at the face of your interrogator; I concentrated on his left earlobe, and he seemed to get used to it—thought I was a little cockeyed, probably. Controlling your emotions is difficult but can be *empowering*. Epictetus: "For it is *within you*, that both your destruction and deliverance lie." Epictetus: "The judgment seat and a prison is each a place, the one high, the other low; but the *attitude of your will* can be kept the same, if you *want* to keep it the same, in either place."

We organized a clandestine society via our wall tap code—a society with our own laws, traditions, customs, even heroes. To explain how it could be that we would order each other into more torture, order each other to refuse to comply with specific demands, intentionally call the bluff of our jailers and in a real sense force them to repeat the full ropes process to get another submission, I'll quote a statement that could have come from at least half of those wonderful competitive flyboys I found myself locked up with: "We are in a spot like we've never been in before. But we deserve to maintain our self-respect, to have the feeling we are fighting back. We can't refuse to do every degrading thing they demand of us, but it's up to you, boss, to pick out things we must all refuse to do unless and until they put us through the ropes again. We deserve to sleep at night. We at least deserve to have the satisfaction that we are hewing to our leader's orders. Give us the list; what are we to take torture for?"

I know this sounds like strange logic, but in a sense it was a first step in claiming what was rightfully *ours*. Epictetus said, "The judge will do some things to you which are thought to be terrifying; but how can he *stop you* from taking the punishment *he threatened*?" That's *my* kind of Stoicism. You have a right to make them hurt you, and they don't like to do that. When my fellow prisoner Ev Alvarez, the very first pilot they captured, was released with the rest of us, the prison commissar told him: "You Americans were nothing like the French; we could count on them to be reasonable." Ha!

I put a lot of thought into what those first orders should be. They would be orders that *could be obeyed*, not a "cover your ass" move of reiterating some U.S. government policy like "name, rank, serial number, and date of birth," which had no chance of standing up in the torture room. My mind-set was "we here under the gun are the experts, we are the masters of our fate, ignore guilt-inducing echoes of hollow edicts, throw out the book and write your own." My orders came out as easy-to-remember acronyms. The principal one was BACK US: Don't Bow in public; stay off the Air; admit no Crimes, never Kiss them goodbye. "US" could be interpreted as United States, but it *really* meant "Unity over Self." Loners make out in an enemy's prison, so my first rule of togetherness in there was that each of us had to work at the lowest common denominator, never negotiating for himself but only for *all*.

Prison life became a crazy mixture of an old regime and a new one. The old was the political prison routine, mainly for dissenters and domestic enemies of the state. It was designed and run by old-fashioned Third World Communists of the Ho Chi Minh cut. It revolved around the idea of "repentance" for your "crimes" of antisocial behavior. American prisoners, street criminals, and domestic political enemies of the state were all in the same prison. We never saw a "POW camp" like the movies show. The communist jail was part psychiatric clinic and part reform school. North Vietnam protocol called for making *all* their inmates demonstrate shame—bowing to all guards, heads low, never looking at the sky, frequent sessions with your interrogator if, for no other reason, to check your *attitude* and, if judged "wrong," then maybe down the torture chute of confession of guilt, of apology, and then the inevitable payoff of atonement.

The new regime, superimposed on the above, was for Americans only. It was a propaganda factory, supervised by English-speaking young bureaucratic army officers with quotas to fill, quotas set by the political arm of the government: press interviews with visiting left-wing Americans, propaganda films to shoot (starring intimidated "American air pirates"), and so on.

An encapsulated history of how this bifurcated prison philosophy fared is that the propaganda footage and interviews started to backfire. Smart American college men were salting their acts with sentences with double meanings, gestures read as funny-obscene by Western audiences, and practical jokes. One of my best friends, tortured to give names of pilots he knew who had turned in their wings in opposition to the war, said there were only two: Lieutenants Clark Kent and Ben Casey (then-popular fictional characters in America). That joke was headlined on the front page of the *San Diego Union*, and somebody sent a copy back to the government in Hanoi. As a result of that friendly gesture from a fellow American, Nels Tanner went into three successive days of rope torture, followed by 123 days in leg stocks, all while isolated of course.

So after several of these stunts, which cost the Vietnamese much loss of face, North Vietnam resorted to getting their propaganda only from the relatively *few* (less than 5 percent) of the Americans they could trust *not* to act up: real loners who, for different reasons, never joined the prisoner organization, never wanted to get into the tap code network, well-known sleazeballs we came to call *finks*. The vast majority of my constituents were enraged by their actions and took it upon themselves to diligently memorize data that would convict them in an American court-martial. But when we got home our government essentially dropped the charges I had preferred.

The great mass of all other Americans in Hanoi were by all standards "honorable prisoners," but that is not to say there was anything like a homogeneous prison regime we all shared. People like to think that because we were all in the Hanoi prison system, we had all these common experiences. It's not so. These *differing* regimes became marked when our prison organization stultified the propaganda efforts of this two-headed monster they called the "Prison Authority." They turned to vengeance against the leadership of my organization and to an effort to break down the morale of the others by baiting them with an amnesty program in which they would compete for early release by being compliant with North Vietnam's wishes.

In May 1967, the public address system blared out: "Those of you who repent, truly repent, will be able to go home before the war is over. Those few diehards who insist on inciting the other criminals to oppose the camp authority will be sent to a special dark place." I immediately put out an order forbidding any American to accept early release, but that is not to say I was a lone man on a white horse. I didn't have to sell that one; it was accepted with obvious relief and spontaneous jubilation by the overwhelming majority.

Guess who went to the "dark place." They isolated my leadership team—me and my cohort of ten top men—and sent us into exile. The Vietnamese worked very hard to learn our habits, and they knew who were the troublemakers and who were "not making any waves." They isolated those I trusted most; everybody had a long record of solitary and rope-mark pedigrees. Not all were seniors; we had seniors in prison who would not even communicate with the man next door. One of my ten was only twenty-four years old—born after I was in the navy. He was a product of my recent shipboard tendencies: "When instincts and rank are out of phase, take the guy with the instincts." All of us stayed in solitary throughout, starting with two years in leg irons in a little high-security prison right beside North Vietnam's "Pentagon"—their Ministry of Defense, a typical old French building. There are chapters upon chapters after that, but what they came down to in my case was a strung-out vengeance fight between the "prison authority" and those of us who refused to quit trying to be our brothers' keepers. The stakes grew to *nervous breakdown* proportions. One of the eleven of us died in that little prison we called Alcatraz, but even including him, there was not a man who wound up with less than three and a half years of solitary, and four of us had more than four years. To give you a sense of proportion on how the total four hundred fared on solo, one hundred had none, more than half of the other three hundred had less than a year, and half of those with less than a year had less than a month. So the average for the four hundred was considerably less than six months.

Howie Rutledge, one of the four of us with more than four years, went back to school and got a master's degree after we got home, and his thesis concentrated on the question of whether long-term erosion of human purpose was more effectively achieved by torture or isolation. He mailed out questionnaires to us (who had also all taken the ropes at least ten times) and others with records of extreme prison abuse. He found that those who had less than two years' isolation and plenty of torture said torture was the trump card; those with more than two years' isolation and plenty of torture said that for long-term modification of behavior, isolation was the way to go. From my viewpoint, you can get used to repeated rope torture—there are some tricks for minimizing your losses in that game. But keep a man, even a very strong-willed man, in isolation for three or more years, and he starts looking for a friend—*any* friend, regardless of nationality or ideology.

Epictetus once gave a lecture to his faculty complaining about the common tendency of new teachers to slight the stark realism of Stoicism's challenges in favor of giving the students an uplifting, rosy picture of how they could meet the harsh requirements of the good life painlessly. Epictetus said:

"Men, the lecture-room of the philosopher is a hospital; students ought not to walk out of it in pleasure, but in pain." If Epictetus's lecture room was a hospital, my prison was a laboratory—a laboratory of human behavior. I chose to test his postulates against the demanding real-life challenges of my laboratory. And as you can tell, I think he passed with flying colors.

It's hard to discuss in public the real-life challenges of that laboratory because people ask all the wrong questions: How was the food? That's always the first one, and in a place like I've been, that's so far down the scale you want to cry. Did they harm you physically? What was the nature of the *device* they used to harm you? Always the device or the truth serum or the electric shock treatment—all of which would totally defeat the purpose of a person seriously trying to break down your will. All those things would give *you* a feeling of moral superiority, which is the last thing he would want to have happen. I'm not talking about brainwashing; there is no such thing. I'm talking about having looked over the brink and seen the bottom of the pit and realized the truth of that linchpin of Stoic thought: that the thing that brings down a man is not *pain* but *shame*!

Why did those men in "cold soak" after their first rope trip eat their hearts out and feel so unworthy when the first American contacted them? Epictetus knew human nature well. In that prison laboratory, I do not know of a single case where a man was able to erase his conscience pangs with some laid-back pop psychology theory of cause and effect. Epictetus emphasizes time and again that a man who lays off the causes of his actions to third parties or forces is not leveling with himself. He must live with his own judgments if he is to be honest with himself. (And the "cold soak" tends to make you honest.) "But if a person subjects me to fear of death, he compels me," says a student. "No," says Epictetus, "It is neither death, nor exile, nor toil, nor any such things that is the cause of your doing, or not doing, *anything*, but only your opinions and the decisions of your Will." "What is the fruit of your doctrines?" someone asked Epictetus. "Tranquility, fearlessness, and freedom," he answered. You can have these only if you are honest and take responsibility for your own actions. You've got to get it *straight*! *You* are in charge of *you*.

Did I preach these things in prison? Certainly not. You soon learned that if the guy next door was doing okay, that meant that he had all his philosophical ducks lined up in his own way. You soon realized that when you dared to spout high-minded philosophical suggestions through the wall, you always got a very reluctant response.

No, I never tapped or mentioned Stoicism once. But some sharp guys read the signs in my actions. After one of my long isolations outside the cell blocks of the prison, I was brought back into signaling range of the fold, and my point of contact was a man named Dave Hatcher. As was standard operating procedure on a first contact after a long separation, we started off not with gushes of news but with first, an agreed-upon danger signal, second, a cover story for each of us if we were caught, and third, a backup communications system if this link was compromised—"slow movin' cagey prisoner" precautions. Hatcher's backup communication for me was a note drop by an old sink near a place we called the Mint, the isolation cell block of Hatcher's "Las Vegas" wing of the prison—a place he rightly guessed I would soon enough be in. Every day we would signal for fifteen minutes over a wall between his cell block and my "no man's land."

Then I got back into trouble. At that time the commissar of prisons had had me isolated and under almost constant surveillance for the year since I had staged a riot in Alcatraz to get us out of leg irons. I was barred from all prisoner cell blocks. I had special handlers, and they caught me with an outbound note that gave leads I knew the interrogators could develop through torture. The result would be to implicate my friends in "black activities" (as the North Vietnamese called them). I had been through those ropes more than a dozen times, and I knew I could *contain* material—*so long as they didn't know I knew it*. But this note would open doors that could lead to more people getting killed in there. We had lost a few in big purges—I think in torture overshoots—and I was getting tired of it. It was the fall of 1969, and I had been in this role for four years and saw nothing left for me to do but check out. I was solo in the main torture room in an isolated part of the prison, the night before what they told me would be my day to spill my guts. There was an eerie mood in the prison. Ho Chi Minh had just died, and his special dirge music was in the air. I was to sit up all night in traveling irons. My chair was near the only paned glass window in the prison. I was able to waddle over and break the window stealthily. I went after my wrist arteries with the big shards. I had knocked the light out, but the patrol guard happened to find me passed out in a pool of blood but still breathing. The Vietnamese sounded the alert, got their doctor, and saved me.

Why? It was not until after I was released years later that I learned that that very week, Sybil had been in Paris demanding humane treatment for prisoners. She was on world news, a public figure, and the last thing the North Vietnamese needed was me dead. There had been a very solemn crowd of senior North Vietnamese officers in that room as I was revived.

Prison torture, *as we had known it in Hanoi*, ended for everybody that night.

Of course it was months before we could be sure that was so. All I knew at the time was that in the morning, after my arms had been dressed and bandaged, the commissar himself brought in a hot cup of sweet tea, told my surveillance guard to take off my leg irons, and asked me to sit at the table with him. "Why did you do this, Sto-dale? You know I sit with the army's General Staff; they've asked for a full report this morning." (It was not unusual for us to talk like that by that time.) But he never once mentioned the note, nor did anybody else thereafter. *That* was unprecedented. After a couple of months in a tiny isolated cell we called Calcutta to let my arms heal, they blindfolded me and walked me right into the Las Vegas cell block. The isolation and special surveillance were over. I was put solo, of course, in the Mint.

Dave Hatcher knew I was back because I was walked under his window, and though he could not peek out, he could listen and over the years had attuned his ear to my walking "signature," my limping gait. Soon enough, the rusty wire over the sink in the washroom was bent to the north—Dave Hatcher's signal for "note in the bottle under the sink for Stockdale." Like an old fighter pilot, I checked my six o'clock, scooped the note up fast, and concealed it in my prison pajama pants, carefully. Back in my cell, after the guard locked the door, I sat on my toilet bucket—where I could stealthily jettison the note if the peephole cover moved—and unfolded Hatcher's sheet of low-grade paper toweling on which, with a rat dropping, he had printed, without comment or signature, the last verse of Ernest Henley's poem *Invictus*:

> It matters not how strait the gate,
> How charged with punishment the scroll,
> I am the master of my fate:
> I am the captain of my soul.

ETHICS BOOK DINNER ⸺⸺⸺

Address to U.S. Naval Academy, Class of 1994,
March 29, 1994.

I NEVER RETURN to this place without my heart thumping with a sense of history. Maybe it gets commonplace, routine, to those who live nearby, but I have never been able to shake the spell. As I walk through the yard and up the steps to Memorial Hall, I sense the ghosts of the great warriors that have gone before us behind every tree and pillar and feel a renewed obligation to be worthy of their company. But, of course, I'm an unabashed romantic, seeing the world the way I wish it to be. But I recommend the viewpoint to you, class of 1994. I don't know how I could have lived such a happy life in the navy had I not clung to it. "Life is a pageant," I was telling myself when I came here as a farm boy fifty-one years ago, "and here is my chance to perform on center stage."

Lots of people don't see it that way, I learned, when I had the great good fortune to be in just the right spot—fighter squadron commander—and right in the eye of the storm, at the start of a war. Things were chaotic—real PT boats to shoot at, phantom PT boats to shoot at—and Washington first not knowing the difference and then not *wanting* to know the difference. What an education! And then a 3 A.M. phone call from the carrier skipper. Washington had laid on their first-ever bombing strike against North Vietnam: "I want you to lead it, Jim. The crew has been up for two hours, bringing up our biggest bombs from *way down* below. Get up and give the executive officer the ordnance loads you want, and help me get this boat turned around to a wartime footing."

God, what a moment! I *loved* it—and right on center stage! But before that day was out, I saw a mixed bag of performances by both junior and senior officers. On deck and in the air, I saw skill, competence, guts, nerve but also careerism, fear, even *cowardice* (I fired a flight leader who wouldn't even cross the beach). And that's where the sense of history comes in; you've got to have a sense of when the drill is over and you're into real life, on center stage, your actions being recorded no longer in *pencil* but in *ink*. Don't get caught in combat without that sense. Remember the old World War I recruiting poster: "Don't *read* history, *make* it!"

And to make history well when the balloon goes up, you've got to develop the habit of you, *yourself alone*, keeping track of the state of play about you, of knowing exactly where the ball is on the playing field. Why? So you can capitalize on the moment! War is episodic. Opportunities don't roll in as a saturating fog bank. They come as *incidents*. And you need *spontaneity* and *instinct* to capture them. Keep those attributes in your operations contingency bag, along with your sense of history.

I improvised with spontaneity and instinct in the airplane world about as far as I dared. I wouldn't have had airplanes equipped to lead that first strike into Vietnam if I hadn't bucked the system on our stateside workup, drawn my own gear, set up my own pilot training syllabus, and made our air-superiority Crusaders and pilots air-to-ground capable: bomb droppers, Zuni rocket shooters. The captain knew that; that's why he called me. But it was in prison, a year and a half later, that I really became my own boss. The situation required it, and there was no other way to go. Survival training had missed the Vietnam predicament by a mile (not a word about the tap code), and the Code of Conduct, though good in most aspects, became an executioner's block for the guillotine of *guilt* in a torture system in which no human being could stick to name, rank, serial number, and date of birth. I figuratively rewrote the book and without abashment.

No, any officer worth his salt, on detached duty and out of communication, has to have the right to sensibly modify the law, issue rules that fit the conditions, and be prepared to defend himself in court. Throughout those years, I figured that *that* was my most important function.

But I'm not here tonight to sell the idea of "letting it all hang out." On the contrary, I intend to make it clear that even in the most detached duty, we warriors must keep foremost in our minds that there *are* boundaries to the prerogatives of leadership, *moral* boundaries.

Napoleon said, "In war, the moral is to the physical as three is to one." To focus on what *moral* meant to those early-nineteenth-century military thinkers who framed modern warfare, I go to Clausewitz: "It is not only the loss in men, horses and guns, but in *order, courage, confidence, cohesion,* and *plan* which come into consideration whether the engagement can still be continued or not. It is principally the *moral* forces which decide here."

Let's stop right there and rejoice to see, in the usage of the *old* warriors, the word *moral* bearing an unmistakably *manly, heroic* connotation. Clausewitz says you cannot continue the offensive unless your forces operate under an ordered morality.

The word seldom appears in dispatches, nowadays being mostly linked to things like sexual abandon or fiscal irresponsibility. Both scurrilous, to be sure, but hardly in the same category with "consideration whether the engagement can still be continued or not." What Clausewitz was saying was that failures of management and engineering are tactical shortcomings that can be fixed but that failures of leadership's *nerve* and *character* are terminal, catastrophic.

Morality *shadows* war. Its echoes were always quietly vibrating even in the corridors of the North Vietnamese prisons. In the ordinary sense, what was moral to our jailers was immoral to us, but the *subject* lurked, always. I am not saying that they honored our moral positions but that, even as they waived them aside, if they detected conviction, consistency, and a sense of personal honor in us, their eyes sometimes betrayed the fact that they were inwardly moved. They winced when you stood your ground and made them send you through the ropes one more time. The commissar later muttered, "You were nothing like the French; we could always count on *them* to be *reasonable*." *Aha*!

Morality lurks in *all* the shadows surrounding our profession. To not only ignore it but fail to embrace it will ultimately *ensure* your failure in the naval service. That's cold turkey. A close reading of my introduction to the book *Ethics for the Junior Officer*, a gift to each of you from the caring generosity of the class of 1964, *tonight*, will make that clear.

But the question of by what route man *partakes* of morality gives way to many viewpoints. Is it an intellectual process? Do you *learn* it? Or are you *born* with a *sense* of morality? And if you are born with it, does it emanate mainly from your *cultural* or your *biological* underpinnings? Thoughts on this vary, but there is no "school solution" as far as I am concerned. It's just that if I am going to be *enthusiastic* about my love affair with morality—and I do have one—I've got to tell you how it seems to come to me. And you would probably choose to do the same in your case. People's natural curiosity demands it.

But for goodness' sake, the important thing is the *partaking* of morality, not the technical details of your friend's idea of its delivery method. Nobody knows *for sure* whether it is an intellectual or natural process and, if it is natural, whether it derives mainly from culture or biology. Those questions go back to the old nature/nurture arguments. So take what I say about *my* case with any grain of salt you want.

The Moral Sense, a book by James Q. Wilson, now a political science professor at the University of California at Los Angeles, formerly at Harvard, infers by its title that the author thinks we have a *moral sense by nature*. For most social scientists in this day and age in the United States, this book comes as a shock! The idea is that though we live in a society whose bookshelves are loaded with skepticisms about the relevance of conscience and the existence of human nature, the overwhelming majority of us persist in employing a moral standard on others and on ourselves. Wilson bravely bucks the relativistic trend: "I think most of us *have* moral sense, even though some of us have tried to talk ourselves out of it."

I bought the book without knowing what was in it. But what quickly got my attention was Wilson's first case study of moral integrity under challenge. He chose to write up a case of a person in a predicament where it is highly unlikely that any adverse comment would come if he totally abandoned his moral responsibility, yet he grabs that moral responsibility, with vigor, knowing it will lead to discomfort and pain and possibly death. The section is called "Duty and Honor in Near Isolation," and all the facts are extracted from Sybil's and my *In Love and War* and my *A Vietnam Experience*. He names me and describes all the trade-offs in each step of my organizing the prisoner underground, the prisoner civilization, the thing we needed most.

My philosophy tutor at Stanford, Phil Rhinelander, spent a whole term trying to psych me out as to what exactly I was looking for in his philosophy class "The Problems of Good and Evil." And he rang the bell when he introduced me to *The Enchiridion* by that first-century former slave and Stoic philosopher Epictetus. I'm sure you've heard me speak of him before.

Epictetus said, "Every one has come into the world with an *innate* conception as to good and evil, noble and shameful, becoming and unbecoming, happiness and unhappiness, fitting and inappropriate, what is right to do and what is wrong." Some would agree with that. Thomas Jefferson would; I grew to. The Stoics cut right to the bone. It was all about the inner man. "Nobody can harm you without your permission." There can be no such thing as a victim; you can only be a victim of yourself. Their interest was almost *exclusively* human conduct, and they believed that every person bore *exclusive* responsibility for his own good and his own evil. To do evil on the excuse that society was letting it all hang out would be, to Epictetus, a cop-out. He believed with all his heart in what I would call the "reliability of retribution of a guilty conscience"—that the perpetrator of evil pays the full price for his misdeeds by suffering the *injury, major injury,* of knowing that he has destroyed the good man within him. "If you violate what Zeus has ordained, you will suffer injury—What kind of injury?" (says the man in the imaginary dialogue). Epictetus replies, "No injury but that of not doing what you ought; to destroy the man of fidelity in you, the man of honor, the man of decent behavior. Do not look for any greater injuries than this."

I would not ask you to buy all that at face value if I had not lived through it. Epictetus believed that, in all men, thought and action start from a single source, *feeling*. Go into the ropes, get a leg broken a second time, puke your guts out while the torture guard stands on your back while you're doubled over, pushing your head down between your feet with his heel, the feeling in your arms *long gone* with the tightness of the ropes, knowing your hands will be useless for weeks. You submit in a flurry of action. Why not kill yourself? How do you get ahold of yourself in that position? You write the damned statement after a fashion, then go into a cold soak, totally alone, for a month, in a dark cell. Does your leg hurt? Very little in comparison to what you *feel* eating your heart out, and what you feel in your heart is the emotion of *guilt*. "I could have resisted longer." Guilt is giving you the third degree; you have just hit the bottom of the barrel.

This was not a onetime thing for us who were the guinea pigs facing the North Vietnamese reaction to the realization that they were in a long-term war. As their top propagandist told me, "We cannot match America's strength on the battlefield, but we will win this war on the streets of New York." They built an extortion system to get from us prisoners propaganda fodder for those streets of New York. On paper, it was foolproof: break American prisoners' spirits by keeping them isolated and overcome by shame. They posted long lists of verboten prisoner actions—"trip wires"—like communicating with another American, which, when we were caught at, put us back in the torture machine and netted them more statements.

The leadership of that country had all been prisoners of the French in the 1930s; they knew the psychology of life behind bars. They wanted statements, and they did *not* want organized resistance. They depended on American senior officers' career ambitions to play into their hands. They knew our Code of Conduct and that propaganda statements blighted our service records. There was a tacit deal: lie low, senior officers, stay aloof from prisoner organizations; you don't bother us, we don't bother you.

I was the senior man at large in the system when I formed the underground, but in succeeding months I found out that several senior to me had arrived and were hiding out, incommunicado in their cells, totally anonymous, never answering wall taps, lying low, preserving a zero-defect service record, never mind the man sobbing and wanting encouragement next door. Talk about violating the moral boundaries of leadership!

Very little of this in the naval service. Although it represented only one-third of the prison's population, prison leadership in the tough years, that is, the four years from fall 1965 through fall 1969, was not exclusively, but certainly predominantly, navy. I and my self-selected top leaders were exiled to a tiny dungeon *inside* the national military headquarters compound for two years, all solo and in leg irons. All good men, but look at the proportions! There were eleven of us: three air force, the senior a major; eight navy, five of us commanders. The old boys of the navy really came through.

Solo time is a good index of prison leadership; they didn't put you alone unless you were making trouble for them. The average navy prisoner had twice the solo time that those in other services had. And the average Naval Academy graduate had half again as much solo time as the average navy prisoner had.

Naval Academy pilots and naval flight officers streamed into Hanoi prisons for eight and a half years! They came from classes 1947 through 1967. No class had more than five prisoners, but that was achieved by *two* classes: 1951 and our hosts tonight, 1964! The 1964 prisoners, in order of shootdown: Charlie Plumb (here tonight from California), Read Mecleary, Dave Carey, Aubrey Nichols, and Ted Triebel.

What was called for in those early and shocking days of the four hard years was a social binding of lost souls. Each of us was at the bottom of a well without a lifeline. Right and wrong were up for grabs—the strongest were reduced to sobbing wrecks—sense had to be made out of our lives. There was no order, we had to make our own, from scratch. I was not a man on a white horse; as James Q. Wilson says, my rules were not so much an imposition as a response to a demand. Trite orders like "obey the Code of Conduct" or "each man must decide for himself how long to hold out" were worse than nothing—they dumped the whole problem right back into the individual's lap. So I said that we must all take torture before we do *this* and *this* and *this*. I was not issuing rules that couldn't be broken; they were rules you couldn't break *until* you submitted in torture. There were lots of questions about what was required before submission, and I was floundering until I found the *right words*: "Not less than *significant pain*." That was it. No more questions. Our lives started making sense, there was a right and a wrong. There was comradeship and love.

When I got home, I tried to encapsule in a few words this complicated process of making order out of chaos: *making law, defining what the good was, teaching, consoling, explaining.* And I came up with more concise words, meaning *just* those things: *jurist, moralist, teacher, steward,* and *philosopher.* I didn't get those words, or what was behind them, behind ivy-covered walls. They were hammered out on the anvil of experience that had elements of every military challenge I know of.

Going back to my morality lecture for the windup, I hasten to say that lest you think I'm leaving you stranded on the subject, with nothing but the speculations of an old coot who lived nearly two thousand years ago, I want to introduce you to the ideas of *another* friend of mine, a living, breathing, first-rate, modern-day *physical scientist* whose conclusions about the origins and functions of the human mind, and the nature of *human* nature, track *well* with the thoughts and intuitions of the old slave.

His name is also Wilson, not James Q. but Edward O. ("E.O.") Wilson. He is a university professor and director of the Museum of Comparative Zoology at Harvard, the job Aristotle would have held at Harvard. E.O. is a biologist, an entomologist, and a geneticist who writes books like *Promethian Fire: Reflections on the Origin of the Human Mind* and *On Human Nature.* I met him for discussions about an odd human trait that pops up here and there, altruism, self-sacrifice without hope of reciprocation. (He uses the citations for Congressional Medals of Honor as a data bank on this.)

E.O. has come to believe that evolution is not just a culture game. (Marxists, anthropologists, and sociologists have long told us that "culture makes the man.") "Social behavior," E.O. tells us, "is at least as much *genetically* determined as culturally determined." He zeros in on what he calls a "gene-culture co-evolution," as a scientist, much as *James Q*. Wilson uses evidence from biology and anthropology, as a humanist. Like Epictetus, he says that if we will just trust them, *we all have great built-in moral choice backup systems within us. What is right and what is wrong are manifested as strong and telltale inner feelings.*

E.O. Wilson describes the process this way:

> Human emotional responses and general *ethical* practices based on them have been programmed to a substantial degree by "natural selections" over thousands of generations. We have inherited emotional guides; we have to choose among them. Our very humanity involves choosing which should be obeyed, and which curtailed. We *sense, feel,* and *measure* our emotional responses to various alternatives as though we were consulting a hidden oracle. That oracle resides in the deep emotional centers of the brain, just beneath the "thinking portion" of the cerebral cortex. To put the matter in somewhat more mechanical terms than is customary for ethical phioliology, you play your scenarios in the conscious mind and note the emotions connected to the alternative courses of action. You *think,* and *feel*—and then choose the most satisfying scenario, knowing you have done the "right" thing.

Feeling *good*, about *yourself*, is what this is all about.

Now, I would like to close on the amusing yet sobering subject of human nature. E.O. says it is mainly genetically driven passions. "It is human nature and *not* pure reason that lifts us above the animals," he stresses. I think this follows from his view of IQ scores. He says they reflect only one component of intelligence. They ignore leadership traits, mental stamina, drive, and creativity. Makes you wonder why we put such emphasis on SAT scores to get into this school.

But as to human nature itself, E.O. says the evolutionary process has stubbornly protected human idiosyncrasy—strong-willed people who decide what hymns to sing, which particular ethical decision to make, always abound:

> Idiosyncratic man follows unexpected and sometimes remarkably ineffi-
> cient procedures in the way he recalls information, judges the merits of

other people, estimates risk, and plans strategy. . . . The nature of humans belies the idea that they are free of all bonds save reason and cultural feedback. The genes have not freed the mind in the special sense of conferring pure cultural transmission or given wholesale license to logical, rational behavior. The genes keep the mind on a tether with a constant eye on the species' continued reproductive capacity and survival.

E.O. puts a particular biological spin on all ideas, which seems to help me account for the otherwise unexplainable quirks of human nature that I've seen and read about. I keep a quotation of T. E. Lawrence, from his *Seven Pillars of Wisdom*, in which he muses about his fighting in the Middle East in the World War I days: "So I sheared off pure reason and plunged into the *biological* factor of command—the 'felt' element in troops, not expressable in figures and had to be guessed at. The greatest Commander of men was he whose *intuitions* most nearly happened. Nine tenths of all tactics are certain enough to be teachable in schools, but the *irrational tenth* was like the king fisher flashing across the pool, and in *it* lay the test of Generals."

Human nature is a frustrating subject. Despite the fact that it *is* "the nature of things," you hear people say, "We've got to rise above it." Here is what Conan Doyle had Sherlock Holmes say to Watson on that subject: "When one tries to rise above nature, one is liable to fall below it. The highest type of man may revert to *the animal*, if he leaves the straight road of destiny. Consider, Watson, that the materialists, the sensualists, the worldly, would all prolong their worthless lives. The *spiritual* would now avoid the call to something higher. It would be the survival of the least fit. What sort of cesspool may not our poor world become?"

No world, with the traditions of this Naval Academy, will ever become a cesspool. Best wishes for happy and productive careers, class of 1994! I started by saying I am a romantic and that I think dreams go well with naval service life. If you choose to have one, stick with it. As Joseph Conrad writes in *Lord Jim*: "A man falls into a dream like he falls into the sea. If he tries to climb out into the air, as inexperienced people endeavor to do, he drowns. The way is to submit yourself, and with the exertions of your hands and feet in the water, make the deep deep sea keep you up. In the destructive element, immerse! Follow the dream, always!"

Thank you.

CONFLICT AND CHARACTER _____

The First Rhinelander Annual Lecture, sponsored by the Stanford University Canterbury Foundation, Stanford Memorial Church, May 5, 1994.

THIS LECTURE IS SPONSORED by the Stanford Canterbury Foundation, which is the Episcopalian ministry here on campus. It is the first in what will be called the Rhinelander Annual Lecture Series, named of course for Philip Hamilton Rhinelander, beloved professor of philosophy here. Phil died in 1987 and is buried in the family plot on their estate on Vinalhaven Island— a rugged, isolated, and beautiful clump of land about thirty miles out into the Atlantic Ocean, off the Maine coast, a place where my wife, Sybil, and I have visited. I was asked to give this first lecture because of our long and deep friendship—as his student, as his coteacher, as his coauthor. At the time of Phil's death, the two of us were under contract to the Stanford Alumni Association to coauthor a book for their Portable Stanford series. It was to have borne the title *Conflict and Character*, the title given this talk.

Our meeting was a chance one, thirty-three years ago. It took place just a few steps from here, across the quad at philosophy corner. I had just turned thirty-eight, and Phil was fifty-three—fifteen years separated us in age. But looking back, I can see that, in upbringing, in education, and perhaps in temperament, our separation was much greater than that of fifteen years in the middle of life. As we met, Phil had been dean of humanities and sciences of this university for six years. I was an overage graduate student filling in a much-appreciated two-year lull in what had been a very active naval career as a carrier-based fighter pilot and shore-based engineering test pilot at the navy's flight test center at Patuxent.

Back in 1954, while I was at Patuxent, the navy had wanted to send me to a three-year aeronautical engineering graduate program, but I begged off because I was so wrapped up in my flight test projects and because I had been assured I would be assigned to the first supersonic fighter squadron in the Pacific Fleet, whenever it was ready to go (I was perfecting the airplane at that time). After pursuing this track, it was six years before I thought I could take a rest from these intense aviation experiences, and by then the only program I was then eligible for was a master's in international relations. I could go either to the Fletcher School at Tufts or Stanford, and I chose the latter.

By the time I had hacked out course work at Stanford for about a year, I came to realize that international relations was a pretty bland subject and that, if I didn't watch out, I was going to leave postgraduate school without any substantive *internal* reward, which set me to thinking: "If I put on the speed I can finish my thesis and all degree requirements six months before I have to leave Stanford: *then,* maybe I'll have time to grasp *something* worth taking away from here. I am continually kidded by my professors for asking questions that are too philosophical and beyond the scope of their course. Maybe I'll take a shot at this philosophy thing."

But I certainly didn't get any encouragement from my adviser. He was an old European who wanted to do right by me but who told me solemnly: "Philosophy is not what you want; you would have to spend a year over there before you got into anything worthwhile."

And in hindsight, I think he would have been *right,* had not the gods smiled on me when, with this adviser's indifferent okay, I ventured into philosophy's halls early in Christmas break 1961 on what we would call in stunt flying a *feel-out pass.*

Those halls were different. They were carpeted, and they were silent. And some of the people I passed looked different. As I crept along, a strong male voice rang out of an open door: "Can I help you?"

"Yes," I said, as I walked in and approached the friendly pipe-smoking gentleman who offered me his hand. I told him that "I have had six years of college, and have never had a course in philosophy and I'd like to try one."

"How can that be?" he asked with astonishment.

I said, "I am a naval officer on a two-year graduate program here."

"Sit down; I was in the navy in World War II. I'm not a regular professor here but just keeping my oar in by teaching a single course I designed myself. It *might* be one you would like!"

"What's the idea of it?"

"It turns out that human beings tend to be born with an *innate* need to believe that on this earth 'the good' will be rewarded and 'the evil' will be punished. But I say, look at the empirical evidence all around us! It shows that there is no such magic balance. Rewards and penalties are totally random; knaves thrive and saints go hungry.

"Now it is my main contention that a properly educated person should not be surprised to suddenly find this out. Literature is replete with tragic stories of shocked individuals who suddenly come upon this lack of a moral economy in the universe by surprise and are just unable to accommodate it. King Lear, for instance, was a good man, a good father, a good king, when suddenly he realized that he was being made the victim of filial ingratitude. [I remember his words like yesterday.] What was Lear's solution? *Insanity!*

On and on, example after example." Phil wrapped it up by saying: "There is as much literature as philosophy in this course. We start with a week on the Book of Job and get his message of how life is not fair and then on through Hume and Kant and Mill and of course Shakespeare, Camus, Dostoyevsky, and other writers of tragedy."

I said to myself right there: "This guy has got information I *need*. This is a course I can *use* in my life." I asked, "What is the name of your course?"

"The Problems of Good and Evil; the students have nicknamed it PG&E. The problem is, it is a two-term course, and without any prior philosophy, you would be at a tremendous disadvantage. Suppose I give you additional readings and then we meet over in my study on Gerona Road once a week for an hour or two of one-on-one discussion?"

I couldn't believe my ears. Of course I accepted, and we wrote down each other's names. That meeting was as close to a miracle as anything I've ever known. It was to change my whole focus, to change my life.

Years later, when we teamed up as teachers, we were sometimes billed as "the man of thought" and "the man of action." Neither of us thought that that was out of line.

What I am saying is that we grew to *celebrate* our differences. It was as impossible for me to be a second Rhinelander—a master of Greek, as he certainly was, three years of it at Kent School and four at Harvard—as it was for him to become an experimental test pilot. The thing was that each of us had a willingness to share the kernels of wisdom we had gleaned from our quite different life experiences and that on matters of aesthetics and moral conviction we grew to think so much alike that both profited from the exchange. I think each of us thoroughly enjoyed sharing the stories of the other's life—sometimes mentally transposing ourselves into that other life we would like to have sampled ourselves.

I'm talking about Phil's life as the son of an Episcopal bishop, as a Boston lawyer, and as a distinguished professor at Both Harvard and Stanford but determined throughout to limit his theorizing to pursuits with practical payoffs. And I'm talking about my life—a farm boy from Illinois who pleased his demanding mother with good grades, good playacting, and good piano music and who found no problem with living out his father's dream of an Annapolis education and a suitably dangerous navy career but determined throughout to make that navy life individualistic, never to be branded "an organization man."

But I'm getting ahead of my story. Those tutorial sessions were golden. Phil was always trying to psych me out. From the expression on his face I could sometimes read this thoughts: "What in the world is this navy-type looking for? He seems so determined to find a polestar to guide him. It's as though he anticipates dangerous waters ahead."

I *was* working hard; I read everything two or three times, had pages of questions prepared for each session. I certainly wasn't working for a grade and he knew that; my degree was already sewed up. I could sense his curiosity about my insistence on taking several hours to get everything straight on David Hume's *Dialogues on Natural Religion*. For some reason, Hume struck a resonant chord with me. Was it that he denied that ethical rules could be deduced from logic? Or that his natural religion shunned all miracles? At that time, I would have found it hard to articulate what exactly was driving me. But I remember thinking that, for the first time in my life, I was surrounded by what I considered worthwhile raw material, these writings of the brightest of men who ever graced the human race. I was privileged to see how often they *departed* from conventional wisdom and to realize how many many different ways there are to skin a cat.

On our last tutorial session Phil, in the casual, gentlemanly, polished, and considerate way I had learned he always followed, looked at me directly and spun around to reach up to one of the top shelves of his book-lined study. "You are a military man as I remember. I want to give you a farewell memento of our many pleasant hours together." He grasped a little, worn, brown book with the name "Hugo" scrawled across the cover and handed it to me. "We have spent this time studying how some of the world's pioneering thinkers conceived of the universe. Here is a book of a man who conceived of it as a buzz saw to which he would never succumb. This is known as *The Enchiridion* of Epictetus. He was born a slave in Asia Minor in the first century A.D., transported to Rome in a slave caravan, and bought at an auction by a freedman in Nero's court. He was a Stoic, indifferent to everything but virtue and vice and in his lifetime became the most forcible and instructive voice in the *inner life* of Rome. He will remind you some of Kant, seeing the essence of the universe as "the starry heavens above, and the moral law within." Frederick the Great never went on a campaign without this book in his knapsack. Take it with you as you return to sea, and remember me."

Phil had it right. After our good-bye, I read *The Enchiridion* and more; the Stoics became my kind of people, and Epictetus, my polestar. Three years from that day, I was shot down and captured in North Vietnam.

During those three years, I had launched on three seven-month aircraft carrier cruises to the waters off Vietnam. On the first, aboard the *Ticonderoga*, we were occupied with general surveillance of the fighting erupting in the south; on the second, aboard the *Ticonderoga and* the *Constellation*, I was the fighter squadron commander and led the first-ever U.S. bombing raids against North Vietnam; and on the third, I was flying in combat almost daily as the CAG of the USS *Oriskany* (CAG is what navy pilots call their wing commander, boss of all flying off their ship; it dates back to when we called air wings *air groups*; the letters stand for Commander of the Air Group.) But on my bedside table, no matter what carrier I was aboard, were my Epictetus books: not only *The Enchiridion* but his (much longer) *Discourses*, Xenophon's *Memorabilia* of Socrates, and *The Iliad* and *The Odyssey*. (Epictetus expected his students to be familiar with Homer's plots.)

I think it was obvious to my close friends, and certainly to me, that I was a changed man and, I have to say, a better man for my time with Phil Rhinelander. I had become a man detached, not aloof but detached—able to throw out the book without the slightest hesitation when it no longer matched the external circumstances. I was able to put juniors over seniors without embarrassment when the juniors' wartime instincts were more reliable. This new abandon, this new built-in flexibility I had gained, was to pay off later in prison.

On September 9, 1965, I was leading a thirty-seven-plane strike against the Dragon's Jaw bridge at Thanh Hoa when the weather turned sour and I diverted all the planes to their secondary targets. Mine was a "milk run," boxcars on a railroad siding between Vinh and Thanh Hoa where the flak had been light to nonexistent the day before. Descending through 10,000 feet, I unsnapped my oxygen mask and let it dangle, giving my pinched face a rest—no reason to stay uncomfortable on this run.

As I glided toward that easy target at treetop level, I felt totally self-satisfied. I had the *top combat job* that a navy pilot can hold, and I was in tune with my environment. I was confident—I knew airplanes and flying inside out. I was comfortable with the people I worked with and knew the trade so well that I often improvised variations in accepted procedures and encouraged others to do the same under my watchful eye. I was on top. I thought I had found every key to success and had no doubt that my Naval Academy, test pilot, and Stanford schooling had provided me with everything I needed in life.

I passed down the middle of those boxcars and smiled as I saw the results of my instinctive timing: a neat pattern—perfection. I was just pulling out of my dive low to the ground when in that *noisy* little cockpit I heard this *other outside* noise I hadn't expected—the boom, boom, boom of a fifty-seven-millimeter gun—and then I saw it, hidden in the trees to my right, and looked right down its barrel, belching those red balls of fire at me. They *had* to have brought it in last night! I was *hit*! All the red lights came on, I was on fire, my control system was going out, and I could barely keep that plane from flying into the ground while I got that damned oxygen mask up to my mouth so I could talk into its mike and tell my wingman that I was ejecting. What rotten luck. And on a milk run.

Suddenly all was quiet as I drifted across the treetops, looking up into my parachute, seeing the rips occur when hit by the rifle shots from down below. I had about thirty seconds to make my last statement in freedom before I landed in the main street of a little village right ahead. And so help me, I whispered to myself, "I am leaving the world of technology and entering the world of Epictetus." I landed in that street as a man with a mission, but quickly I found myself a man in deep trouble, as I was gang tackled by a mob, a bone broken in my back, and a left leg shattered in a way that made me know on the spot that I would be crippled for life.

As an insider, I knew the whole setup—that the North Vietnamese already held about twenty-five prisoners, all air crewmen, probably in Hanoi, that I was the only wing commander to survive an ejection, and that I would be their senior, their commanding officer, and would remain so, very likely, throughout this war. And here I was, starting off crippled and flat on my back.

Epictetus had said, "Remember, you are an actor in a drama of such sort as the Author chooses—if short, then in a short one; if long, then in a long one. If it be his pleasure that you should enact a poor man, or a *cripple*, or a ruler, see that you act it well. For this is your business—to act well the given part, but to *choose* it belongs to Another." (The upper-case As on Author and Another make them Stoic code words for God.) And I remembered, too, what he said about broken legs: "Lameness is an impediment to the leg, but not to the *will*."

Epictetus was right about lameness. After a crude operation, I was on crutches within a couple of months, and the crooked leg, healing itself, was strong enough to hold me up without the crutches in less than a year. All told, it was only a temporary setback from things that *were* important to me, and being cast in the role as the sovereign head of an American expatriate colony that was destined to remain autonomous, out of communication with Washington for years on end, was *very* important to me. I was forty-two years old, still on crutches, dragging a leg, at considerably less than my normal weight, with hair down near my shoulders, my body unbathed since my last shipboard shower months before, a beard that had not seen a razor since I arrived, when I took command (clandestinely, of course, the North Vietnamese would never acknowledge our rank) of about seventy-five Americans. That expatriate colony would grow over the next seven years to nearly five hundred. I was determined to "play well the given part."

The key word for all of us at first was *fragile*. A good clue to the fallout of everybody being forced to recognize his own fragility right off the bat was the fact that never in that prison system did I ever hear anybody lash out at someone he considered a wimp. It was this sort of mood that captured my imagination as ideas of how to lead under the circumstances started crashing through my head. Several things were obvious. Primarily, we had been saddled at home with an interpretation of Eisenhower's Code of Conduct that was a breeder of unwarranted despondency: "When questioned, should I become a prisoner of war, I am bound to give only name, rank, service number, and date of birth."

(General S. L. A. ["Slam"] Marshall, the author of the code, told me after the war that he borrowed the language from nineteenth-century international law and that it meant that the prisoner was *not obliged* to give anything beyond these four items. International law *required* that you give the four but *required* nothing else. In the years between Korea and Vietnam, our service chiefs first misinterpreted Marshall's words—substituting the idea that anything beyond these four items was *prohibited*—and then competed among themselves to see who could write the most stringent directive about how silence was golden in prison, a totally misguided idea. This was *absurd* in view of the real-life situation we faced and very *destabilizing* to the naive prisoner.)

The fact was, nobody could beat the ropes. The three-cornered squeeze play—the *anxiety* of having the blood circulation stopped in your arms and upper torso by bindings, the *pain* of having your shoulders sometimes dislocated and always *nearly* dislocated, and the *claustrophobia* and vomiting resulting from being bent double by a man standing on your back, your head stuffed down between your feet—could reduce every member of Stanford's defensive line to a sobbing, compliant, self-loathing wreck in fifteen minutes.

We first had to establish *the tradition* (*order* was hardly the word for anything in there) of freely reporting to your prison mates the key material you had given up in the ropes—note hiding places and so forth. This had a tactical rationale—protecting your friends from walking into a booby trap— but more important, a *psychological* rationale. We had to openly admit how we all fared in this circumstance to defuse the guilt feelings, else some would freeze up, eat their hearts out, grow distrustful of others, and become vulnerable loners. We were in a place where in mere months or even weeks, men made or destroyed their lifetime reputations. We seemed to be scanning reams of data on the problems of good and evil in fast time. The extortion system could *quickly* drive to the surface weaknesses of moral integrity, which at the pace of normal life could take years to fester and erupt into public view. Epictetus said that the *invincible* man was the one whom nothing that happens *outside* the sphere of his moral purpose can dismay. Here, we had to check dismay *within* his sphere of moral purpose, too.

I remember Phil Rhinelander telling me one time that Professor Mark Van Dorn of Columbia had said that a man with a proper education could, should the necessity arise, *refound* his own civilization. That's right where we were—the job was not marshaling people into line but founding a prison civilization within which they could keep their bearings. We as a group had to develop the confidence to disregard bogus orders from home; we had to become the center of our *own* world where we could bring out the *best* in *ourselves*. We had to have our *own* laws, our *own* customs, maybe our *own* heroes. We had nothing but one another, and nothing surpassed the importance of trusting one another. Never was there a more appropriate place to call up what Phil Rhinelander called "the morality of character" and let it overshadow "the morality of laws." Solzhenitsyn has told us that a "letter of the law" mentality "paralyzes men's noblest impulses" and is "unworthy of man." Aristotle distinguished between the ethics of character and the ethics of acts by suggesting that society's main objective is to instill *virtue* in its citizenry and that specific laws are a secondary concern.

The leadership problem was how to define "the good" in an environment where we were defenseless against the ropes and at the mercy of the whims of a propaganda machine in which our reputations and words were its raw material. "Identify the mood, and work through it; identify the mood and work through it," I kept telling myself. And the mood in those whispered and soon wall-tapped conversations, I can put into an apocryphal statement that could have come from at least half of those wonderful competitive flyboys who were my comrades: "CAG, we are in a spot like we've never been in before. But we deserve to maintain our self-respect, to have the feeling we are fighting back. We can't refuse to do every degrading thing they demand of us, but it's up to you, boss, to pick out the things we must all refuse to do unless and until they put us through the ropes again. We deserve to sleep at night. We at least deserve to have the satisfaction that we are responsive to our CAG's orders. Give us the list, CAG; what are we to take torture for?" (Nobody actually said that, but I grew to know that that was exactly the way they felt.)

The good became individual self-sacrifice in defying our jailers. Rational? Of course not. But reason was a poor guide in this world we had staked out for ourselves. What was important here, was *will, willpower*. Quoting Dostoyevsky, the old prisoner of nineteenth-century Siberia: "You see, gentlemen, reason, gentlemen, is an excellent thing, there is no disputing that, but reason is only reason and can only satisfy man's rational faculty [just one of the human mind's *many* useful techniques, says E.O. Wilson, my sociobiology friend from Harvard], while *will* is a manifestation of all life, that is, of all human life, including reason as *well as all the impulses!*" In the Hanoi dungeons we had to capitalize on "all the impulses."

So our good took the form of my list of things to take torture for. Epictetus: "Where, then, does the great evil and the great good lie in man?— In the attitude of his *will*; and if that element stands firm and neither his *self respect*, nor his *faithfulness*, nor his *intelligence* be destroyed, then the man is also preserved; but if *any* of these qualities are destroyed or taken by storm, then the man also is destroyed."

I was not issuing rules that couldn't be broken; they were rules you couldn't break *until* you submitted to torture. "Make them hurt you," I said. "To what degree?" they asked. "To not less than significant pain; they don't like to do that. Make them work for it." And I did not neglect to follow historian John Keegan's fifth imperative of command: showing by my every move and whole being that I subscribed to the principle that those who impose risk should be seen to share it. I took the ropes a dozen more times and spent four years in solitary.

I put my first of many "take torture for" lists in acronym form: *BACK US*. Don't *B*ow in public; stay off the *A*ir; admit no *C*rimes; never *K*iss them good-bye; *US* could be interpreted as United States, but it really meant our bedrock highest value: Unity over Self. Loners make out, so my first rule of togetherness was to stress that no prisoner negotiates any deals for himself but only for all.

In 1969, in the middle of all this, the *American Political Science Review* printed an article by Harvard professor Michael Walzer entitled "Prisoners of War: Does the Fight Continue after the Battle?" His answer was no, and the argument behind that answer was that it was unjust to force the individual to be subject to the orders of two masters (in this case, the Vietnamese and me). How wrong he was. If we had followed his advice and become passive stooges of our captors, half of us would have wound up guilt-ridden and been hauled away to the psycho ward as soon as we were released. I concluded in prison that the pincers of *fear and guilt* are the destroyers of men. Nothing else. Primitive men knew that, too. We endured the longest imprisonment, and certainly one of the harshest, in our country's military history. And we brought home *no* psychotics. More than 95 percent came home feeling good about themselves. When I later became president of the Naval War College (and took pride in being the first president since Alfred Thayer Mahan to teach a regular lecture course—Foundations of Moral Obligation was its name), I used this Walzer article to demonstrate the degree of *impractical* advice that *can* come from behind the ivy-covered walls of cloistered academia. One of the many former Ivy League professors on my faculty at Newport had been a colleague of Walzer's at Harvard, and I asked him how he got that way. "I'll just say this: he used to teach Hobbes, and you know as well as I do that Hobbes taught not to trust anybody but yourself." I thought that was very telling. The common thread through that 5 percent whose prison experience was less than satisfactory was that they were all *loners* who couldn't bring themselves to trust their comrades. That was my big lesson from the experience. And my exposure to Phil Rhinelander's mental discipline and incisive practicality taught me to observe and learn things like that. Phil was nothing if not a trusting and generous Christian gentleman whose disciplined mind always focused on those *practical* payoffs.

I came up here to Stanford to see him as soon as I could after I got out of prison. He had gone emeritus by that time and proudly told me that he had received an honorary doctorate from the West Coast's Episcopal Seminary in Berkeley, California. He contrasted this to the experience of an old European spinster, who after a lifetime of service to the church, was called before the bishop and given the Order of Chastity, Second Class. Phil said his was definitely first class.

As president of the Naval War College, I appointed Phil to our Academic Advisory Board, which meant a couple of good visits a year to Rhode Island and lots of good advice on our curriculum. There were several Rhinelander relatives in Newport. In fact Phil's parents are buried there, and Phil and Virginia agreed to come back and spend a semester while Phil taught a course, very like The Problems of Good and Evil, to the navy captains and army and air force colonels having their one-year strategy and policy sabbatical there.

But it was a couple of years later, after my Citadel presidency, when I took the appointment at the Hoover Institution, that we really got back in the swing of old times again. Phil filled me in on his past. He had finished as a classics major at Harvard in 1929 and Harvard Law School in 1932. While with a Boston law firm, he became disturbed about the Hitler-Chamberlain pact of 1938 and signed up with the naval reserve. (At that time he had his wife, Virginia, several kids and the old World War II spirit.) He was called up for duty in the spring of 1941 as a lieutenant commander in naval intelligence and was so involved until after the war. He dropped the profession of law and forthwith reentered Harvard as a Ph.D candidate in philosophy. There he became a close friend of Harvard president Conant. It was through this friendship that Phil generated his intense interest in teaching classes for what he called *nonconcentrators*. By this he meant courses that brought out worthwhile lessons of life in fields outside the majors of those in attendance. President Conant, world-class educator and chemist, led the way by every year carrying a two-term senior course he called Natural Science 4, Science for Nonscientists. When Phil joined his faculty, Conant set up Rhinelander (philosopher) and Hugo (professor of literature whose name was scrawled on my little *Enchiridion*) to team teach the two-term Humanities 4, Ideas of Good and Evil.

These were the leading courses in a whole group of cross-pollination courses at Harvard, which Conant named General Studies, and Phil was only forty-one years old when President Conant put him in charge of the whole General Studies program. (Phil's cousin told me that Phil was a bright star in the Harvard faculty in those days and accepted a bid to become dean at Stanford only after he was sure he was not to take Conant's job when the latter stepped down in 1953.) Phil's Philosophy 6 at Stanford was a follow-on from his Humanities 4 at Harvard, only he did it all alone, playing Hugo's and his instruments both.

These were happy times for Phil and me on the Stanford campus. There was the *course* we taught together—Moral Dilemmas of War and Peace—often attended by as many as a hundred, including visitors. We started off alternating lectures, he one day and I the next. But as time wore on, Phil and I became so familiar with each other's thinking, and with the subject matter, that we would spontaneously trade places up front when the questions or subject matter favored the expertise of one or the other of us. There were good social times together, and there was the contract signing of the Portable Stanford book we were to coauthor.

Then suddenly, in late 1986, on Phil's routine annual physical with no aches or pains or known illnesses, it was discovered that he had developed an incurable liver cancer and had only a few months to live. It was then that Phil showed us all his true mettle as a human being. He seldom mentioned his physical problem, never felt sorry for himself, continued to come by my office with his yellow legal pad and discuss lines of thought he thought our book should contain. As we talked about the lessons of my experience, how his education of me played into that, we more or less simultaneously came up with a radical idea involving Philosophy 6. It sort of fell out of Epictetus's proclamation that "difficulties are what show men's character. Therefore, when a difficult crisis meets you, remember that you are the raw youth with whom God the trainer is wrestling." But our bottom line was this: *The challenge of education is not to prepare people for success but to prepare them for failure.* I think that it's in hardship and failure that the heroes and the bums really get sorted out.

It started to look like the book was doomed as Phil weakened, despite the great voluntary editorial and research assistance we were receiving from Phil's favorite doctoral advisee, Diane Harvey, by then mother of a family and professor of philosophy at Menlo College. In the winter late afternoons of early 1987, Diane and I alternated bedside sessions with Phil, and he continued to talk lucidly and read his philosophical notes of the day from the ever-present yellow legal pad at his bedside. By mid-March he was failing rapidly; his children and grandchildren began arriving from the East Coast.

But the big lovely campus house was *never* a sad place. Phil was on top of things, breezy and pleasant as his death approached. Diane Harvey was with him on the afternoon of the final night. I will always remember her excited, happy explanation of how it all seemed as she left the house. The family had all gathered around Phil in his bed, and he was chatting amiably and softly with them all as she silently left by the front door. "It was a scene almost like the death of Socrates," she told me.

It's been a pleasure to recall the unique and important association Phil Rhinelander and I shared. As a great teacher, a great human being, and a key figure in establishing this chaplaincy, he would be very pleased to know that the Stanford Canterbury Foundation plans an annual lecture in his name every year.

ARRIAN'S *ENCHIRIDION* AND *THE DISCOURSES* OF EPICTETUS _____

Lecture given to Stanford freshmen as a part of their Cultures, Ideas, and Values Program, November 30, 1994.

PROFESSOR IVANHOE HAS INVITED ME to introduce you to this little book—*The Enchiridion.* It is a *compendium*, a brief summary of a larger work of a philosopher I'm going to talk about this morning. If you read the handout, you'll know I first saw it when I was given a copy by a philosophy professor here at Stanford years ago. You'll also know that I was no kid when I got it. The navy had sent me to graduate school when I was thirty-seven years old, after I had spent fifteen years as a fighter pilot, experimental test pilot, and made dozens of cruises flying off aircraft carriers. The idea was to get some nontechnical education into my head to broaden me for what was looking like a successful career up the road.

I had spent a year and a half studying international relations here and had all the course work and most of my master's thesis done when I realized I was about to leave Stanford without *taking on anything* I would call *wisdom.* By that I mean, inspiration, a polestar to guide me. I had simply been processing tedious material about how nations organized and governed themselves. I was too old for that. I knew how political systems operated; I had been beating political systems for years.

The navy had given me a blank check for two full years on campus, and in the coming final six months, I was determined to find something that would sustain me in times of peril, which I felt in my bones were coming. It was 1962, and Vietnam was creeping into the back pages of the newspapers. I knew that part of the world and all of its enigmas well, and I sensed the stage being set for war.

It was my lucky day when I met Phil Rhinelander. He was Stanford's dean of humanities and sciences and had been in the navy in World War II. I told him of my feelings, that I had six more months of navy sponsorship at Stanford, and he invited me to take the course he was giving down there in the Philosophy Department: The Problems of Good and Evil. "What's the idea of it?" I asked. I'll never forget his reply: "The course is a meld of philosophy and literature. It addresses the problem of man seemingly having an underlying need to believe that virtue is rewarded and evil punished on this earth, when the *evidence* is overwhelming that *there is no moral economy in the universe!*"

"The statistics are out there," he said, "people good and evil routinely coming to random ends—riches or poverty, health or illness, plush living or concentration camps. But that does not seem to relieve man's subconscious feeling that the world works the other way. And when an unwary person is suddenly smitten by what he considers an unjustified evil, he frequently comes unhinged. We read about cases like that. For instance, what was King Lear's solution for his problem of filial ingratitude? [He was a good father and good king whose children betrayed him.] He went insane! And so on to other cases. It is my belief that an educated person should *not* be caught short when he first comes upon the hard evidence that there is no moral economy in the universe, and that is why I originated the course."

Well, you might imagine what was going through my head. This was the kind of information I *needed!* Then Rhinelander made me a surprising and wonderful offer: "Without any background in philosophy, you deserve to have special help to bring you up to speed. I would meet with you in my study at my campus home on Gerona Road weekly, for *a one*-hour, one-on-one tutorial."

Believe me, those hours we spent together in his study were golden, and I could tell you of many things that I finally got straight in my head there, but I'll jump right to our last tutorial. As I was about to leave, he reached up to his top shelf and pulled down a very worn little brown booklet and handed it to me. It was *The Enchiridion.*

Phil said, "Here is a little book to remember me by. This copy is the one I always used at Harvard when I taught Humanities 4. This is kind of an executive summary—a handbook for the busy man. In the Greek language, *Enchiridion* means something like 'ready at hand,' some of the main content of the teachings and conversations of a unique person. He is called Epictetus, born a slave to a Greek woman in a town in Asia Minor in the year A.D. 50. He became a Stoic. The religion of the Stoics was a *natural* one, and I remember your great interest as we discussed David Hume's *Dialogues Concerning Natural Religion*. Also, you're a military man, and you'll see in the preface that Frederick the Great never failed to take the *The Enchiridion* with him on his campaigns."

Professor Rhinelander gave me more background on Epictetus and Stoicism, and then we said goodbye. I was not to see him for another twelve years. Three years after that, I was shot down and was in a communist political prison, to stay there eight years, to live four years in solitary confinement, to be in leg irons for two of them, to have bones broken, and so on. Who would have ever predicted that?

But now, I want to tell you more about the life of Epictetus and how he got into print. As a young slave he had many masters, some cruel; he was permanently crippled by one early in his life. He was eventually taken to Rome in a slave caravan and bought at auction by a freed slave named Epaphroditus, a secretary to Emperor Nero. Epaphroditus was at Nero's side as the army was breaking down the door to arrest the emperor as a public enemy when the latter tried to cut his own throat, muffed it, and Epaphroditus finished the job.

Through this fluke, Epaphroditus forever thereafter living under a cloud, Epictetus just took to the streets of the city of Rome. A high-minded, intelligent young man, who learned Greek at his mother's knee, he started attending the philosophy lectures given in the public parks. And in those days in Rome, "philosophy" was synonymous with "Stoicism." The turning point in his life was to be adopted by Musonius Rufus, the best teacher of philosophy in first-century Rome. Although Epictetus was still technically a slave, Rufus, an Etruscan knight, took him as a student. His tutelage ran on for ten years, and then Rufus launched him on his career as a bona fide philosopher of Rome.

Epictetus, like all philosophers in Rome, was exiled by Emperor Domitian in the year A.D. 89, and he picked out the little town of Nicopolis, on the Adriatic coast of Greece, as a place to found a school. My favorite authorities set the date of his death at A.D. 138 at age eighty-eight. I've come across nothing about his "retirement," so I think of him starting his school in about A.D. 90 at the age of forty and teaching there for another forty or forty-five years. This little book is only selected exerpts from eight volumes of Epictetus's lectures and conversations, all given—we think—in *the year 108*. He was talking to basically rich young men from formidable families, mostly from Athens and Rome. It was the Socrates scene all over again, five hundred years later—the same students, same age (mid-twenties), the same type of dialogue.

Epictetus, a bachelor until his very late years, when he took a wife his age to help him care for an infant he rescued from death by exposure, was a natural, extraordinarily gifted teacher. He was gregarious, loved the Olympic games, which were conducted only about fifty miles from his school. He and his friends would go there together and harangue the crowds. His manner of speaking was *not* that of your typical prissy moralist, though he focused explicitly and almost entirely on *conduct*. He and his philosophic protégé, the seventy-one years younger Emperor Marcus Aurelius, went down in history as *practicing* Stoics, not boring theoreticians. Both were disinterested in the "intellectual paraphernalia" of most "philosophies," including their own—Stoic physics, Stoic logic, and so on. "What do I care?" asked Epictetus, "whether all existing things are composed of atoms, or of indivisibles, or of fire or earth? Is it not enough to learn the true nature of the good and the evil?"

The religious possibilities of Stoicism were developed further by Epictetus than by any of his Stoic predecessors over the previous four hundred years. He often phrased his pithy remarks in athletic or military metaphors: "Difficulties are what show men's character. Therefore when a difficult crisis meets you, remember that you are as the raw youth, with whom God-the-trainer is wrestling. . . . If Thou sendest me to a place where men have no means of living in accordance with nature, I shall depart this life, not in disobedience to Thee, but as though Thou were sounding for me the recall."

And he was funny.

He asks and answers the question: What do you do for friends, as you ascend the ladder of intellectual sophistication? Do you hang in with your old pals or concentrate on intellectual peers? "If you do not drink with old friends as you used to drink with them, you cannot be loved by them as much. So choose whether you want to be a boozer and likeable to them, or sober and not likeable." (Then he makes it clear that in *his* mind, satisfaction and self-respect are best served by escalating friendships apace with your education.) "But if that does not please you, turn about the whole of you, to the opposite; become one of the addicts to unnatural vice, one of the adulterers, and act in corresponding fashion. Yes, and jump up and shout your applause to the dancer!"

To the painfully shy and reticent students: "As the good chorus-singers do not render solos, but sing perfectly well with a number of other voices, so some men cannot walk around by themselves. Man, if you are anybody, both walk around by yourself, and talk to yourself, and don't hide yourself in the chorus. Let yourself be laughed at sometimes, look about you, shake yourself up, so as to at least find out who you actually are!"

Now neither these eight volumes of Epictetus's lectures, hallway talk, and private conversations *nor* their "executive summary" were compiled by Epictetus. He couldn't have cared less about being in print. They were taken down in some kind of frantic shorthand by a twenty-three-year-old student, a remarkable man, Flavius Arrianus, usually known as Arrian. He was an aristocratic Greek born in a Black Sea province of Asia Minor. You can't help but imagine what it took for him to improvise this shorthand and follow the old man around and take down all that material. After getting a load of Epictetus and his "living" speech, he must have said something like, "Wow, we've got to get this guy down on papyrus!" In his dedication of his final manuscript to a friend, he writes: "Whatever I heard him say, I used to write down, word for word, as best I could, endeavouring to preserve it as a memorial, for my own future use, of his way of thinking and the frankness of his speech."

History gives us snapshots of Arrian's illustrious career. After leaving Epictetus's school and a term as a successful Roman army officer, we find him in Athens lecturing in about A.D. 120 and there meeting the Roman emperor Hadrian, who was on a five-year tour of the empire following his investiture in 117. Epictetus figured into two fallouts of Arrian's presence in Athens at that time. First, in A.D 130, Hadrian appointed Arrian consul for a year, followed by six years as governor of the large province of Cappadocia in Asia Minor. Arrian introduced Epictetus to Hadrian, and they became lifetime friends. Second, when Arrian vacated his lectureship in Athens for politics, he was relieved by Q. Janius Rusticus, who later became the tutor of the young Marcus Aurelius. Emperor Aurelius acknowledges in his later book *Meditations* his adminration for Epictetus, having been assigned his eight volumes by Rusticus. Arrian lived in Athens after his political career and there wrote several books, including his definitive text on Alexander the Great's expedition to the east: *The Anabasis of Alexander*.

Sometime after Arrian's death, four of his eight volumes of Epictetus disappeared. The four that remained were put together during the Middle Ages and bound as *The Discourses*. So you'll find things from the four lost books in *Enchiridion* that are not in *Discourses*. But *The Discourses* give us lots of background material that helps us better understand *Enchiridion*.

The time between Stanford and prison was a very eventful period in my life. I started a war (dropped the first-ever American bombs on North Vietnam) and led good men in more than 130 aerial combat missions in flak; throughout three seven-month cruises to Vietnam I had not only *Enchiridion* but *The Discourses* on my bedside table on each of the *three* aircraft carriers I flew from. And I read them.

On the 9th of September 1965, I flew right into a flak trap, at treetop level, 500 knots, in a little A-4 airplane—cockpit walls not even three feet apart—which I couldn't steer after it was on fire, control system shot out. After ejection I had about 30 seconds to make my last statement in freedom before I landed on the main street of that little village right ahead. And so help me, I whispered to myself: "Five years down there, at least. I'm leaving the world of technology and entering the world of Epictetus."

I want to step off the chronology escalator for just a minute and explain what memories of *The Enchiridion* I *did* have "ready at hand" when I ejected from that airplane. What I had in hand was the understanding that a Stoic always keeps *separate* files in his mind for (A) those things that are up to him and (B) those things that are not up to him or, another way of saying it, (A) those things that are within his power and (B) those things that are beyond his power or, still another way of saying it, (A) those things that are within the grasp of his will, his free will, and (B) those things that are beyond it. Among the relatively few things that are up to me, within my power, within my will, are my opinions, my aims, my aversions, my own grief, my own joy, my attitude toward what is going on, my own good, and my own evil.

Now I'm talking like a preacher here for a bit. Please understand that I'm not trying to *sell* anything; it's just the most efficient way to explain it. Stoicism is one of those things that, when described analytically, sounds horrible to some modern people. Stoic scholars agree that, to describe it effectively, the teacher must become, for the time being at least, a Stoic.

For instance, to give you a better feel for why your own good and your own evil are on that list, I want to quote Aleksandr Solzhenitsyn from his book *Gulag Archipelago*, when he talks about that point in prison when he gets his act together, realizes his residual powers, and starts what I know as "ascending," riding the updrafts of occasional euphoria as you realize you are getting to know yourself and the world for the first time.

> It was only when I lay there on the rotting prison straw that I sensed within myself the first stirrings of *good*. Gradually it was disclosed to me that the line separating good and evil passes not between states nor between social classes nor between political parties, but right through every human heart, through all human hearts. And that is why I turn back to the years of my imprisonment and say, sometimes to the *astonishment* of those about me, "Bless you, prison, for having been a part of my life."

I *understand* that.

He learned, as I and many others have learned, that good and evil are not just abstractions that you kick around and give lectures about and attribute to this person and that. The only good and evil that means anything is right in your own heart—within your will, within your power, where it's up to you. What the Stoics say is, "You take care of that, and you'll have your hands full."

What is not up to you? beyond your power? not subject to your will in the last instance? For starters, let's take your station in life. As I glide down toward that little town on my short parachute ride, I'm just about to learn how negligible *is* my control over my station in life. It's not at all up to me. Of course, I'm going right now from being the wing commander of a thousand pilots, crewmen, maintenance men, a hundred airplanes, and all sorts of symbolic status and goodwill to being an object of contempt. "Criminal," I'll be known as. But that's not *half* the revelation that is the realization of your own *fragility*—that you can be reduced by the natural elements or *men* to a helpless, sobbing wreck, unable to control even your own bowels, in a matter of minutes. And more than even that, you're going to face fragilities you never before let yourself believe could be true. Like after mere minutes, in a flurry of action while being knocked down and then sat up to be bound with tourniquet-tight ropes, with care, by a professional, hands cuffed behind, jackknifed forward, head pushed down between your ankles held secure in lugs attached to a heavy iron bar, that with the onrush of anxiety, knowing your upper-body blood circulation has been stopped and feeling the ever-growing pain and the ever-closing in of claustrophobia as the man standing on your back gives your head one last shove down with his heel and you start to gasp and vomit, *that* you can be made to blurt out answers, probably correct answers, to questions about anything they know you know. (I'm not going to pull you through that explanation again; I'll just call it "taking the ropes.")

No, station in life can be changed from that of a dignified and competent gentleman of culture to that of a panic-stricken, sobbing, self-loathing wreck, maybe a *permanent* wreck if you have no *will*, in less than an hour. So what? So after you work a lifetime to get yourself all set up and then delude yourself into thinking that you have some kind of ownership claim on your station in life, you're riding for a fall. You're asking for disappointment. To avoid that, stop kidding yourself, just do the best you can on a commonsense basis to make your station in life what you want it to be, but never get *hooked* on it. Make sure in your heart of hearts, in your inner self, that you treat your station in life with *indifference*. Not with contempt, only with indifference.

And so on to a long list of things that some unreflective people assume they're assured of controlling to the last instance: your reputation, for example. Do what you will, it's at least as fickle as your station in life. *Others* decide what your reputation is. Try to make it as good as possible, but *again*, don't get *hooked* on it. In your heart, when you get out the key and open up that old rolltop desk where you really keep your stuff, don't let "reputation" get mixed up with what's within your *moral purpose*, what's within the power of your *will*, in other words, what's up to *you*. Make sure it's in the bottom drawer, filed under "matters of indifference." And so too with your *health*, your *wealth*, your *pleasure*, your *pain*, your *fame*, your *disrepute*, your *life*, your *death*. They are all externals, all outside your control in the last instance, all outside the power of where you really live. And where you really live is confined to the regime of your moral purpose, confined to matters that can be projected by your acts of will: like desires, aims, aversions, judgments, attitudes, and, of course, your good and your evil. For a human, the moral purpose, the will, is the *only* repository of things of absolute value. Whether they are projected wisely or foolishly, for good or for evil, is up to you. When his will is set on the right course, a man becomes good; when it's on a foul course, he becomes evil. With the right course comes good luck and happiness, and with the foul course, bad luck and misery. To a Stoic, bad luck is your fault; you've become addicted to externals. Epictetus: "What are tragedies, but the portrayal in tragic verse of the sufferings of men who have admired things external?" Not even God will intercede in your decisions. Epictetus: "God gives you attributes, like magnanimity, courage, and endurance, to enable you to bear whatever happens. These are given *free* of all restraint, compulsion, or hindrance; He has put the whole matter under *your* control without reserving even for Himself *any* power to prevent or hinder." Your deliverance and your destruction are 100 percent *up to you.*

I know the difficulties of gulping all this down right away. You keep thinking of practical problems. Everybody has to play the game of life. You can't just walk around saying, "I don't care about my health or wealth or my reputation or whether I'm sent to prison or not." Epictetus was a great teacher because he could draw a word picture that cleared the way to look at what he was talking about.

In this case, Epictetus said everybody should play the game of life—that the best play it with "skill, form, speed and grace." But like most games, you play it with a ball. Your team devotes all its energies to getting the ball across the line. But after the game, what do you do with the ball? Nobody much cares. It's not worth anything. The competition, the game, was the thing. The ball was just used to make the game possible, so just roll it under the porch and forget it—let it wait for the next game. Most important of all, don't *covet* it, don't *seek* it, don't *set your heart* on it. Doing so makes externals dangerous, makes them the route to slavery. First you covet or ahbor things and then along comes he who can confer or remove them. I quote *Enchiridion* 14: "A man's master is he who is able to confer or remove whatever that man *seeks* or *shuns.* Whoever then would be free, let him wish nothing, let him decline nothing, which depends on others; else he must *necessarily* become a slave."

So I took those core thoughts into prison; I also remembered a lot of attitude-shaping remarks from the *Enchiridion* on how not to kid yourself into thinking that you can somehow stand aloof, be an "observer of the passing scene," aloof from the prisoner underground organization: *Enchiridion* 17: "Remember that you are an actor in a drama of such sort as the Author chooses—if short, then in a short one; if long, then in a long one. If it be his pleasure that you should enact a poor man, or a cripple, or a ruler, or a private citizen, see that you act it well. For this is your business—to act well the given part. But to choose it belongs to Another." (The capital As on Author and Another are Stoic code markings for another name for God.)

Another attitude-shaping remark on when in tight straits, *how you should stifle* what's in you of that student body president personality, of give and take, openness, being responsive, offering counteroptions rather than outright refusal to go along. We called people like that "players" in prison and tried to prevent them from digging their own graves. *Enchiridion* 28: "If a person had delivered up your body to some passer-by, you would certainly be angry. And do you feel no shame in delivering up your own mind to any reviler?"

All that, over the previous three years, I had put away for the future.

Right now (and I'm back on chronology), it's very *quiet* in the parachute, and I can hear the rifle shots down below and match them up with rips occurring in the parachute canopy above me. Then I can hear the noontime shouting and see the fists waving in the town as my chute hooks a tree but deposits me on the main street in good shape. With two quick-release fastener flips, I'm free of the chute and immediately gang tackled by the ten or fifteen town roughnecks I had seen in my peripheral vision, pounding up the street from my right. It felt to me like the quarterback sack of the century; I don't want to make a big thing of this or indicate that I was surprised at my reception, but by the time the tackling and pummeling and twisting and wrenching were over, and it lasted for three or more minutes before the guy in the pith helmet got there to blow his whistle, I had a badly broken leg that I felt sure would be with me for life. And that hunch turned out to be right. And I'll have to say that I felt only minor relief when I hazily recalled Epictetus's admonition in *Enchiridion* 9: "Lameness is an impediment of the leg, but not to the *will*; and say this to yourself with regard to everything that happens. For you will find it to be an impediment to something else, but not truly to *yourself*."

As an insider, I knew the whole setup on prisoners of war—that the North Vietnamese already held about thirty prisoners in that early September 1965, probably up in Hanoi, that I was the only wing commander to survive an ejection, and that I would be their senior, their commanding officer, and would remain so, very likely, throughout this war that I felt sure would last at least five years. And here I was starting off crippled and flat on my back.

Well, Epictetus turned out to be right. After a very crude operation just to get my lock-kneed and splayed leg under me, I was on crutches within a couple of months, and the crooked leg, healing itself, was strong enough to hold me up without crutches in a few more. I took command (clandestinely, of course) of the by-then seventy-five pilots—due to grow to nearly five hundred over the eight years—determined "to play well the given part."

I'll drop the prison chronology right there and concentrate on bringing to light as many more interesting wrinkles of Epictetus and his Stoicism as time will allow.

I would like to say straight off that I have read through and studied *The Discourses* at least ten times, to say nothing of my many excursions into

Enchiridion, and I have never found a single inconsistency in Epictetus's code of tenets. It is a put-together package, free of contradictions. The old boy may or may not appeal to you, but if he turns you off, don't blame it on incoherence; Epictetus has no problem with logic.

I think more needs to be said about good and evil. After all, the Stoic is indifferent to *everything but* good and evil. In Stoic thought, our good and our evil come from the same locus. "Vice and virtue reside in the will alone." "The essence of good and evil lies in *an attitude* of the will." Solzhenitsyn locates it in the heart, and Epictetus would buy that—*or* will *or* moral purpose *or* character *or* soul—he's not a nitpicker about things like that. What he bears down on is that your good and your evil are the essence of *you.* He says you *are* moral purpose, you *are* rational will. You are not hair, you are not skin, you are moral purpose—get that beautiful, and you will be beautiful.

That was revealed to Solzhenitsyn when he felt within himself the first stirrings of good. And in that chapter the old Russian elaborated other truths about good and evil; the line separating them does *not* pass between political or cultural or ethnic groupings, but it does pass right through every human heart, through *all* human hearts. He adds that for any individual over the years, this separation line within the heart shifts, oscillates somewhat, that even in hearts *overwhelmed* by evil, one small bridgehead to *good* is retained. And even in the *best* of all hearts, there remain an *un-uprooted* small corner of evil. There is some good and some evil in all of us. In that same chapter, Solzhenitsyn comments: "If only there were evil people somewhere insidiously committing evil deeds, and it were necessary only to separate them from the rest of us and destroy them. But the line dividing good and evil cuts through the heart of every human being, and who is willing to destroy a piece of his own heart?"

I just want you to know I connect with that. In a crucible like a torture prison, you reflect, you silently study what makes those about you tick. Once I had taken the measure of my torture guard, watched his eyes as he worked, watched him move, *felt* him move as he stood on my slumped-over back and cinched up the ropes pulling my shoulders together, I came to know that there was good in him. (That was ironic because when he first came in with the new commissar, when torture was instigated after I got there, I had nicknamed him "Pigeye" because of the total vacancy of the stare of the one eye he presented as he peeked through cell door peepholes.) He was my age, balding and wiry, quick, lithe, and strong, like an athletic trainer. He was totally emotionless—thus his emotionless eyes. Under orders, he put me through the ropes fifteen times over the years and rebroke my bad leg once, I feel sure inadvertently. It was a court-martial scene, and he was having to give me the ropes before a board of North Vietnamese officers; I could tell he was nervous, and he pressed me flat over my bad leg instead of the good one he had always put the tension on before. The healing knee cartilage gave way with a loud pop, and everybody but the two of us got up and left the room.

In all those years, we probably had no more than twenty hours, one on one, together. But neither of us ever broke the code of an unvaryingly strict line of duty relationship. He never tricked me, always played it straight, and I begged no mercy. I admired that in him, and I could tell he did in me. And when people say, "He was a torturer, didn't you *hate* him?" I say, like Solzhenitsyn, "to the astonishment of those about me," "No, he was a good soldier, never overstepped his line of duty."

By that time, I had learned that *fear and guilt* are the real pincers that break men's wills. I would chant under my breath as I was marched to interrogation, knowing that I must refuse to comply and take the ropes, "Your eyes must show no fear; they must show no guilt." The North Vietnamese had learned never to take a prisoner "downtown"—to the payoff for what our whole treatment regime was about, public propaganda exploitation—unless he was truly intimidated, unless they were *sure* he felt *fear*. They had suffered the political damage of several, including myself, who had acted up, spoken up, and blurted out the truth to the handpicked audience of foreigners at the press conference. Book 4 of *The Discourses*: "When a man who has set his will neither on dying nor upon living *at any cost*, comes into the presence of the tyrant, what is there to prevent him from being without fear?—Nothing." Fear is an emotion, and to Stoics, *all* emotions are acts of *will!* You fear because you *want* to fear. Refuse to want to fear, and you start acquiring a constancy of character that makes it impossible for another to do you wrong. Threats have no effect unless you *fear*. Learning to take charge of your emotions is *empowering*. When you get there, *Enchiridion* 30 applies: "No one can harm you without your permission."

What are some of the guidelines to identifying the good and the evil in Stoic thought? Well, first, Stoicism goes back to the idea that nature is God's body and that it doesn't do to try to improve on it. In fact God and nature are two aspects of the same thing. God's soul is the mind of the universe, and nature is his body. All humans are not only a part of nature but a part of the mind. (The mind is like a flame, and our individual consciousnesses are sparks in it.) Just as the mind is the active and nature is the passive, so our minds are active and our bodies passive. Mind over matter—it all happens in your head, so don't worry about your body. The perfect man models himself on this operation of the universe. Nothing is ever lost. All remains in the care of Providence. Just as the universe, in which the mind of God is imminent and indwelling and moves in a manner self-sufficient and self-ruling, *so the good man is independent, autonomous, a law unto himself and a follower of the eternal guidance of duty and conscience.*

You probably gasped back there when I said that even God would decline to intercede as you made self-destructive decisions. That comes from this idea that each man must remain autonomous, a law unto himself. That's the way the Stoics said the system works.

All this got started back in fifth-century B.C. Athens as a backlash against a preoccupation with inuring everybody to the perfect society. Diogenes of Sinope, a friend of both Aristotle and Alexander the Great (they all knew each other, and all died within a two-year period), struck out on *his* campaign, not to conquer the east as did Alexander, not to stamp out ignorance as did Aristotle, but to do something about man's condition as a mere cog in a machine, where he had no way to fight back against his slavery to his *fears and his desires.* He had to take command of himself, control himself. The Stoic goal was not the good society but the good *man.*

But the Stoics were good citizens. In politics the Stoic would love his country and hold himself ready to die at any time to avert *its* disgrace *or his own.* But a man's conscience was to be higher than *any* law. A right of man is to be self-ruling!

So on good and evil, where does that leave us? Nothing that is natural can be evil. Death cannot be evil. Disease cannot be evil. Natural disasters cannot be evil. Nothing *inevitable* can be evil. The universe as a whole is perfect, and everything in it has a place in the overall design. Inevitability is produced by the workings of this divine mechanism.

Neither good nor evil can be abstractions. Epictetus said, "Where do I look for the good and for the evil? Within me, in that which is my own. But in that which is another's *never* employ the words 'good' or 'evil,' or anything of the sort. Goods or evils can never be things others do *to* you or *for* you."

Why not make health or life be good? Because man deserves the good, and it's better that he not deserve anything he does not control. Otherwise, he will go after what is not his, and this is the start of crime, wars, you name it.

Another thing. You do not control God. You must not refer to him as good or evil. Why not? If you pin these mundane labels on him, reciting "God is good," people may become tempted, when things God controls run counter to what they're trying to do—weather being unfavorable for farmers or the wind being from the wrong direction for sailors—to start calling him evil, too. And that's impious. "Remember," says Epictetus, "piety must be preserved. Unless piety and self-interest be conjoined, piety cannot be maintained in any man."

Now for some other things that follow from the assumptions of Stoicism that you might not have thought of:

The Stoics say that the invincible man is he who cannot be dismayed by any happening outside his span of control, outside his will, his moral purpose. Does this sound irresponsible to you? Here you have a man who pays no attention as the world blows up around him, so long as he had no part in causing it.

The answer to that depends on whether or not you believe in *collective guilt*. The Stoics do not. Here is what *The Encyclopedia of Philosohy* (Macmillan) says about collective guilt: "If guilt, in the proper sense, turns on deliberate wrongdoing, it seems that no one can be guilty for the act of another person—there can be no shared or collective or universal guilt. Guilt is incurred by the free choice of the individual. . . . But many have questioned this. Among them are some sociologists who misrepresent in this way the dependence of the individual on society. [At their urging we delight in shouting 'We should all feel guilty about the conditions of our schools. We should all feel guilty about our dropping the bomb on Hiroshima.'] But the main location of the idea of collective guilt is religion—many forms of doctrines of original sin and universal sin regard guilt as a pervasive state of mankind as a whole."

Speaking for myself, I think of collective guilt as a manipulative tool. It reminds me of the communist "criticism/self-criticism" technique. Many of the precepts of the Stoics *depend on* an abhorrence of the concept of collective guilt.

As you know, the Stoics believe that every man bears the exclusive responsibility *himself* for his own good and own evil. That leads to their further conclusion that *it is impossible to imagine a moral order in which one person does the wrong and another, the innocent, suffers*. Now add all that to Epictetus's firm belief that we are all born with an *innate* conception of what is good and evil, what is noble and shameful, what is becoming and unbecoming, fitting and inappropriate, what is right to do and what is wrong. And further, remembering that all Stoic talk refers to the inner man, what is going on "way down here," it follows that the perpetrator of evil pays the full price for his misdeeds in suffering the injury of knowing that he has destroyed the good man within him.

This self-knowledge that you have betrayed yourself, destroyed yourself, is the very worst harm that can befall a Stoic. Epictetus says:

- No one comes to his fall because of another's deed.
- No one is evil without loss or damage.
- No man can do wrong with impunity.

I call this whole personal guilt package that Epictetus relied upon "the reliability of the retribution of the guilty conscience." As I sometimes say,

"There can be no such thing as a 'victim'; you can only be a *victim* of yourself."

This collective guilt issue comes up in *The Discourses* in a very stark way. It is in book 1, chapter 28, entitled "Concerning what things are small and what things are great among men." This gets into a discussion about Homer's *Iliad*, but where I start there is a cross-fire conversation between Epictetus and one of his students about "impressions of the mind."

The Stoics gave that name to those bursts of suggestion that flash on the screen of your mind, usually when you're in tight straits, wooing you to believe that a crisis is imminent and that you should accede to the suggestion immediately and take counteraction. Stoics place great stock in man's obligation to exercise *stringent judgment* on whether to accept this suggestion at face value or use caution, play for time, and see if what you first believed you were being told was an exaggeration. Your response is both a judgmental and a moral act.

Inner tranquility is a *goal* of the Stoics—mainly so your soul can be *calm* as you judge the impressions of your mind. The soul is like a bowl of water, the impression like a ray of light that falls on it. When the water is disturbed, the ray of light is distorted. If you judge an impression while your soul is agitated, your judgment cannot be relied on because you are suffering from vertigo. The emotions of grief, pity, and even affection are well-known disturbers of the soul.

Grief is the most offensive; Epictetus considered the suffering of grief an act of evil. It is a willful act, going against the will of God to have all men share happiness. In book 3 he says: "Now another's grief is no concern of mine, but my own grief is. Therefore, I will put an end at all costs to what is my own concern, for *it* is under my control. And that which is another's concern I will endeavour to check to the best of my ability. But my effort to do so will *not* be made at all costs. Otherwise, I shall be fighting against God. And the wages of fighting against God and this disobedience will be paid by me, by day and by night." He is more pliable, however, in *Enchiridion* 16: "When you see anyone weeping for grief, do not disdain to accommodate yourself to him and, if need be, to groan with him. Take heed, however, not to groan inwardly, too."

Pity is also an evil; a Stoic would allow it sometimes but only for the person with self-inflicted wounds, like the man who knows he destroyed the good man within him. Affection gets the widest tolerance of the three; if you can love as a man with a noble spirit, okay, but if the relationship requires you to be a slave and miserable, it does not profit you to be affectionate.

Once you accept the impression, it becomes your conviction, subject to your will and control. You inherit all its problems. *Enchiridion* 1 advises us to first ascertain if the suggestion involves things that are up to us and if not, reject it.

The rest of the dialogue focuses on the *Iliad*. Epictetus makes the point to his student that both Paris's urge to steal Helen and her urge to let him get away with it resulted from each of them accepting an "impression" that should have been rejected. And if King Menelaus, husband of Helen, had used his head and read *his* impression of all this properly (i.e., that it would be a *gain* to be rid of a wife like Helen), there would have been no Trojan War.

The student was astounded that such great matters (the Trojan War) could depend on something so small as how one judged an impression. Epictetus, of course, takes exception and thinks the student has it backward. The world's truly great matters, he insists, rest in things like how a man judges his impressions, not on wars, unless you bear personal blame. He pooh-poohs the idea of being indignant about routine evolutions of mankind—revolutions, wars, famines—that lie "out there" as abstractions. He says it's like getting all upset because animals stampede, when it's just their nature.

The student asks: In what way does man differ from a horse?

He differs in understanding what he does, in his faculty for social action, in his faithfulness, in his self-respect, his steadfastness, his intelligence.

Where then is man's good and evil, in the true sense, to be found?

Just where the difference is; and if that element wherein the difference lies be preserved and stands firm and well fortified on every side, and neither a man's self-respect, nor his faithfulness, nor his intelligence be destroyed, then the man is also preserved; but if any one of these qualities be destroyed or taken by storm, then the man also is destroyed. And it is on this that great events depend.

Did not Paris come to his great fall when the Hellenes assailed Troy with their ships, and when they were devastating the land and when his brothers were dying?

Not at all, for no one comes to his fall because of another's deed. He came to his fall when he lost his self-respect, his faithfulness, his decency of behavior.

When did Achilles fall? Was it when Patroclus died?

God forbid; it was when he was angry, when he cried for a trumpery maiden, when he forgot that he was there not to win lady-loves, but to make war. These are men's failures, this is their seige, this is their razed city, when their right judgments are broken to the ground, and when they are destroyed. What else happened to Agamemnon or Achilles, but that they should do and suffer such evils because they followed their impres-

sions? What name do we give to those who follow everything that comes to their head?

Madmen

Well, is that not what so many men do?

Men get what they deserve. If they do evil, they pay; if they misjudge their impressions, they pay. *Eureka*! There *is* a moral economy in the universe! How ironic, totally ironic, that I should be drawn to Phil Rhinelander's class by my fascination with his theory that no moral economy existed, and then, years later, after several trips around the world, after becoming enamored of the book that I was to remember him by, through it, I come to a conclusion that is the exact antithesis of his original proposition!

I exaggerate. It's easy to explain. It's the difference of point of view. His hypothesis rested on the distribution of riches versus poverty, health versus illness, plush living versus prison living. All externals. All what a true Stoic is indifferent to. What the Stoic is interested in is all "inside" his breast; the man in the street is interested in what is outside—material things. "What is the fruit of your doctrines?" Epictetus was asked. His reply was three crisp words: "Tranquility, Fearlessness, and Freedom." I'll never let go of that. I've moved "inside."

After I came home from prison, I was on a speakers' program with the philosopher Will Durant. We had several good conversations that weekend, and he was quite interested in my taking up Stoicism. He thought I had it right. I'll close with a quotation from his *Life of Greece* (New York: Simon & Schuster, 1939).

> Stoicism was a noble philosophy and proved more practicable than a modern cynic would expect. It brought together all the elements of Greek thought in a final effort of the pagan mind to create a system of morals acceptable to the classes that had abandoned the ancient creed; and though it naturally won only a small minority to its standards, those few were *everywhere the best*. Like its Christian counterparts, Calvinism and Puritanism, it produced the *strongest characters of its time*. Theoretically it was a monstrous doctrine of an isolated and pitiless perfectionism. Actually it created men of courage, and saintliness, and goodwill, like Marcus Aurelius, Epictetus, Cato the Younger. It influenced Roman jurisprudence and the building of a law of nations, and it helped to hold ancient society together until a new faith came.

Thank you.

1994 INTERVIEW WITH ADMIRAL STOCKDALE

First appeared in the Hoover Institution Newsletter, *summer 1994.*

Q: The first week in August this year will mark the 30th anniversary of the Tonkin Gulf events that President Lyndon B. Johnson used as the basis of his Tonkin Gulf Resolution. Both houses of Congress promptly passed it, and the Johnson administration thereafter used it as "the functional equivalent of a Declaration of War." The events of that fateful week centered on three air actions, all of which you led. In your book *In Love and War* you charge that the Tonkin Gulf Resolution was a falsification of events that you and others saw and reported to Washington during and after the battles— that America launched a war under false pretenses. Do you persist in your charge?

A: Yes, I persist, and, of course, I am right. People who are not acquainted with the mass of evidence that confirms government falsification on this matter tend to describe my dissent as being based on what I saw versus what somebody else saw. On that pivotal night of August 4, *nobody* on either of the two U.S. destroyers, nor any American in the air, saw any signs of enemy craft, surface or air. This was made clear that night in a message sent to Washington by Captain John Herrick, the destroyer division commander and senior officer on the scene. Both aircraft carriers confirmed this with clear messages that none of their pilots made any sightings.

It was after my "reprisal" raids that were ordered the following day that Washington realized that it had not a shred of on-scene evidence to justify the retaliation. A "flash" message was sent to the commanders of all the units involved in the fiasco of the night of August 4. It said, "An urgent requirement exists for proof and evidence of a second attack by North Vietnam naval units against the destroyers *Maddox* and *Joy* on the night of 4 August. . . . Material must be of the type which will convince United Nations organization that the attack did in fact occur. . . . It would be helpful if materials could be in format appropriate for transmission to the State Department."

I was not shown the message because it was clear that I was not a good candidate for collaboration in this scheme. However, when I returned home from the prisoner-of-war camps nine years later (I was shot down 13 months after these Tonkin Gulf flights), I found accounts of that long-ago night littered with quotations of sightings from men with whom I had sat in the immediate postaction debriefings. I had heard these men deny any sightings.

I buttonholed several of these fellow officers and sailors who had obviously made false, after-the-fact statements and found them in general to be a devastated lot. The government had asked for false statements, and they were suckered in and, by the time I got to them, wallowing in guilt feelings. How low can a government get? And this matter of government solicitation of false statements is only one of the several particulars.

One of the better histories of that war was written by Stanley Karnow, *Vietnam: A History* (first edition, 1983). A few years ago, Stan called me in my Hoover office and said that he had read *In Love and War* with dismay because it had come out just after his book had gone to press and that though he deeply suspected that events of that first week in August 1964 was much as I described them, my specifics would have greatly strengthened his case. He was now writing a second edition; could he come out and talk over my experience and materials so he could incorporate them this time. "Of course," I said.

After we had our session at Hoover, I said something like, "As strongly as I know I am right, it's hard to fight both the government and half the historical profession at the same time." Stan said, "Relax; I don't think there is a serious historian in America who does not go along with you on this, 100 percent."

Q: Regarding Vietnam, earlier this year, under the sponsorship of the Stanford Alumni Association, you and your wife, Sybil, led a group to Hanoi where you had been held for eight years as a prisoner of war. In fact, this was the first time you have traveled to the area since your release. Can you share some of your thoughts and observations about the trip?

A: Here at home, everybody seemed to think I was in for some great emotional event in Vietnam. It didn't happen because so much over there was the same. The government is still hard-line communist, and they say so with emphasis, even in their English-language handouts. "There will be no talk of pluralism or second political parties." (This may erode with cross-effects of their "new look" in economics, but it will take lots of time.)

I told the Alumni Association that though I would very much like to take the whole cruise group through Hoa Lo prison, I was not going to make the request of the Hanoi government. I learned over there, with that government, to hew closely to the advice of Epictetus: "A man's master is he who is able to confer or remove what that man seeks or shuns. Whoever then would be free, let him wish nothing, let him decline nothing, which depends on others; else he must necessarily be a slave."

Stanford's travel director was able to get the Vietnam Tourist Bureau to make the request, which it did, and it was approved.

The day we arrived in Hanoi, we were notified that the agreement had been summarily canceled. "So what's new?" said I to myself. It was just as I had left it—the authoritarianism, the smells throughout the city (particularly within a block of the prison), and the Tijuana-like look of the place.

There were some French buildings in the central city—all now mildewed and looking their age (1880 vintage). But Sybil and I, though we looked hard, could find not one brick in the whole inner city displaced an inch by anything that looked like the force of a bomb explosion. Not one bit of bomb damage in a city that stateside bleeding hearts wailed about during our happiest days in prison—Christmas 1972, when we knew it was "time to pack, we're going home!" (The bombs, of course, were out in the rail yards, as we said they were.)

Q: The issue of ethical conduct has been a focus for much of your writing. Last year, the Hoover Institution Press published your essay on the philosopher Epictetus, whom you have studied for some time and to whom you previously referred. What exactly does Epictetus, for instance, have to say in these times to people of the twentieth and twenty-first centuries?

A: Epictetus tells people of all centuries what I've come to believe is the truth: That the essence of yourself, your inner self, is totally what *you make it*. Your moral purpose is of your own making. Your good and your evil are of your own making. And so it is with your deliverance and your destruction. No buck passing.

I know we're told by some that our cultures and our genes have a lot to do with all of this, but Epictetus would probably say that if you have the willpower you should, you probably can override both.

As many of you know, Dr. Phil Rhinelander gave me a book by Epictetus as a farewell gift when I left graduate school here at Stanford, and I had just three years to consider and absorb it before I found myself crippled and in a political, torturing, solitary confinement prison. Epictetus was crippled (same leg—his left), and he had been a slave for years before he won his freedom as a Stoic philosopher.

There is something wrong with the word *ethics* when you apply it to teaching about the thought processes of a man like Epictetus. You don't have to learn a bunch of rules of behavior from him—you learn how to rebuild yourself to have "greatness of soul and nobility of character."

There is nothing old fashioned or out of date about him; you find just as many applications for what he says while in a dogfight in a supersonic jet as you can in a classroom talking about the nature of evil in the world. But he urges us to acquire a constancy of character that will *make it impossible for another to do you wrong*. And to get that invulnerability, that inner invulnerability, requires mastering the ability to be continually conscious of whether you are dealing with something you control or something that in the last instance you do not control. The only good things of absolute value are those that lie within your own control. And they are relatively few: things like thought, impulse, our opinions, our desires, our aversions, what we conceive of, what we choose, and so on. Who is the invincible man? He who *cannot be dismayed* by *any* happening beyond his control.

Things not in your control he calls *externals*, and you are to be indifferent to them. By that he means you are not to become obssessed with having them for their own sake. To have your heart set on something you do not control is to invite slavery, for he who does control it, knowing of your hunger for it, can make you perform like a monkey on a string. Invulnerability is staying off such hooks.

All this means so much to me because it is an exercise in prison smarts on how to "stay off the hook." And at its center is an idea that centers on dignity and the quality of life. In an age when so many seem to cherish the idea that they are "victims" of this or that, it's nice to hear an old man explain why there should really be no such thing as a victim, that you can only become a victim of yourself. As Epictetus says, "No one can harm you without your permission."